America's Inequality Trap

Chicago Studies in American Politics

A series edited by Benjamin I. Page, Susan Herbst, Lawrence R. Jacobs,
Adam J. Berinsky, and Frances Lee

Also in the series:

America's Inequality Trap

NATHAN J. KELLY

The University of Chicago Press
Chicago and London

The University of Chicago Press, Chicago 60637
The University of Chicago Press, Ltd., London
© 2019 by The University of Chicago
All rights reserved. No part of this book may be used or reproduced in any
manner whatsoever without written permission, except in the case of brief
quotations in critical articles and reviews. For more information, contact the
University of Chicago Press, 1427 E. 60th St., Chicago, IL 60637.
Published 2019
Printed in the United States of America

28 27 26 25 24 23 22 21 20 19   1 2 3 4 5

ISBN-13: 978-0-226-66547-4 (cloth)
ISBN-13: 978-0-226-66550-4 (paper)
ISBN-13: 978-0-226-66564-1 (e-book)
DOI: https://doi.org/10.7208/chicago/9780226665641.001.0001

Library of Congress Cataloging-in-Publication Data

Names: Kelly, Nathan J., author.
Title: America's inequality trap / Nathan J. Kelly.
Other titles: Chicago studies in American politics.
Description: Chicago : The University of Chicago Press, 2019. | Series: Chicago
    studies in American politics | Includes bibliographical references and index.
Identifiers: LCCN 2019032051 | ISBN 9780226665474 (cloth) |
    ISBN 9780226665504 (paperback) | ISBN 9780226665641 (ebook)
Subjects: LCSH: Income distribution—Political aspects—United States. |
    Wealth—Political aspects—United States. | Equality—Political Aspects—
    United States. | Elections—United States—Economic aspects. | United
    States—Politics and government—2009–2017.
Classification: LCC HC110.I5 K45 2019 | DDC 339.2/20973—dc23
LC record available at https://lccn.loc.gov/2019032051

♾ This paper meets the requirements of ANSI/NISO Z39.48-1992
(Permanence of Paper).

To Arwen Hope Morgan Kelly, whose life gives joy every day and renders it both easier and more essential to imagine the world as it should be

CONTENTS

ONE

Contemporary Politics and the Perpetuation of Inequality

As returns started coming in on the evening of the 2016 presidential election, Democrats were prepared for celebration. With the election coming on the heels of two terms with Barack Obama in the White House, most indicators were pointing to another four years of Democratic control. The polls had Hillary Clinton in the lead. The prediction models suggested that Donald Trump had only a moderate chance for success. It even seemed possible that Democrats might capture at least one chamber of Congress, increasing their ability to make progress on their policy goals.

As more precincts across more states reported results, however, it became clear that Donald Trump was exceeding expectations. By around ten o'clock that night it was apparent that Democratic optimism for another presidential victory had been misplaced and that a Republican would be elected president for the first time since the 2007 financial crisis. It was a close race, and Clinton in fact won the national popular vote just as many of the forecasts had predicted. But Trump won in the states where he needed to, particularly in working-class areas of the country that were assumed to be stable bastions of Democratic support.

Many analysts were completely befuddled. Trump was, after all, best known as a reality TV star and real estate mogul with a history of questionable business dealings. He had no political experience and demonstrated little policy knowledge. The campaign had revealed numerous potential scandals in Trump's past and featured dozens of major gaffes and inflammatory statements from the candidate. But he won anyway. How could this happen?

After time for reflection, the 2016 election might best be described as a combination of rigid partisanship and rising economic and racial resentment. In large part, mainstream Republican elites continued to support Trump regardless of his latest campaign shenanigans. The alternative was a Hillary

Clinton presidency, and that outcome was impossible for committed Republican partisans to stomach. It probably wasn't difficult for them to imagine that a political neophyte like Trump could be controlled once in office, and Trump's policy statements were sufficiently vague to allow Republicans to project their preferred positions onto the candidate. Any Republican in the White House would be preferred to a Democrat in these politically polarized times. So, with some important exceptions, mainstream Republican elites did not oppose Trump once he became the party's nominee, and many lent him active support. Republicans in the mass public basically followed their lead.

Winning the votes of core Republican voters would not have been enough to win, of course. Some combination of the following had to happen for a Republican victory in 2016: converting Obama voters into Trump voters, convincing Obama voters to stay home, or getting former nonvoters off the sidelines to vote for Trump. This is where some combination of racial and economic resentment played an important role. Pundits and analysts continue to debate the role of racial bias and economic discontent in Trump's victory. Those debates, fruitlessly in my view, aim to nail down whether racism or economic conditions were the driving factor. It was likely both (and the role of sexism should also not be dismissed). A handful of scholars were pointing to these factors almost in real time during the election. In particular, Katherine Cramer's (2016) study of resentment in rural Wisconsin uncovered the type of anti-elite, anticity, anti-academic, anti-immigrant, antiminority attitudes that played a central role in Trump's pitch for the presidency. And Arlie Hochschild's (2016) work pointed to similar dynamics in a deep dive into life in rural Louisiana. For those who were aware of the dynamics that these studies were describing and believed them to be part of a larger pattern, the outcome of the 2016 election was certainly understandable and, to some extent, anticipated.

Like most observers, though, I thought Hillary Clinton would win. It seemed to me she had an ample cushion in the pre-election polls, that the economic fundamentals were favorable enough for the Democrats, and that Trump was a sufficiently troubled candidate to ensure a Democratic victory. But I also had in my mind the work I was doing for this book. And it was not hard to see how Trump's victory represented a continuation of the historical patterns I was uncovering as part of this project.

Election 2016: The Inequality Trap Redux

This book is about how economic inequality and American politics are linked—in particular how the concentration of economic power shapes political power in ways that reinforce the gap between the rich and the rest. I argue, essentially, that income concentration is connected to politics in ways that tend to reinforce the gap between the rich and the poor.

My focus is the political ramifications of increasing income concentration. The core question is whether a rising concentration of economic resources changes politics in ways that make reducing inequality more difficult. I find that the consequences of rising economic inequality are not just economic. The concentration of money at the top also leads to a concentration of economic and political power that creates a sort of self-perpetuating plutocracy. I examine how institutional features of American politics and behavior within those institutions respond to rising resource concentration, and I present evidence of an "inequality trap" in which an increase in the level of inequality affects politics in ways that make future reductions in inequality less likely.

Viewing our current political situation through the lens of an inequality trap suggests that what we are observing now is simply the latest iteration of patterns that have been in place for some time. As the 2016 presidential campaign unfolded, the United States was living in one of the most unequal periods in its history. We can see this clearly in figure 1.1, which depicts the share of income going to the top 0.01 percent from 1913 to 2015.

After reaching a high point of just over 4 percent prior to the Great Depression, the income share of the top 0.01 percent of incomes declined fairly steadily until the mid-1970s. This was an era known as the Great Compression. Incomes were growing for rich and poor alike, but the most substantial

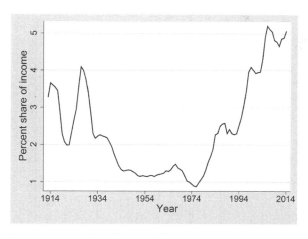

1.1. Top 0.01 percent share of income, five-year moving average, 1913–2014.
Source: Author's calculations from World Inequality Database.

gains accrued to the middle and bottom of the income distribution. The middle class was growing. Economic prosperity was broadly shared.

The late 1970s marked a complete reversal, and the income share of the ultrarich increased steadily for the next thirty years. After a brief downward blip following the Great Recession, income shares for the top 0.01 percent are now hovering around 5 percent. It's hard to put in perspective exactly how much inequality this represents, but here goes. In 2014, 5 percent of total national income went to 0.01 percent of tax units. That's five hundred times the income share that would go to a group that size in a perfectly equal society. It represents a minimum income among the top 0.01 percent of nearly $7 million. Compare that to a median income of just over $50,000. It is a staggering differential. Before the end of business on January 3, someone in the top 0.01 percent has made what the average American makes in a year. Let that sink in. It's part of the context for the 2016 election and everything that has happened since.

In this context of extreme inequality, the 2016 election produced unified Republican control with a billionaire in the White House. It is at first blush confusing how this could happen. After all, while both parties have contributed to policies that exacerbate economic inequality, it is clear that Republicans are much more favorable to those at the top than to those at the bottom. Electing more Republicans is not the path toward more egalitarian outcomes. People are expressing more frustration than ever with economic and other elites—this was in full view during the 2016 election—and yet Republicans won across the board.

It turns out that this was no mere anomaly. Rather, the result is consistent with how public opinion and election outcomes have responded to changes in inequality for decades. The core message of chapter 3 is that a portion of the public responds to rising inequality not by becoming more supportive of redistribution but by shifting in a conservative direction that makes egalitarian policy making less likely. That is, the feedback pathway between inequality and public opinion is one source of the inequality trap in American politics. Based on an examination of more than five decades of public opinion data, my analysis suggests that economic inequality and racial animus act jointly to depress progressive economic policy preferences—mostly among the poor. And this has been the case for decades. High inequality makes racial tensions more politically relevant, and Donald Trump played on this quite effectively by concurrently activating racial animus in stunningly explicit ways and channeling the frustration among those left behind economically.

Election outcomes are the focus of chapter 4. Here again, the results from the 2016 election are quite consistent with long-running patterns that implicate feedback between election outcomes and inequality as a source of an inequality trap. Simply stated, rising inequality advantages Republicans and undermines Democrats. Of course there are myriad other dynamics at play, and Democrats can win even when inequality is very high (the 2008 Democratic victories in the midst of an economic crisis under a Republican president is a perfect example). But generally speaking, I show in chapter 4 that high levels of inequality help Republicans and hurt Democrats. This is seen in over one hundred years of aggregate election outcomes in which the composition of Congress has tended to shift toward Republicans as inequality moves higher. It is also seen in analysis of individual-level voting decisions, where voters with inegalitarian racial views are less likely to support Democratic candidates during periods of higher inequality.

Now that we've had some time to observe the aftermath of the 2016 election, the impact of the results has been largely unsurprising in terms of distributionally relevant policy choices. The largest single policy accomplishment during unified Republican control was the package of tax cuts passed at the end of 2017. The distributional consequences of those tax cuts are clear—more money for those at the top and the same or less for those at the bottom. It is an upward redistribution of income that was enacted in the face of some of the highest levels of income concentration our country has ever experienced. That policy was purely the work of Republicans, and it showed that despite some of Trump's populist rhetoric, he is more than willing to go along with the traditional Republican objective of reducing taxes on the rich.[1] But we have also seen a willingness of some Democrats to join Republicans in inequality-enhancing policies, such as efforts to weaken finance sector regulations. These patterns, also, are not new and can be linked to rising inequality. This partisan convergence on prorich policy is the focus of chapter 5, where I use a combination of qualitative and quantitative evidence to show that Democrats became increasingly supportive of deregulatory policy changes that would contribute to higher inequality as income concentration increased in the 1980s and 1990s. This points to inegalitarian partisan convergence as another form of feedback between inequality and politics that contributes to the inequality trap.

It is important to note, of course, that a Democrat held the White House for two terms prior to Donald Trump's election in 2016. And for the first two of those years, Democrats had a majority in both chambers of Congress as well. Passing legislation like the Affordable Care Act was no small feat, and the economic progressivity of the ACA—most prominent in its expansion of Medicaid and its revenue-generating provisions—has often been underappreciated. But the fact is that when Barack Obama was elected in 2008, inequality was about as high as it's ever been. And when Barack Obama left office in 2017, it still was. Not much was accomplished to equalize the economic playing field in the eight years prior to Donald Trump's victory. This pattern of policy inaction and its income-concentrating effects marks a continuation of patterns that have been at play for a long time. Those historical trends are explored in more detail in chapter 6, which examines the role of status quo bias and policy stagnation in America's inequality trap.

Together, I explore four potential feedback pathways for an inequality trap in American politics—public opinion (chapter 3), elections (chapter 4), inegalitarian policy convergence (chapter 5), and policy stagnation (chapter 6). I find evidence that each of these pathways contributes to an inequality trap. When economic inequality rises, several parts of the political system respond in ways that perpetuate inequality.

As income has become more concentrated in a smaller proportion of hands, Republicans and Democrats have become more likely to find agreement on a small sliver of inegalitarian policy programs. The inegalitarian effects of policy inaction have also been ratcheted up as inequality has become more extreme. Elections and public opinion have not done much to push back against these trends. Instead, Democrats, who are generally more supportive of policies to combat rising inequality than their Republican opponents are, perform worse when inequality is higher, and the public does not become more supportive of redistributive policies when national-level inequality increases. To the contrary, those at the lower end of the economic ladder actually become *less* supportive of redistributive policies as inequality rises. The analysis leading to these conclusions is largely based on data for years prior to Donald Trump's 2016 victory. But the dynamics of that election and what we have witnessed since are consistent with a continuation and even a deepening of the broader patterns uncovered here.

A Preview of What's to Come

In a sense, I have started with the conclusion of the story—that inequality continues to perpetuate itself in contemporary American politics. Now I want to go back to the beginning and explain how the book will unfold. In chapter 2, I turn to the theoretical underpinnings of an inequality trap, discuss initial evidence of that trap, and lay out a guide to the core analytical decisions made in the remainder of the book. Each of the substantive chapters is informed by existing theory and analysis that is specific to the aspects of American politics that are analyzed. But the overarching theoretical framework emphasizes how economic power places the rich in a politically powerful position that allows the perpetuation of economic in-equality through multiple forms of political decision making. While the particular mechanisms through which this power is exercised are specific to the US context, the overarching dynamic through which economic power begets political power that then reinforces economic power is likely to be a more general phenomenon.

Chapters 3 through 6 represent the heart of the analysis, with each chapter assessing a separate pathway through which economic inequality is reinforced in American politics. Below, I summarize each chapter, and table 1.1 represents a more succinct visual depiction of the core conclusions from each chapter.

Chapter 3 examines feedback between public opinion and income con-centration. One of the central findings in this chapter is that an increase in inequality does not generate a progressive backlash against inegalitar-ian outcomes. This nonresponse helps to maintain high levels of inequal-ity. Furthermore, I find that those who are poorer and more racially biased against blacks have become less supportive of redistribution as inequality at the national level has risen. Those with the most racially egalitarian views re-spond quite differently to rising inequality, becoming more supportive of re-distribution. These countervailing responses to rising inequality essentially cancel each other out at the aggregate level but point to patterns consistent with a dynamic feedback loop between public opinion and distributional outcomes among a subset of Americans. Economic inequality and racial at-titudes have effects on public opinion that magnify each other. Racial bias generates opposition to redistribution, and that effect is exacerbated when inequality is high. Economic inequality is often unrelated to support for redistributive policies, but among those who have biased racial attitudes, economic inequality undermines support for the very policies that would reduce gaps between the rich and the poor.

Chapter 4 focuses on elections and income inequality. When Republi-cans gain power in Washington, inequality rises more than it does when Democrats are in power. And as inequality rises, Republican electoral vic-tories become more likely. The general pattern here is of self-reinforcing feedback between inequality and election outcomes. People are more likely to support Republican candidates when inequality is higher. This connec-tion is (as with public opinion) the result of a combination of racial bias and rising inequality. This suggests that inequality has both direct effects on election outcomes as well as moderator effects in which inequality changes the relevance of racial attitudes in the voting calculus.

Chapters 5 and 6 shift from a focus on political attitudes and behavior

Table 1.1: Summarizing the Substantive Results

Chapter	Summary of Findings
Chapter 3	Assesses feedback between public opinion and economic inequality
	Public opinion in general does not become more liberal or supportive of redistributive policy when inequality rises
	Those with low levels of racial bias respond to rising inequality by supporting redistributive policy, but those with moderate to high levels of racial bias become more conservative and less supportive of redistributive policy when inequality is higher
	Public opinion fails to serve as a check on rising inequality
Chapter 4	Assesses feedback between election outcomes and economic inequality
	Republicans become more successful in presidential, House, and Senate races as inequality rises
	Those with moderate to high levels of racial bias are most strongly affected by rising inequality, becoming more supportive of Republican candidates as inequality rises, while those with low levels of racial bias evidence a different voting response to higher inequality, becoming more supportive of Democrats
	The core conclusion is that the party most likely to pursue inequality-reducing policies finds it harder to achieve power as inequality rises
Chapter 5	Explores how rising inequality shapes the policymaking process, focusing on how efforts to deregulate the finance industry were simplified by rising inequality
	Isolated partisan convergence can occur when the parties reach sufficient consensus on a policy change in a general context of high partisan polarization
	When inequality is high, these areas of convergence are most likely to occur around inegalitarian policy changes
	Democrats became more supportive of financial deregulation, though far from universally so as inequality moved higher
Chapter 6	Examines the relationship between economic inequality and policy stagnation
	Policy stagnation does not always lead to greater inequality, but when inequality is high policy stagnation exacerbates inequality
	Core conclusion is that the institutions of American government that bias outcomes toward the status quo serve the interests of the rich and contribute to America's inequality trap

to policy-making institutions and processes. In chapter 5 I argue that rising inequality provides opportunities for bipartisan agreement on inegalitarian policy outcomes. In a detailed discussion of the legislative history of financial deregulation, I show how regulation of the finance sector became easier to undermine as income concentration increased. And, of course, financial deregulation contributed in important ways to fueling further increases in inequality. We see deregulation move onto the agenda of conservative reformers, and as inequality rose, Democrats had incentives to allow deregulatory changes to move ahead.

Chapter 6 focuses on the role of policy inaction in contributing to an inequality trap. I find that the effect of policy stagnation on inequality varies depending on how high inequality already is. When inequality is low, policy stagnation has no effect on inequality. It does not necessarily keep inequality low, but neither does it increase inequality. But as inequality rises, the distributional consequences of policy inaction change, making future increases in inequality more likely. In this sense policy inaction contributes to a dynamic inequality trap, in which rising inequality is further reinforced by policy stagnation. But this effect happens because inequality exacerbates the inegalitarian consequences of policy inaction, not because policy inaction always leads to more inequality.

In the final chapter I discuss some of the broader implications of the analysis. In particular, I discuss how and why the political response to high inequality prior to the Great Depression differed so greatly from the response to the Great Recession, which also occurred during a period of extremely high inequality. Building on this discussion, I suggest possible strategies for escaping the inequality trap. Let's move now to a more detailed discussion of how and why an inequality trap might arise in the first place.

TWO

An Inescapable Plutocracy?

To start down the path of a more systematic analysis of America's inequality trap, I devote this chapter to definitions and foundations of my argument: What is an inequality trap, and why might the relationships between economic inequality and the political system give rise to such a trap? I also present some preliminary empirical evidence of an inequality trap and provide an overview of the more detailed analysis to come.

The key definition first. An inequality trap is a situation in which increasing levels of inequality make future reductions in inequality less likely. There are two potential versions of an inequality trap. In the first version, when inequality rises it stays at the new level and does not fall in the future. This is what most of us probably think of when we think of a trap—traps latch on to prey and don't let go. Once the prey is in the trap it is simply stuck and cannot extricate itself from its trapped state. I will refer to this scenario as a static trap. In the second version of an inequality trap, inequality rises and then continues to rise in the future in a self-reinforcing upward spiral. This enhanced version of a trap acts more like a black hole than a mouse-trap. When an object moves too close to a black hole in outer space, it is trapped to be sure, as it will not be able to return to its previous location without some major outside intervention. But once ensnared, it also continues to move toward the black hole. Initial movement in the direction of the trap is reinforced by the pull of the trap once the object is ensnared. I will refer to this scenario as a dynamic trap since it implies reinforced *movement* rather than reinforced *stasis*.

Both versions of the inequality trap are consistent with the general definition above. In one version, an increase in inequality is sticky. That is, an increase is not naturally followed by a decrease because of characteristics of the political system. In the other, an increase is self-reinforcing. Once an increase happens, politics changes in ways that make future increases more likely. In either scenario an increase in inequality today makes reductions in the future less likely, though the black hole version of an inequality trap is clearly more serious than the classic version of a trap. I consider the possibility that either or both of these versions of an inequality trap could be operative in the United States, finding evidence for one or both in each of the four feedback pathways that I analyze.

The idea of feedback is clearly essential to understanding an inequality trap and coming to grips with the empirical signature of such a trap. Such a feedback system has at least two components. When one component of the system changes, it affects itself because of feedback from the other component of the system. It is therefore a requirement that the relationship goes in both directions (see figure 2.1a). If the relationship goes only one way then the feedback system ceases to exist and a change in one component of the system does not affect itself—it affects only the other component of the system (or has no effects within the system at all). When there is a feedback relationship in place, that feedback can be either self-reinforcing or self-correcting. In a self-reinforcing feedback system, an increase in one component creates further increases in that component (see figure 2.1b).[1] In a self-correcting feedback system, an increase in one component of the system decreases that component via feedback (see figure 2.1c).[2]

If economic inequality is part of a feedback process, a self-reinforcing feedback system would generate an inequality trap. It is worth pointing out that feedback systems can be more complicated, with multiple mechanisms through which the system can operate. In the context of economic inequality, there are several candidates for factors that could be part of a positive feedback loop. Inequality might change the way the economy functions so that the rich can maintain their relative advantage, for instance, by generating increased returns on capital (Piketty 2014). Inequality could also generate demographic changes, such as spatial economic segregation, that make it harder for those with low incomes to move up the economic ladder.

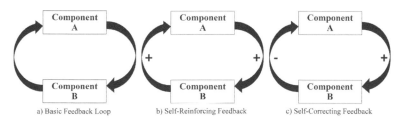

a) Basic Feedback Loop   b) Self-Reinforcing Feedback   c) Self-Correcting Feedback

2.1. Describing feedback processes.

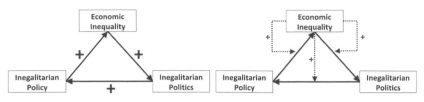

a) Direct Feedback Loop from Inequality to Politics   b) Feedback Via Moderating Effects

2.2. Two versions of a political inequality trap.

While these economic and demographic pathways are interesting in their own right, I am concerned with such pathways only to the extent that they play a role in changing the political landscape. My goal is to identify and test *political* components of a feedback system that contribute to an inequality trap. I begin here by describing in general terms how politics and policy could contribute to an inequality trap.

Imagine a hypothetical feedback system with three components—economic inequality, politics, and policy. This is obviously a dramatic simplification since "politics" here would represent myriad aspects of partisan and ideological conflict in the process that leads to policy outcomes, and "policy" is shorthand for hundreds of specific policies as well as the process of policy implementation. A straightforward reinforcing cycle might look something like figure 2.2a—rising economic inequality produces inegalitarian shifts in the political process, which generate inegalitarian policy outcomes, which further exacerbate economic inequality. This is clearly a reinforcing feedback system that fits the definition of an inequality trap.

There is also a second, perhaps more subtle way that a self-reinforcing feedback loop between inequality and politics could emerge. Rather than the direct connections between inequality and politics from figure 2.2a, income concentration could change the nature of the relationships between the components in the system. Figure 2.2b depicts this sort of feedback. Instead of focusing on the solid lines connecting inequality, politics, and policy, here the focus is on the dotted lines running from inequality to the solid arrows. The dotted lines represent what are known as moderator effects. That is, one component of the system either enhances or diminishes the connections between other aspects of the system. A positive moderator makes an effect more positive while a negative moderator makes an effect more negative. For example, economic inequality might strengthen the relationship (i.e., make a positive relationship more positive) between inegalitarian political factors such as Republican control of policy-making institutions and inegalitarian policy outcomes. If Republican control of policy-making institutions is more likely to produce inegalitarian policy outcomes as inequality increases, this represents another way that economic inequality might reinforce itself by shaping the political system.

One of the key foundations of this conception of an inequality trap is that economic inequality is not like most other economic indicators. It is easy to lump income inequality together with indicators like GDP growth, unemployment, inflation, or home sales. But inequality is different. Inequality should not be viewed as a disembodied actor that can be dismissed as a mere aggregate statistic. Rather, income inequality reflects not only an economic reality but also a political power structure. Economic inequalities matter for people's *political* lives, not just their economic ones.[3] When someone in the top 0.01 percent makes as much in a day as an average earner makes in four months, there are obvious implications for the sorts of goods and services that those two people can afford to purchase. But this gap also has implications for political, economic, and social power that are too often either ignored or assumed depending on which side of the political spectrum one is on. As Tilly (1998) argues persuasively, people in positions of higher relative status have myriad opportunities to utilize their advantage in a self-perpetuating way. A high-quality education, whether by paying directly to a private institution or through buying more expensive real estate for access to public options, is not cheap. But it does help to transfer advantage from one generation to the next. This is just one example of what Tilly (1998) calls opportunity hoarding. In examining the potential feedback of economic inequality on the political system, my goal is to neither ignore nor assume how inequality might intersect with the political reality of peoples' lives. Instead, I seek to analyze such relationships as critically and systematically as I can.

To reiterate, for an inequality trap to exist there has to be a two-way relationship between politics and inequality. Politics and policy must influence inequality. Inequality must also affect politics and policy. Otherwise, there is no closed feedback loop characteristic of a trap. Moreover, the nature of those relationships must be consistent with the models of self-reinforcing feedback discussed above—more inequality must produce changes in politics that make it harder to reduce inequality. I move now to a discussion of the theoretical underpinnings of a feedback relationship between economic inequality and politics.

The Political Underpinnings of Economic Inequality

We saw in chapter 1 how the gap between the rich and other Americans has shifted over time. One of the key turning points appears to have come sometime in the mid-1970s, when after several decades of falling inequality and broadly shared prosperity, the gains from economic growth became increasingly concentrated among the very rich.

The steady rise in inequality in the fifteen years between 1975 and 1990 grabbed the attention of scholars who were becoming energized to understand the underlying dynamics of rising inequality, and who began a new research agenda with roots in numerous classic academic studies of social class, economic stratification, and poverty (Dahrendorf 1959, Durkheim 1933, Lindblom 1977, Okun 1975, Schattschneider 1960, Weber 1968). These efforts to understand why inequality was rising focused on structural economic and demographic changes pertaining to deindustrialization, globalization, aging, union decline, and skill-biased technological change (Berman, Bound, and Machin 1998, Bound, Johnson, et al. 1992, Danziger and Gottschalk 1995, Goldin and Katz 2008, Nielsen and Alderson 1997). This work in large part placed distributional outcomes outside the political process. Some scholars nodded to the fact that government policies might matter at the margins. But this early work on contemporary US inequality leads easily to the conclusion articulated by Secretary of the Treasury Henry Paulson that income inequality is "simply an economic reality, and it is neither fair nor useful to blame any political party" (Paulson 2006).

But in the past ten years, a distinct narrative has emerged placing *politics* center stage in understanding economic inequality. Among the most impactful of these studies is Larry Bartels's *Unequal Democracy* (2008). He presents evidence that the relative prosperity of the rich and poor is shaped by partisan politics and the divergent policy choices made under different constellations of partisan power. In this account the policies favored by Republicans and Democrats differ dramatically, and inequality is reduced when Democrats, who more strongly support a variety of egalitarian policies, attain power in national policy-making institutions. This aspect of his work makes clear that the actions of the welfare state are an important and all too often neglected element of explaining the distribution of income.[4]

My own previous work provides additional support for the conclusion that party politics shapes distributional outcomes (Kelly 2009). In an analysis of more than fifty years of data on inequality, election outcomes, public policy, and public opinion, I find several connections between American politics and income inequality. One of the core conclusions is that distributional outcomes are a product of the US macro political system. Income concentration increases more when public opinion becomes more conservative, when Republicans gain power in national policy-making institutions, and when policy shifts to the right. When the macro political system shifts toward the left, however, economic inequality moves lower than it would have otherwise. Importantly, I find evidence that it is not just tax and transfer policy that connects politics to income inequality. Government policies that set the rules of the game for market competition also affect inequality in important ways. In fact, I find that these "market-conditioning" activities of government provide a stronger link between politics and income inequality in the United States than the more traditional tax and transfer policies that are usually the focus of discussions about public policy and income inequality.

Jacob Hacker and Paul Pierson (2010) also push beyond a focus on redistributive policy to examine the broader governmental framework that sets the rules of political conflict and shapes market interactions. They develop an impressive historical narrative showing how key policy actions (and nonactions resulting from institutional rules that make shifting from the status quo very difficult in the US system) helped to skew the market economy to advantage the superrich. The core message of these and several other studies is that choices made through the American democratic process served to transform an economic system of broadly shared prosperity into one where the gains from economic growth go almost entirely to those at the very top.[5]

The evidence is pretty clear at this point. Economic inequality is at least in part an outcome of American politics. This is one essential requirement for the existence of an inequality trap. But the relationship has to go the other way as well for there to be a self-reinforcing feedback loop that generates an inequality trap. While the latest wave of research on income inequality in America has probed the political underpinnings of distributional outcomes, this work has not yet engaged with the broader literature about the self-reinforcing nature of power. Because recent work on the political economy of American inequality has not sufficiently grappled with ways that both political and economic power are intertwined and can take on a life of their own, the possibility of an inequality trap as I have proposed has not been seriously explored. In the next section, I seek to introduce some of the existing work that points out how an unequal economy undermines equal political power in ways that can generate a self-reinforcing link between economic inequality and politics.

Democratic Politics in the Face of Economic Inequality

An inequality trap is rooted in the idea that economic (and other social) inequalities perpetuate themselves, and this idea has a long history. Tocqueville (2000) argued that there is an inherent connection between social, economic, and political *equality*. To the extent that America was equal economically, it served to change social organization in a way that helped to broaden and perpetuate that equality. But by implication, shifting away from equality in the social, economic, or political domain would undermine inequality in the other domains. Even in this very early work on American society, we see the skeleton of an argument suggesting that various forms of inequality (or equality) can be self-perpetuating. Rising or falling inequality in one domain can affect inequality in other domains in ways that produce a self-reinforcing pattern over time.

More recently, connections between economic inequality and democratic politics have become a growing thread in the American political economy literature. L. Jacobs and Soss (2010) provide a succinct and useful overview of research on American inequality in the context of broader political economy traditions. As they point out, how American democracy incorporates and processes divergent economic interests and deals with fundamental economic changes was at the heart of early studies of American politics. Scholars such as Wilson (1908), Herring (1940), Key (1949), Easton (1953), Dahl (1961), Schattschneider (1960), Lowi (1969), and Lindblom (1977) were all interested in the distribution and organization of power in the United States, and they brought various theoretical lenses to bear on a wide variety of questions about the connection between American politics and economics.

My interest in an inequality trap, or an ongoing system of feedback between economic inequality and the American political system, is very much an outgrowth of these long-running debates. The typology of frameworks for analyzing the American political economy developed by L. Jacobs and Soss (2010) points out that one of the key disagreements across these theories is about the extent to which inequalities, including economic inequality, are durable in the context of American democracy or whether American institutions create a more felicitous circle of progress. Using my terminology, the debate is whether an inequality trap exists in American politics and, if so, which institutional and behavioral aspects of American democracy generate this trap.

Electoral Democracy as Remedy to Economic Inequality

In the monarchies, oligarchies, and feudal societies of medieval Europe it is unsurprising that economic inequality was the norm. In such systems, economic and political power reside in a relatively small set of hands, and this leads quite naturally to a society of haves and have-nots. America was to be different. And democracy, of course, is supposedly the key aspect of American life that would serve to perpetuate economic, social, and political equality. In fact, from democracy's earliest foundations, one of the key concerns of economic elites has been that the equality at the core of democratic politics would imperil private property and allow the masses to use the power of the state to expropriate wealth in order to equalize economic outcomes through redistribution. Fear of economic redistribution among economic elites is often cited as a core source of resistance to democratization (Ansell and Samuels 2014, Boix 2003).

The logic of this perspective is straightforward and enticing. In an economically unequal society, those who are lower on the economic ladder will benefit from the downward redistribution of economic resources. Seeing such benefits, the poor will be more supportive of redistributive policies than the rich. Since democratic systems incorporate a wider swath of the economic spectrum into the political decision-making process, democracy will lead to redistribution. This happens because the pivotal actor shifts from one less supportive of redistribution (in a more oligarchic system where economic elites have power) to one more supportive of redistribution (in a democratic system in which more citizens have power).

One of the classic statements of this redistributive version of democracy is Meltzer and Richard (1981). Building on median voter models (Downs 1957, Hotelling 1929), Meltzer and Richard develop a formal model predicting increased support for redistribution as economic inequality increases. Their model implies both that democracies will redistribute more than nondemocracies and that support for redistribution will be higher within democracies as inequality rises. The Meltzer-Richard model is quite stylized and focused exclusively on the domain of tax and transfer policy, but the model has clear connections to a long line of research in the pluralist tradition. L. Jacobs and Soss (2010, 349), in fact, call this model a "particularly essentialist" version of median voter theory and the pluralist tradition in which it is rooted.

The pluralist view of democracy envisions a political system in which there are no permanent winners or losers (Dahl 1961, Dahl 1971). Pluralists see American democracy as highly fragmented, with various types of resources having relevance for influencing the policy-making process. Economic resources are certainly one important contributor to political influence, but there are other forms of influence as well. And for pluralists, competing groups are advantaged and disadvantaged in different ways on different resource dimensions at different points in time. What is an advantage at one time may become a disadvantage later (Dahl 1961, Dahl 1971,

Truman 1951). This is what Dahl calls "polyarchy," and it forms the basis for a substantial body of later research examining public opinion, elections, interest groups, and policy outcomes in the United States.

Analysis in the pluralist tradition is most clearly associated with studies of interest groups. Truman (1951), for example, argued that organized interests are essential to democracy in the United States and that groups organize naturally around competing ideas to give voice to divergent interests. The preferences communicated via the interest system, under this view, are a fairly faithful aggregation of the will of the public, and elected officials respond to the signals sent via the interest system. While certain interest segments may be advantaged in terms of economic resources, other segments of the interest system are advantaged in other ways. Business interests may have certain structural advantages, but labor unions are a countervailing interest with other sorts of advantages. In support of this argument, scholars such as Vogel (1989) and K. Smith and Rademaker (1999) find that the influence of business has fluctuated over time and that the interests of the broader public are routinely enacted over the objections of business.

Models that place the median voter and elections at the heart of American politics are also an important outgrowth of pluralist democratic theory. One of the core implications of the median voter model is that policy outcomes will follow the preferences of the average American and not be dramatically skewed by those with extreme preferences (Downs 1957). While there is ample evidence that individual voters are largely uninformed about politics and unable or unwilling to connect the dots between their economic interests and the policies proposed by candidates for office (Bartels 2005, Converse 1964, Carpini and Keeter 1997, Lupia 2015), there is reason to believe that the electorate as a whole may behave much more predictably. Even if individuals are largely uninformed, movement over time in aggregate preferences may be quite systematic if the preferences of the uninformed shift randomly while the preferences of the informed shift systematically. If this is correct, there may be a meaningful signal in aggregate opinion shifts even if there is a great deal of noise in individual preferences (Popkin 1991). We see this dynamic play out in analyses of aggregate public opinion and policy responsiveness over time, with the public responding sensibly to changing policy outcomes and economic conditions and politicians producing policy change that generally aligns with the shifting sentiments of the public (Erikson, MacKuen, and Stimson 2002, B. Page and Shapiro 1983, Stimson, MacKuen, and Erikson 1995, Stimson 1999, Stimson 2004).

The pluralist perspective paints a rosy picture of American democracy. Citizen preferences align at least reasonably well with their economic interests. Election outcomes are strongly influenced by the policy preferences of citizens as well as citizen evaluations of the past and/or anticipated future performance of candidates. A wide variety of preferences are represented in the interest group system, and these groups compete on a basically equal playing field. Policy outcomes are often responsive to mass rather than elite preferences and interests. Most relevant to the theme of this book, there is nothing like an inequality trap in the pluralist line of thought.

The Reality of Democracy and the Persistence of Inequalities

There are several alternative ideas, however, that do suggest the possibility of an inequality trap. These perspectives suggest multiple pathways through which inequality might feed back into the political system in ways that reinforce economic inequality. Some of these competing perspectives adopt aspects of the core logic of pluralism but argue that certain empirical realities within America's mostly pluralist system fail to prevent the self-reinforcing accumulation of power that pluralism fundamentally rejects. Others view the logic of pluralism as fundamentally flawed and see political competition of a wholly different variety in American democracy.

Preference Formation and Elections

Pluralist theories focus on linkages between voters, interest groups, elections, and policy outcomes, arguing that the interest aggregation systems of American democracy do a reasonably good job of translating the will of the citizenry into policy outcomes. One set of objections to the rosy conclusions of pluralism arises from research on opinion formation. This view maintains a focus on the same interest aggregation connections as pluralism and does not necessarily reject the idea that citizen preferences are translated at least roughly into policy outcomes. However, the way that citizens form preferences and express those preferences in their political behavior undermines the pluralist vision of a system in which the interests of the have-nots are on more or less equal footing with the haves. The problem for pluralism under this view is that citizen preferences often diverge widely from their economic interests, and even when preferences and interests are tightly intertwined there can be a gulf between citizens' economically motivated policy preferences and their electoral choices.

This situation can arise for a variety of reasons. Enduring partisan ties may prevent a voter from abandoning a party when that party's policies no longer serve the voter's economic interests (Angus Campbell, Converse, Miller, and Stokes 1960). These same partisan ties also fundamentally shape perceptions of the political world, generating a form of partisan-motivated reasoning that makes voters less likely to notice political and economic realities that would undermine their partisan identity and less likely to blame their preferred party for economic problems (Enns, Kellstedt, and McAvoy 2012, Gerber and Huber 2010, Nyhan and Reifler 2010, Taber and Lodge 2006, Tilley and Hobolt 2011, Zaller 1992). Aside from partisanship, voters often form general economic preferences as well as preferences for redistribution based on racial and ethnic prejudice rather than material self-interest (Alesina, Baqir, and Easterly 1999, Gilens 2000, Glazer 2003, Morgan and Kelly 2017). Shapiro (2002) goes so far as to call Meltzer and Richard's model of support for redistribution, which is rooted in pluralist theories of democracy, "one thesis that history has roundly refuted" (118). He goes on to cite the issues discussed here as well as many other problems with the psychological assumptions of the Meltzer-Richard model (and pluralism more generally) as the primary reason for the theory's predictive weakness (Shapiro 2002).

The issues raised to this point, however, do not lead naturally to suspecting the existence of an inequality trap. Many of these individual psychological processes are at least *considered* in system-level analyses of the links between opinion, elections, and policy outcomes (Easton 1953, Erikson, MacKuen, and Stimson 2002). Importantly, while there is often a disconnect between economic interests, policy preferences, and voting behavior at the individual level, this line of scholarship does not of necessity imply that these same disconnects exist at the aggregate level. It is quite possible that the lack of linkage between opinion, elections, and policy outcomes disappears through the miracle of aggregation, and when it comes to assessments of general economic performance there is evidence that it does (MacKuen, Erikson, and Stimson 1993).

Other research, however, goes further, arguing that certain features of opinion formation and political behavior undermine aspects of the pluralist account of American democracy and form the foundation for more pervasive problems, including the possibility of what I call an inequality trap. Here again, this work still accepts much of the logic of a pluralist system that acts to tally up preferences across society in a way that approximates a faithful representation of citizen preferences. Bénabou (1996), for instance, starts with many of the same essentially pluralist assumptions as Meltzer and Richard about how elections and the policy process are connected to citizen preferences. But Bénabou's (1996) model diverges dramatically on the question of how preferences for redistribution respond to rising inequality, predicting *less* support for redistribution as inequality rises rather than more.

It is also important to note that citizen preferences do not form in a political vacuum. The way parties, campaigns, elected officials, policy experts, and the media discuss political issues and frame policy choices can have important effects on opinion formation (Druckman 2004, L. Jacobs and Shapiro 2000, Zaller 1992). Edelman (1964) argued that economic elites can use their power to manipulate the beliefs and preferences of citizens. Elite proponents of particular policy choices have clear incentives to shape the information environment in ways that would mold public opinion in favor of their preferred outcomes (Gaventa 1982). An excellent example of this in action is the long-running effort of antigovernment conservatives to encourage university and think-tank research supportive of libertarian goals and to work at the grassroots level to mobilize these ideas in states and localities (Mayer 2016, Skocpol and Hertel-Fernandez 2016, Skocpol and Hertel-Fernandez forthcoming). Bartels's (2005) analysis of public attitudes toward regressive tax cuts under the George W. Bush administration suggests that such efforts sometimes bear fruit (see also Achen and Bartels 2016, Bartels 2008).

With this scholarship as backdrop, it is possible to see the first indications of how an inequality trap could form. Inequality rises, and support for the redistributive policies that would reduce inequality declines either by some reasonable "natural" process (Bénabou 1996) or by changes in power dynamics that make it possible for the rich to manipulate the opinions of poorer citizens. Then, even if the interest system and elections perfectly translate citizen preferences into policy outcomes, redistributive policy becomes less likely in the future. Such a pattern would coincide with an inequality trap because an increase in inequality at one point in time would reduce the likelihood of a future reduction in inequality and may even make future increases more likely. Chapters 3 and 4 analyze in more detail the effects of rising inequality on public opinion and election outcomes in the United States, finding patterns in both domains that are consistent with the existence of an inequality trap.

Interest Aggregation and Policy Making

The discussion above fits nicely into what Hacker and Pierson (2010, 100) call "politics as electoral spectacle," where public opinion and elections are at the core of understanding American democracy. But electoral democracy may serve as at best a limited check on rising inequality. Many of the limitations of elections are rooted in the characteristics of citizens—they are only episodically interested in politics (Carpini and Keeter 1997), they struggle to connect their objective economic interests to preferred policies (Bartels 2005), they often vote for candidates who do not align with their policy preferences (Bartels 2008), they fail to hold elected officials accountable for their policy decisions (Achen and Bartels 2016), and they often blame policy makers for circumstances that are entirely out of the policy makers' control (Achen and Bartels 2016). While the miracle of aggregation can partially ameliorate some of these concerns, they are far from completely removed. And when election outcomes are tight, idiosyncrasies rooted in factors other than electoral accountability can determine outcomes.

But research on interest groups rooted in the pluralist perspective might suggest that all is not lost (Berry 1999, Lowery and Gray 1995, Truman 1951). Although individual voters and even the electorate as a whole may be essentially incapable of or unwilling to counteract rising inequality, interest groups might step into this void. There are several steps between elections and policy outcomes, and organized interests play a substantial role. A pluralist interest system in which numerous competing perspectives are influential in the detailed work of policy making might ensure that economic inequality does not become self-perpetuating.

Yet other work suggests that the more central groups are to our conception of American political conflict, the more likely an inequality trap may be. For example, Hacker and Pierson (2010, 100) call American democracy "politics as organized combat." Their emphasis on groups leads them to suspect that processes similar to those I call an inequality trap are in place, with self-reinforcing feedback between economic inequality and American politics. As Schattschneider (1960) famously noted: "The flaw in the pluralist heaven [of interest groups] is that the heavenly chorus sings with a strong upper-class accent" (35). Under this view, there is a bias in the interest group system toward those who can successfully overcome the collective action problems that stand in the way of organization (Olson 1965). Monetary resources provide a means to bypass the collective action problem, meaning groups representing those with more economic means are likely to be overrepresented.

Over the past ten years, scholars have become increasingly attentive to the question of whose interests are reflected in public policy. The results are not encouraging. When those at the top want something different from others,[6] the rich are much more likely to get what they want than everyone else (Gilens 2012, Gilens 2009, Gilens and Page 2014, Bartels 2008). Senate roll-call voting is quite responsive to the views of high-income constituents, but much less so to the views of others (Bartels 2008). Other work has shown even more stark contrasts in the responsiveness of policy makers to the rich and the poor. Gilens and Page (2014) conclude "the preferences of the average American appear to have only a miniscule, near-zero, statistically non-significant impact upon public policy" (575).

Some of the clearest evidence that moneyed interests have a distinct advantage in the interest system has been developed by Schlozman, Verba, and Brady (2012), who use both mass survey data and information about political advocacy organizations to show that the affluent are much more active and organized in the political realm. Similarly, Hacker and Pierson (2010) note that the affluent and business interests have capitalized on their resource advantages to organize in favor of ultimately successful policy initiatives that have contributed powerfully to income concentration. Johnson and Kwak (2010), Phillips (2002), and C. Ferguson (2012) argue that the US is dominated by a "financial oligarchy," while Winters and Page (2009, 731) state that "in the U.S. context, as elsewhere, the central question is whether and how the wealthiest citizens deploy unique and concentrated power resources to defend their unique minority interests." The most important minority interest of oligarchs is likely "wealth defense" (Enns, Kelly, Morgan, and Witko 2016, Winters and Page 2009, Winters 2011). An oligarchic system would look like figure 2.3, with economic inequality affecting the political system in ways that produce unequal political power, which in turn generates policy outcomes that maintain high levels of inequality. This is quite consistent with the idea of an inequality trap, and figure 2.3 looks very similar to the earlier figures I presented depicting a positive feedback loop between inequality and politics.

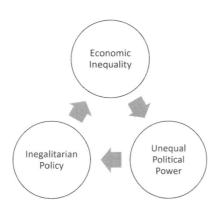

2.3. A simple model of American oligarchy.

Oligarchies are political systems dominated by a minority of individuals and families (oligarchs) who possess a concentration of material resources and who use a fraction of those resources for the political defense of their income and wealth.[7] Oligarchs can utilize material resources (whether individually owned or not) to protect their economic and social status by using "wealth for wealth's defense" (Winters 2011, 2). In societies where property rights are not as clearly secured by the state, oligarchs may engage in direct rule. In advanced capitalist societies like the United States, where property rights are strongly and reliably defended by the state, oligarchs are more likely to engage in indirect rule such as influencing political actors and policies that impinge on their ability to accumulate larger shares of income and wealth (Winters 2011).

Other work also implies a link between economic means and political power in capitalist democracies (Domhoff 2010, T. Ferguson 1995, Tilly 1998). Those in higher-status groups, Tilly (1998) argues, seek to maintain their status advantage through the mechanisms of exploitation and opportunity hoarding. While both of these mechanisms go far beyond the realm of politics and policy making, the policy-making process provides a potential target and vehicle for both exploitation (in which the advantaged generate increased returns for themselves by organizing others who are not fully compensated for their effort) and opportunity hoarding (when the advantaged gain access to a valuable resource and exclude others from access to that resource). Those who have vast material wealth can advance the "narrow and short-run policy concerns of wealthy families," influencing policy through funding think tanks, foundations, and charities; owning media outlets; and promoting their preferences by shaping elections and investing in the political process (Domhoff 1990, 16; T. Ferguson 1995).

In sum, a focus on the relative power of competing groups in the policy-making process further suggests the possibility of an inequality trap. Here, as inequality rises, the power of those at the top increases relative to those at the bottom. As the political power of the financial elite increases, their ability to achieve policy victories and prevent policy defeats intensifies. If the efforts of those at the top of the economic heap are focused on maintaining their relative economic position, their enhanced power in the political realm will undermine the likelihood of egalitarian policy change and increase the likelihood of inegalitarian change. Such policy outcomes would make reductions in future inequality less likely, which closes the feedback loop needed to generate an inequality trap. In Chapters 5 and 6 I examine in more detail how economic inequality feeds back into the policy-making process in ways that perpetuate inequality. I show that rising inequality exacerbates the inegalitarian consequences of policy inaction and makes bipartisan agreement on inequality-enhancing policies more likely.

The more unequal an economy is, the more economic resources are concentrated among economic elites. My argument is that this has implications for American politics, with those implications tending to perpetuate the gap between the rich and the rest.[8] Those with money have advantages in the political system. Some of those advantages become evident in the brute exercise of political force. Money means making campaign contributions, being present in networks that interact with elected officials on a regular basis, hiring professional lobbyists, owning media companies, and bankrolling organizational influence. This brute political force is relevant in the process of policy creation, adoption, and implementation. And America's policy-making institutions help to turbo-charge the influence of these sorts of activity, which is most likely at work within the halls of government. But some of the advantages that the rich gain when inequality rises happen out in the mass public and likely have something to do with deeply rooted psychological responses to social and economic conditions as well as the intentional actions of those at the top. These effects will be seen in opinion responses and election outcomes in contexts of rising inequality. The bottom line is that America's political system provides many pathways for the unequal political power offered by an unequal economy to produce an inequality trap.

Initial Evidence of an Inequality Trap

The above discussion emphasizes how various lines of thinking in previous research suggest a feedback relationship between economic inequality and politics that could generate an inequality trap. While there has been much speculation about the existence of such feedback mechanisms, there has been relatively little systematic analysis of the relationships that would form the feedback connections needed to generate an inequality trap. To the extent that previous analyses have addressed this possibility, the evidence has been circumstantial and largely based on inferring temporal feedback relationships from static analysis. Nevertheless, there is certainly suggestive evidence in existing work.

Over twenty years ago, Paul Krugman (1996) talked about a "spiral of inequality." Krugman takes note of the astronomical levels of inequality that had developed since the 1970s (and the income share of the top 0.01 percent was *only* 3 percent then instead of about 5 percent now) and suggests several ways that a formerly middle-class nation changes when "whole segments of society live in vastly different economic universes." He gives a fair amount of attention to how economic inequality changes politics, for instance by shifting the balance of political power toward the wealthy and generating ever more divergent preferences between the rich and the poor. But Krugman's story of an inequality spiral is largely based on speculation—the spiral of inequality is assumed.

Much more recently, Benjamin Page and Martin Gilens (2017) identify several ways that democracy and inequality are tied together. They argue, based on a broad swath of political science research as well as their own original analysis, that inequality undermines democracy and democracy undermines inequality. They trace several ways that American democracy, defined as equal policy responsiveness to all citizens, has been undermined by rising inequality. And they encourage broad reforms aimed at deepening American democracy as a way to reduce economic inequality.[9] Research pointing to rising inequality as both a cause and an effect of labor union decline (Western 1997) and Krueger's (2012) argument that rising inequality leads to declining economic opportunity also suggest that America is in an inequality trap. But there is still little to no direct evidence that such an inequality trap exists.

At this point I want to take a very preliminary first step toward an analysis of how feedback between economic inequality and politics contributes to an inequality trap in America by asking simply if rising economic inequality today tends to be followed by rising inequality in the future. I set aside the question of whether politics might contribute to such a pattern, coming back to those issues in later chapters. But there really isn't any point of trying to figure out if inequality shapes politics in self-reinforcing ways if the most basic empirical signature of an inequality trap is not present. Thus, I assess whether that empirical signature exists here.

Throughout the book, my focus will be on top income shares—the share of income going to a group no larger than the top 1 percent. I focus most of my analysis on top income shares for two reasons, one theoretical and one empirical. The theoretical underpinnings of an inequality trap discussed earlier in this chapter point to concern about a politically dominant economic elite that hoard power and use their political influence to maintain their economic advantages. I need a measure that can credibly serve as an indicator of elite economic power. Since my ultimate interest is in how economic inequality shapes the political system, the gap between the very rich and other Americans is the most theoretically relevant. This is certainly not to say that other aspects of inequality don't matter. In fact, top income shares move mostly in tandem with many other measures of the general income distribution. And what is happening at the top has implications for those throughout the income distribution. But given my focus on feedback between economic inequality and politics, most of the analysis uses top income shares to measure inequality.[10]

Empirically, I focus on top income shares because the underlying data measuring this outcome are based on tax returns as opposed to census data. Data on top income shares were compiled as part of Piketty's important work that culminated in his publication of *Capital in the Twenty-First Century* (Piketty 2014). Prior to Piketty's effort to compile income shares based on income tax returns, the best information we had about income in the United States came from Census Bureau surveys. The two big problems with census income data are that (1) it relies on people's recollection of their income (which tends to be much more flawed than what they report to the IRS under potential legal penalties for inaccurate reporting) and (2) the richest among us are all lumped into a single income group through a procedure called top-coding.[11] Whether you make $5 million or $1 million, your income is lumped together in the same category in census income data. Piketty's data mark an important step forward because these problems were overcome, allowing a more complete picture of what is happening at the very top of the income distribution.

Recalling that an inequality trap implies that current increases in inequality make future reductions in inequality less likely, simply looking at the path of inequality over time can provide a first hint as to whether this pattern is present. In figure 1.1 at the beginning of the previous chapter, I charted the share of income going to the top 0.01 percent. That measure of inequality declined steadily from the late 1930s through the mid-1970s and then has increased steadily since, which looks like a self-reinforcing pattern. The dual intervention of the Great Depression and World War II produced economic changes that pushed in the direction of equality. Those egalitarian economic shifts then appear to have become self-reinforcing in a downward direction. The economic changes underway in the 1970s, such as technological innovations making returns to education higher (Goldin and Katz 2008), were inequality inducing. Those changes seem to have set in motion an upward spiral of inequality. For some, simply observing this pattern over time seems sufficient to conclude that inequality is indeed self-reinforcing (Krugman 1996).[12]

In figure 2.4 I take a slightly more systematic look at the future effects of a change in inequality. Based on a regression analysis that relies on over-time covariation between current and previous values of inequality, I estimate how a shift in top income shares at one point in time affects future values of

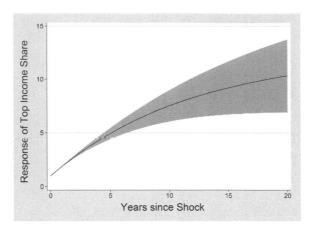

2.4. Effect of income concentration on future values of inequality.
Source: Author's calculations.

inequality.[13] Figure 2.4 takes the estimates from that regression analysis and simulates how future values of inequality would be affected by a one unit increase in inequality. In this case, a one unit increase is a 1 percentage point increase in the share of income going to the top 0.01 percent. Based on this analysis, an initial percentage point increase in top income shares would translate into an eventual ten percentage point increase in top shares twenty years later if nothing else changes over that period.[14] I would not advocate taking the specific estimate here too seriously given the univariate nature of the model, but the main conclusion is that once inequality increases (or decreases), it is likely to stay on that path for years to come.[15] This result is consistent with the story of an inequality trap. However, a great deal of work remains to see whether this self-reinforcing pattern holds up to additional scrutiny and whether politics plays a role.

An Overview of Evidence to Come

The analysis in the coming chapters has several moving parts. First, each chapter analyzes a separate aspect of politics, from political behavior to policy-making institutions, as potential contributors to a spiral of inequality. Second, the nature of the evidence brought to bear in different parts of the analysis ranges from aggregate time series data, to individual responses to cross-sectional surveys, to a qualitative policy case study. Each chapter includes some combination of levels and approaches to analysis. Third, since there are two potential forms of an inequality trap—discussed above as static and dynamic traps—each portion of the analysis considers the possibility of both types. Finally, inequality can feed back into the political system by directly changing political outcomes, by moderating the relationship between various parts of the political system as well as the distributional consequences of politics and policy, or by both. In an effort to distill what is a complicated and varied set of analyses, I provide a guide in table 2.1 focused on the analytical approaches implemented in each of the next four chapters.

Let's quickly walk through this guide. Chapter 3, which examines the connection between public opinion and the income gap, utilizes a combination of aggregate time series and micro-level survey data. Aggregate time series analysis suggests that a static inequality trap is the best way to characterize the temporal relationship between public preferences and income inequality.[16] That is, the opinion response to rising inequality is not likely to further exacerbate inequality. But neither is it likely to undermine existing levels of inequality. Additional analysis of individual-level opinions helps to flesh out what is happening in the aggregate results, with a particular focus on whether individuals with different characteristics respond differently to economic inequality. The analysis in this chapter examines variation over time as well as across individuals and considers both general and specific attitudes.

Chapter 4, which examines the role of election outcomes in the inequality trap, parallels the analysis in chapter 3. Analysis of movement over time in election results and distributional outcomes uncovers a dynamic inequality trap with direct connections between inequality and elections. Whether the outcome is presidential, Senate, or House elections, the same general patterns emerge with varying degrees of strength. As inequality rises, the electoral fortunes of Republicans improve, thereby increasing the likelihood of even higher inequality. The micro-level results bolster the aggregate results and provide a bit more nuance.

Chapters 5 and 6 examine the role of policy-making institutions and processes in the inequality trap. In chapter 5, I conduct a detailed case study of the legislative history of financial deregulation. This case study is rooted in a qualitative analysis of the legislative record as well as quantitative time series analysis of policy outcomes in this domain. The analysis suggests a dynamic inequality trap with both direct effects of inequality on policy making and moderator effects in which inequality changes existing connections between partisan politics and policy outcomes. Chapter 6 uses time series analysis as well as data on roll-call voting in Congress to examine connections between inequality, polarization, and status quo bias. Policy inaction contributes to

Table 2.1: A Guide to the Analysis and Results

Chapter	Pathway of Feedback	Type of Analysis	Type of Trap	Nature of Feedback
Chapter 3	Public opinion	Aggregate time series of general ideological preferences	Static	Direct
		Micro-level opinions on general redistribution, variation in inequality is temporal	Dynamic	Direct+ moderator
		Micro-level opinions on specific redistributive policies, variation in inequality is spatial	Dynamic	Direct+ moderator
Chapter 4	Elections	Aggregate time series of partisan power in Congress and presidency	Dynamic	Direct
		Micro-level vote choice in congressional elections, variation in inequality is temporal	Dynamic	Direct+ moderator
		Micro-level vote choice in presidential election, variation in inequality is spatial	Dynamic	Direct+ moderator
Chapter 5	Policy action	Historical account of finance sector regulation	Dynamic	Moderator
		Aggregate time series of financial deregulation	Dynamic	Direct+ moderator
Chapter 6	Policy stagnation	Aggregate time series of policy inaction and status quo bias	Dynamic	Moderator
		Aggregate time series of party polarization	None	NA
		Individual legislator roll-call voting	None	NA

Note: "Static" trap refers to a trap in which inequality increases and is maintained. "Dynamic" trap refers to a trap in which inequality increases and then continues rising. "Direct" feedback indicates that inequality feeds back on itself through a direct effect via the specified pathway. "Moderator" feedback indicates that inequality feeds back via the pathway by changing how the political factor affects inequality rather than affecting the political factor directly.

a dynamic inequality trap, in which rising inequality is further reinforced by policy stagnation. Despite previous research (McCarty, Poole, and Rosenthal 2006), I find little evidence that party polarization contributes to an inequality trap in any straightforward way.

As the discussion above indicates, much of the evidence I will bring to bear throughout the remainder of the book examines change over time. I focus on temporal variation for a couple reasons. First, the very idea of an inequality trap is temporal in nature. A shift in inequality is quite unlikely to have immediate, contemporaneous effects on the political system. And it is essentially impossible to imagine a scenario in which economic inequality could feed back on itself instantaneously. Instead, the feedback effects of economic inequality—on politics and then on itself—unfold over time. A current increase in inequality shapes how politics works in the future, which then affects the future path of inequality. It is a process that is temporally dispersed. The theoretical foundations of an inequality trap require an examination of change over time. And time series analysis provides the most direct strategy for testing the core empirical implications of an inequality trap.

The second reason I focus on change over time is to strengthen causal claims. One of the key challenges in this project is sorting out causation in a system in which feedback is a core theoretical expectation. The question of whether politics influences inequality, inequality influences politics, or whether the relationship goes both ways will be key. Existing literature in this area typically assumes that causation flows in only one direction or the other. Applying time series analysis to as much as one hundred years of annual data offers the advantage of temporal ordering, which aids in identifying the direction of association. But this approach only establishes the *potential* for causation that is implied by association. Therefore, I also utilize individual level cross-sectional data and time series cross-sectional data to assess a wider variety of empirical predictions flowing from the inequality trap model, some of which are less prone to problems of reverse causation. My research design does not attempt to establish causation by relying on any single critical test of each mechanism. Rather, by thinking through micro-level, macro-level, cross-sectional, time series, and historical implications of the theoretical model and testing these theoretical claims using a variety of data sources and methodological approaches, I triangulate toward a cumulative case for causation.

While the remainder of the book deploys several analytical strategies, a particular technique that crops up repeatedly is vector autoregression (VAR) analysis of annual time series data followed by impulse response functions (IRFs) to visualize the effects. This book focuses on questions that are inherently dynamic in nature—they imply a process that unfolds over time. To capture such processes, it is essential to observe the world through a temporal lens, which is precisely what time series data and analysis allow us to do. VAR is a regression technique that is rooted in observing association between multiple variables as they move through time. In traditional time series regression models, one variable is identified as an outcome and other variables are labeled as causes, with effects running in only one direction. This framework, of course, will not work here since an inequality trap by definition involves an ongoing feedback loop. A VAR is designed for such feedback loop situations, not forcing the designation of some variables as causes and others as outcomes. All the variables in a VAR are both outcomes and explanations.

IRFs will be used repeatedly to aid in the interpretation of the VAR models estimated. An IRF reports the effect of some hypothetical increase in one variable on another variable over an extended period of time. Looking at an IRF chart can tell you how much one variable will affect another and for how long, based on VAR model estimates. I generally will report cumulative IRFs in which the effects are added up over time. So the effect on an outcome in year 4 after an initial increase in an explanatory variable is the effect in years 1 through 4 combined. This means that if initial increases in the outcome are followed later by decreases, the cumulative IRF will capture that. And these IRFs account for both direct effects of one variable on another as well as indirect effects that a variable has via other variables in the system. For those interested in more details about VAR models, there is an extended discussion in online appendix A. I have also attempted to provide details of modeling choices in notes throughout the analysis for those who want to take a deeper dive. In many of those notes I refer readers to portions of the online appendixes where I present results under alternative specifications or using different assumptions.[17]

To conclude, I want to be clear that many of the mechanisms that I see as creating an inequality trap were not consciously created or even intentionally utilized to maintain economic inequality. In fact, the very same factors that create an inequality trap can only be described in this way because we currently have high levels of inequality. When inequality is low or falling, the inequality trap could easily transform itself into a barricade against inequality. Equally important, the story of America's inequality trap is not one of well-intentioned efforts to reduce inequality that backfired in ways that were unanticipated. In my view, the inequality trap is in large part a function of two broad factors: (1) inequality interacting with US political institutions in ways that highlight institutional features perpetuating inequality and (2) behavior within these political institutions that are in some sense routine and predictable responses to rising inequality.

THREE

Public Preferences and Economic Inequality

Democracy is a multifaceted system of government, defined by the existence of certain rights, free and fair elections, inclusion of competing groups, and individual dignity for all. But the core of democracy is a relationship between the state and the people—an ongoing "two-way communication between government and the governed" (Stimson 2004, 170). For there to be such two-way communication, members of the public need to have preferences that respond to what government does, and the government needs to respond to changing preferences. This back and forth between citizen preferences and government action is an essential ingredient of democratic accountability, in which the governed are empowered to generate change when government is not responsive or acts outside its scope. Discussing American democracy means discussing public opinion.

There are, of course, several competing theories about the precise role that public opinion plays in American democracy. Median voter models envision citizens who are highly informed about policy and hold elected officials accountable in elections by replacing politicians who stray too far from the voter's preferred policy position (Downs 1957). Pluralist models posit that interest groups faithfully aggregate the preferences of individual citizens, communicate those preferences to elected officials, and play an important role in holding politicians accountable during elections (Dahl 1961, Truman 1951). The macro politics model considers several components of the American governing system and finds that public opinion responds meaningfully and (in large part) reasonably to economic and political events, election outcomes are influenced in important ways by shifts in public policy sentiment, and public opinion plays a key role in shaping policy outcomes (Erikson, MacKuen, and Stimson 2002, Stimson, MacKuen, and Erikson 1995, Stimson 2004).

Other theories, however, argue that public opinion has little to no independent effect on the policies that government pursues. Contrary to median voter models, there is evidence that most Americans are uninformed and generally inattentive to the political happenings around them (Carpini and Keeter 1997, Lupia 2015) and that political opinions are so unstable that it may be inappropriate to even describe most citizens as having meaningful policy preferences (Converse 1964, Zaller 1992). Voters' social identity appears to be a more important determinant of who they vote for than their policy preferences (Achen and Bartels 2016), which undermines the idea that elections serve as a useful mechanism of policy-oriented accountability. A variety of antipluralist perspectives argue that some citizens have more power than others, so it is not the preferences of the *public* that matter so much as the preferences of a powerful *subset of the public* (Domhoff 2010, Gilens 2012, Gilens and Page 2014, Schattschneider 1960). In this same vein, Hacker and Pierson (2010) point out that it is organization that matters most in politics, and they identify "the decline in the reach and clout of organizations representing moderate-income Americans [as] the most fundamental aspect of [the emergence of a winner-take-all society]" (150). Under this view, public opinion is really a sideshow, with the real action happening via "organized political combat" (Hacker and Pierson 2010, 100–102) in which certain segments of the population are at an extraordinary disadvantage.

America's system of government is supposedly designed to prevent social and political outcomes from moving too extremely in one direction or the other. The policy-making process is strongly biased toward the status quo (a factor that I will examine as a contributor to the spiral of inequality in chapter 6). This means that a high degree of consensus is required for policy change. It also makes it hard for even a fairly large majority of lawmakers to move the dial quickly and substantially toward their preferred policy outcomes. This protects against wild swings in policy and the social outcomes they influence. And in a sense, these protections are antidemocratic, with a small "d."

Even if such wild swings somehow occur, the more democratic aspects of the system have the potential to reign things back in. As Erikson, MacKuen, and Stimson (2002) argue, public opinion and election outcomes typically provide a backlash in response to extreme outcomes. Johnson's Great Society produced a public response in the conservative direction. Reagan's drive toward the right eventually made Democrats more popular and conservative policies less desirable. The public, by giving politicians negative feedback when lawmakers take things too far, provides an additional backstop against extreme outcomes. In the broadest strokes, there appears to be good evidence in support of this view (Erikson, MacKuen, and Stimson 2002, M. Smith 2000, Stimson, MacKuen, and Erikson 1995, Wlezien 1995).

But as we've seen, income concentration has become extreme. It's been moving essentially in the same direction for over forty years. While there have been a handful of efforts to address rising inequality through policy, those efforts have been small in comparison with the scale of change. How has the public responded? Casual observation doesn't suggest there has been a backlash, at least not to this point. The Occupy Wall Street movement expressed frustration with income concentration. But that movement ended up not amounting to much. The Tea Party had some strains that were superficially concerned with an unfair economy that advantaged those already at the top. But the policy prescriptions favored in that movement are designed to further *increase* economic inequality. So no real backlash there.

In fact, for at least some subset of Americans, it seems possible that rising inequality has actually depressed their appetite for the policies and politicians most likely to do something about high inequality. Cramer's (2016) *Politics of Resentment* takes a close look at people outside of urban centers in Wisconsin politics. Her work goes far beyond people's perceptions of economic and political inequality, of course, but one of the implications seems to be that as economic gains have become increasingly concentrated in cities, those outside of urban centers have become resentful. Instead of demanding more action by the government to ameliorate these unequal outcomes, they have lost faith in government altogether. These people seem to think government helps only other people, not them. So shrinking government is the best hope for the "undeserving" (people of color, politicians, academics, etc.) to be taken down a peg. Hochschild (2016) develops quite similar themes in her examination of life in rural Louisiana, and there has been no shortage of journalistic coverage in the aftermath of Trump's 2016 victory seeking to understand how so many poor white people were willing to support a wealthy real estate mogul for president. This work all points to a different form of backlash in response to rising inequality. Instead of a backlash to ameliorate inequality, there could be an inequality-reinforcing backlash.

In these next two chapters, I examine two key pillars of American democracy—public opinion and elections. The question is how these two aspects of the democratic system respond, if at all, to changes in income concentration. I start in this chapter with public opinion. The core disagreement about the role of public opinion in American democracy can be boiled down to divergent answers to the following two questions: (1) Where does public opinion come from? and (2) What are the effects of public opinion?

This chapter examines both of those questions by analyzing the interplay between the concentration of income in the hands of a few and the preferences of the mass public. The primary focus is on how changes in income concentration shape opinion formation. I also discuss how public opinion affects the concentration of income.

This chapter and the next are not intended to answer the broadest questions about public opinion, democracy, and electoral accountability. Instead, the focus is more specifically on the reciprocal relationship between political behavior (opinion and vote choice) and income inequality. The question is not so much whether public opinion contributes to electoral accountability in this context as whether public opinion serves as a check on rising inequality or not.

Nevertheless, the analysis both draws on and informs broader debates about public opinion and democratic accountability. I begin below with a discussion of thermostatic public opinion and dynamic representation, which I see as the two core components of a modernized median voter model. Discussing these two models and then applying them to income concentration provides the foundation for a self-correcting feedback relationship between public opinion and income inequality. Such a self-correcting relationship would run counter to what we expect if public opinion contributes to the inequality trap. I then introduce a series of arguments that suggest a breakdown in the self-correcting inequality-opinion relationship suggested by the thermostatic model. Many of these arguments are connected to antipluralist theories and suggest that as income is concentrated in the hands of a few and political power is concentrated in those same hands, mass preferences are likely to shift against the very policies that could level the economic playing field. I then present an analysis that combines macro-level time series and individual-level data. To preview the results, I find evidence of a self-reinforcing opinion-inequality link among a subset of Americans. For these people, rising inequality appears to trigger less support for the very policies that would reduce income inequality. Those who don't respond to rising inequality in a self-reinforcing fashion basically don't respond at all. There is no public backlash to rising inequality, meaning that the public provides at best a flawed backstop against extreme levels of inequality.

Thermostatic Preferences, Dynamic Representation, and Income Concentration

The thermostatic model of public opinion addresses the question of what drives public opinion. The answer, according to the model, is at least in part government policies. The core insight of the model is that aggregate public opinion responds meaningfully to political outcomes. Wlezien (1995) focuses on the public's response to government spending. He observes that when spending in a certain policy domain increases, public support for spending in that domain goes down. Surveys often ask people whether they want the government to do or spend more, less, or stay the same, and survey items such as this are often utilized in tests of the thermostatic model.[1]

The public, considered collectively, has a preferred outcome—levels of spending in this case—that can shift over time. At any given moment, actual spending is likely above or below the collective target, but this is theoretically inconsequential. The main point is that if spending increases, some people who previously wanted government to spend more are now satisfied, meaning that they would no longer want government to "spend more" in that area. This produces a decline in aggregate support for spending in that area. It also creates an interesting thermostatic dynamic between public opinion and policy outputs. When government does more, the public responds by adjusting its preference downward. When government does less, the public responds by asking for more.

Stimson (1999) and Erikson, MacKuen, and Stimson (2002) extend the logic of the thermostatic model across issue domains and beyond preferences for spending. Stimson's (1999) measure of public mood taps the overall public sentiment on matters of domestic policy across a wide variety of policy domains, from abortion to Social Security. Mood creates a gauge of how "left" or "right" public opinion is at any given time.

If we glance quickly at the path of mood over time, we can easily craft a story about a dynamic cycle between political events and outcomes on the one hand and public opinion on the other that is broadly consistent with the view that public opinion is the great thermostat of American democracy (see figure 3.1). Throughout the 1950s, with Republican Dwight D. Eisenhower in the presidency, public opinion moved toward the left. After the passage of a series of liberal proposals in the 1960s, opinion moves in the other direction until the election of Ronald Reagan. This marks another turning point, with opinion moving toward the left again during the Reagan and Bush presidencies. After Bill Clinton's election in 1992, there is a more modest shift back to the right, and then opinion moves toward the left again during the George W. Bush administration. More systematic evidence indeed supports the conclusion that the public responds to changes in partisan control of government and the ideological tenor of policy making (Erikson, MacKuen, and Stimson 2002).

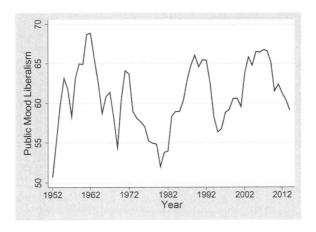

3.1. Liberalism of public opinion.
Source: http://stimson.web.unc.edu/data/, accessed January 21, 2016.

Soroka and Wlezien (2010) argue that this thermostatic response of public opinion to policy outcomes is an essential ingredient of democratic accountability. If public preferences are not informed by government action, then there can be no accountability because what people say they want is independent of what government does. Accountability requires communication between citizens and policy makers that goes both ways: citizens need to respond to what policy makers do and policy makers need to react to what the public wants.

Some of the same studies that establish a predictable thermostatic response of public opinion to political events also demonstrate that election outcomes and policy making respond systematically to shifts in public opinion. When the public moves toward the left, Democrats are more likely to win national office, and more liberal policies are enacted (Erikson, MacKuen, and Stimson 2002, Erikson, MacKuen, and Stimson 1995, Wlezien 2004). The opposite occurs, of course, when opinion shifts to the right. This means that public opinion's thermostatic response to political events actually serves as a meaningful signal to policy makers and that policy makers appear to respond. This closes the loop between public opinion and policy outcomes in a way that prevents policy from drifting too far from what the public wants. But how does this connect to income inequality, if at all?

My previous work has explicitly sought to link distributional outcomes with the macropolitics framework of which the thermostatic model and dynamic representation are an important part. When focusing on income inequality as an outcome of politics, I found evidence that changes in public

opinion produce election outcomes and policy changes that have systematic and predictable effects on income inequality (Kelly 2009, Kelly 2005).
When the public mood shifts toward the right, Republicans gain power and
enact conservative policies that tend to exacerbate the gap between the rich
and the poor. When public opinion shifts to the left, policy interventions
tend to produce lower levels of inequality than would exist otherwise.

Earlier work on the thermostatic model along with my work on inequality as an outcome of politics and policy could mean that rising inequality
is in part self-correcting. If rightward opinion shifts produce conservative
policies that increase inequality, those conservative policy shifts will push
public opinion toward the left. That leftward shift in opinion, then, would
shift election outcomes toward the Democrats and more liberal policies that
reduce inequality. These potential implications have not been explicitly addressed in previous work, but this is the picture that emerges if one pieces
together existing bits of analysis. This picture is, in fact, far from complete.
In particular, existing studies generally ignore possible opinion responses
to inequality itself.

There is a substantial literature in political economy devoted specifically to understanding attitudes toward redistribution, and this literature
provides a direct point of connection between the thermostatic model of
opinion and economic inequality. Meltzer and Richard (1981) argue that
when inequality increases, the mass public responds by requesting more
government activity, which government then enacts by increasing redistributive welfare state programs. Feedback from economic inequality to public
opinion is at the heart of the model. The key insight of the Meltzer-Richard
model is that those with below-average incomes favor at least some degree
of redistribution while those above the mean do not. An increase in inequality, by definition, shifts mean income upward and away from median
income. As inequality increases, then, the number of people with income
below the mean increases. This leads to the central prediction of the Meltzer-
Richard model—that increases in income inequality produce increased
public support for redistribution. This model is wholly consistent with the
idea of self-correcting inequality. When inequality goes up, it pushes opinion toward support for redistribution, which then produces policies that
reduce inequality.

The thermostatic model of public opinion did not incorporate economic
inequality when initially developed. The model focuses solely on the public's response to shifting public policy. But when we consider the evidence
that distributional outcomes are, in fact, a fundamental outcome of policy
choices, it is not a large leap to think that inequality might fit into a sys-

tem of thermostatic feedback.[2] Combining insights from political economy models of redistribution with analysis in the macropolitics tradition points toward a system in which inequality is self-correcting.

It seems highly unlikely, however, that we live in a world of self-correcting inequality. We have already seen how the trajectory of income concentration tends to move for decades at a time in one direction or the other. And despite some of the highest levels inequality in modern history, voters awarded control of both houses of Congress to the party with a history of tax cuts for the rich. Of course there are numerous potential explanations for such patterns that go beyond the response of public opinion to rising inequality. But there are several strands of recent scholarly literature that raise serious questions about thermostatic connections between inequality and public opinion. I turn to that discussion now.

A Broken Thermostat?

An extended version of the thermostatic model in concert with the Meltzer-Richard model of support for redistribution paints a comforting picture of American democracy. If this story is correct, then feedback from economic inequality to public opinion would undermine an inequality trap rather than contribute to it. But thermostatic feedback from inequality to public opinion requires the existence of at least two conditions. First, the public as a whole must accurately perceive the changes in inequality. They need to notice when inequality goes up or down. Second, people must make a connection between inequality and egalitarian policies and respond in a thermostatic fashion by supporting egalitarian policies when inequality rises. Problems with any aspect of this chain would undermine the public's thermostatic response to inequality.

Regarding the ability of citizens to accurately perceive and react sensibly to changes in inequality, it would be an impossible case to make if we had to rely solely on individual-level theory and evidence. Most citizens most of the time are relatively uninformed about politics and economics. To the extent that they are informed, it is based on gut-level reasoning that can easily go astray. While Popkin (1991) shows that individuals can gather a large degree of useful economic information from their local context based simply on their lived experience, this is not likely the case with regard to inequality. As geographic economic segregation has increased, it has likely become more challenging for people to accurately perceive inequality based on their local experience. Economic segregation in some ways hides inequality for the local-level observer. Furthermore, even if people have observed rising inequality at the local level, it is inequality between rather than within communities that is likely to matter most when it comes to the political power differentials that income concentration can produce. This suggests that the local level inequality that people are most likely to observe directly from firsthand experience is likely the least politically relevant, and inequality at higher levels of analysis (like the state or national level) is more meaningful.

We don't, however, have to focus solely on individual-level theory and evidence. While most of the people most of the time are nearly oblivious to the economic and political world outside their personal domain, some people some of the time are paying careful attention. That is all it takes to raise the possibility that the public as a whole is sufficiently tuned in to the ebb and flow of inequality to accurately identify changes in inequality over time.

The news media is the primary source of information about inequality for these attentive citizens (be they numerous or few). While studies of media coverage related to income concentration are few and far between, McCall (2013) analyzes print-media coverage of inequality and finds substantial attention to the issue of economic inequality going back to at least the early 1990s. As data on rising income concentration have become increasingly available and reliable, and as the levels of inequality identified by these measures have skyrocketed, media coverage of inequality has become even more ubiquitous. There is little question that an attentive person would have access to information depicting rising inequality at the national level via the news media.

The opportunity to be knowledgeable about and attentive to economic inequality, however, is a far cry from demonstrating that such knowledge is sufficiently widespread to produce a public that accurately perceives how inequality has changed over time. McCall and Kenworthy (2009) examine just about the entirety of survey evidence tapping into attitudes toward inequality (see also McCall 2013). They challenge the notion that Americans don't care about or notice changes in income concentration. General Social Survey (GSS) data shows that Americans generally perceive income differences as too large and have become at least slightly more concerned about inequality in the United States as income concentration has risen (McCall and Kenworthy 2009, 463).

Furthermore, both McCall (2016) and Kelly and Enns (2010) show evidence that people are able to perceive broad changes in the wage distribution, even if they tend to consistently underestimate inequality at any particular point in time. When people were asked to identify the earnings for people in several occupations, the perceived ratio of the highest to the lowest-paid occupation was about twenty to one in 1987.[3] In 2000, that same value increased to just over seventy-four to one. This gives at least a rough indication that people in fact perceived the substantial increase in inequality that happened over this time period.

There are certainly scholars who argue that people are simply uninformed about inequality, fail to perceive increasing income concentration, or don't care about inequality (e.g., Bartels 2005, Bartels 2008, Hacker and Pierson 2010, Ladd and Bowman 1998). This view is likely correct if we focus on individuals at a particular snapshot in time. But the aggregate time series evidence suggests that the public as a whole, while consistently underestimating inequality (and this could certainly have important consequences), does seem to notice the broad dynamics of income concentration. This suggests that at least the first condition for a thermostatic relationship between public opinion and inequality is in place—people do seem to notice when inequality goes up or down.

The second requirement for a thermostatic relationship is that people must link income concentration, and their position within the income distribution, to the policies that can change the distribution of income. Broadly speaking, there are two sets of policies that can shape the income distribution—explicit redistribution through taxes and transfers, and market conditioning policies that change the market distribution of wages and investment income (Hacker and Pierson 2010, Kelly 2009, McCall and Kenworthy 2009). Existing studies suggest that people are more willing to connect rising inequality to policies that focus on generating opportunity (market conditioning policies) than they are to connect rising inequality to tax and transfer policies.

Bartels (2005) analyzes attitudes toward the 2001 Bush tax cuts. These tax cuts reduced tax progressivity and were substantially more beneficial to the rich than to the poor.[4] Yet Bartels finds that low-income Americans were largely ignorant of the distributional consequences of this policy. Moreover, the poor were more likely than the rich to support this upward redistribution of income though changes in the tax code. McCall (2013) finds a link between concern for inequality and broad-based policies to enhance economic opportunity (market conditioning policies). But that support does not extend to more straightforward redistributive policies. This still provides a substantial political opportunity for reducing inequality since interventions that work by generating opportunity for those at the middle and bottom as well as more explicit redistributive programs have similar effects on distributional outcomes. And as it turns out, the Democratic Party is on the egalitarian side of the policy debate relative to Republicans on both the economic opportunity and explicit redistribution fronts (Kelly 2009).

But the existing evidence strongly suggests a breakdown in the self-correcting opinion inequality thermostat when it comes to connecting public policy to distributional outcomes in the minds of citizens. The core issue is that people, even in the aggregate, have a difficult time linking their economic self-interest to changes in the aggregate distribution of economic resources. As Chong, Citrin, and Conley (2001) demonstrate, it is counterproductive to assume that self-interest is the default motivation of individual citizens or even the public as a whole in the domain of politics. They argue that symbolic factors such as social identity and partisanship are likely dominant except in unusual circumstances. And we can see this logic applied to the realm of redistributive policy in Franko, Tolbert, and Witko's (2013) analysis of attitudes toward a ballot initiative in Washington state. They find that in an information environment and partisan context in which the redistributive dimension of a proposed policy is emphasized and the benefits of the policy are clearly linked to economic self-interest, people connect their self-interest to the redistributive proposal. While it is not the norm for citizens to connect redistributive policy proposals to their self-interest and their concerns about economic inequality, this apparently can happen in the unusual circumstance in which the redistributive consequences of the policy are both *crystal clear* and *emphasized in political debate* (Franko, Tolbert, and Witko 2013).[5]

This points to the central importance of the media and political elites in framing redistributive issues and shaping the information environment in which citizens reside. Economic elites and others who are ideologically opposed to government interventions to equalize opportunities and outcomes clearly have strong incentives to muddle the discussion of redistributive policies. Republicans very effectively framed the 2001 Bush tax cut as benefiting everyone despite the fact that the tax cut was upwardly redistributive with the lion's share of the benefits going to those already at the top (Bartels 2005). McCall (2016) also emphasizes the role of the media and political elites in shaping how the public thinks about and responds to rising inequality. She argues that it is commonplace for elites to discuss unequal opportunity, but it is less common to explicitly focus on equal outcomes. This suggests that progressive politicians could find success in generating support for redistributive policies by more explicitly connecting unequal outcomes to unequal opportunities, in essence attempting to break down the implicit dichotomy between support for equalizing opportunity and support for equalizing outcomes. Notably, however, as income concentration has risen and politicians have become increasingly reliant on campaign contributions from wealthy donors, they appear to have become less willing to discuss economic inequality in a way that would help citizens link rising inequality to the most straightforwardly egalitarian policy interventions (Enns, Kelly, Morgan, and Witko 2016).

The discussion to this point has focused on whether or not the public accurately perceives inequality and correctly understands their self-interest and the distributional effects of policy options. If the public fails to perceive inequality and/or link rising inequality to redistributional policies that would be in their economic interest, then the thermostatic connection between inequality and public opinion would be interrupted. Essentially, we would expect no relationship between inequality and public opinion.

It may be, however, that the feedback connection between opinion and inequality is perfectly well intact, but that the nature of the feedback is self-reinforcing rather than thermostatic. Even if people understand which policies are in their economic self-interest and they are attentive to shifts in inequality, there are many factors not directly related to economic self-interest that could generate a nonthermostatic, self-reinforcing opinion response to changes in inequality. Emotion, identity, and a host of psychological factors may be relevant to understanding any relationship between inequality and public opinion. In other words, the fixation on perceptions of inequality and the self-interest motivation assumed in the Meltzer-Richard model may be entirely misguided. In the thermostatic analogy, this is a more grave situation. Here we have a thermostat that is doing exactly the *opposite* of what it is supposed to do. Instead of reining an outcome in when it goes too far in one direction or the other, the thermostat (of public opinion) is reinforcing that outcome and actively preventing corrective reversals of the outcome.

There are at least four mechanisms that might serve to generate a self-reinforcing relationship between inequality and public preferences. I will call the first factor diversionary ethnonationalism. This perspective is laid out quite nicely by Solt (2011). As inequality rises, those at the top of the economic ladder have strong incentives to maintain the status quo. Plutocrats, essentially, become better and better off as the gap between the rich and the poor increases. Politicians whose policy goals align with those of the wealthy (and oppose egalitarian policies) likely recognize that rising inequality may undermine their ability to maintain power.

Such leaders can make nationalist and/or ethnically based appeals in an effort to undermine class identity and to erode support for redistributive benefits. Activating racism and nationalism can help focus middle- and low-income voters on something other than economic inequality. Emphasizing nationalist or race- and ethnicity-based appeals encourages citizens to define their identity in terms other than economic class (Alesina and Glaeser

2004, Glaeser 2005, Scheve and Stasavage 2006). Citizens are primed to think about the interests of the nation as a whole or the majority ethnic group as opposed to subsets of the population defined by economic means. Taken together, this makes attention to inequality less likely and undermines support for redistribution even if the public is attentive to distributional outcomes. Cross-national analysis of mass nationalist attitudes supports the claim that rising inequality generates nationalism (Solt 2011) and that nationalist sentiment reduces support for redistribution (Shayo 2009). Edsall and Edsall (1992) argue that this dynamic played a key role in Reagan's success in cutting taxes in the 1980s.

In fact, recent research in social psychology suggests that politicians and economic elites don't even need to stoke xenophobia, racism, or nationalism in a context of rising inequality. Rather, such psychological responses may commonly occur simply by priming thoughts about scarcity. Krosch and Amodio (2014) conduct a series of experiments in which they show that subjects who are placed in an experimental context in which resources are more scarce are more likely to perceive African Americans as blacker and behaving as more stereotypically black. Based on what we know from research on racial attitudes and welfare attitudes, such a response would readily translate into lower support for a variety redistributive programs (Gilens 2000, Kellstedt 2003, Winter 2006). Older studies show that people in environments of scarcity are less likely to see others as worthy of receiving resources and more likely to distribute resources in a discriminatory fashion (Brewer and Silver 1978, LeVine and Campbell 1972, Ross and Ellard 1986, Sherif 1966, Skitka and Tetlock 1992). Exposure to an increasingly unequal economy in which one is not at the top of the economic heap might prime such a psychological focus on scarcity, which could then reduce support for egalitarian policies.

A second factor that could serve to generate a self-reinforcing link between inequality and public opinion relates to trust in government. The basis for this argument begins with Hetherington's (2005) work on trust in government and policy attitudes. He argues that trust and mistrust of government has far-reaching consequences for public opinion. The core result of his analysis is that declining trust in government is a key factor undermining support for progressive public policy. He also argues that race is a critical element of trust and distrust of government. Those who have negative views of blacks are much less supportive of progressive policy when trust is low. But the policy attitudes of those with more positive views toward blacks are much less affected by trust. So, here again, racial attitudes enter the story even though the focus is on trust in government and support for redistributive policies.

Trust in the institutions of American government has been declining since the 1960s, over the same time frame that inequality has been rising. If institutional trust and economic inequality are related to one another, then the fact that declining trust undermines support for progressive policies is another pathway through which inequality might reinforce itself through public opinion. Uslaner and Brown (2005) present evidence from the American states showing that the correlation between inequality and trust is not mere happenstance. High levels of inequality appear to reduce feelings of efficacy and undermine the ability of people to have a positive outlook on life generally (Alesina and Glaeser 2004), which is then translated into less interpersonal and institutional trust. This, then, completes a potential pathway connecting rising inequality to declining trust to reduced support for progressive policies including redistribution.

Third, economic elites could strategically manipulate discourse and the information environment in ways that would undermine support for redistribution (Edelman 1971). At first glance this may seem to suggest only a lack of connection between rising inequality and support for redistribution. And that is quite possible. After all, economic elites may always attempt such manipulations in order to depress support for redistribution. There are two reasons why this type of behavior might create a conservative opinion shift in response to rising inequality. One factor at play is that economic elites face stronger incentives to protect their relative position as they increasingly pull away from others economically. That is, there is more to lose if you are at the top of a very unequal society than a relatively egalitarian one. A second factor at work is that such elite efforts at manipulation might be more effective as inequality rises. With more resources to devote to these efforts and more economic power relative to other actors, economic elites may have better luck with these strategies as income becomes more concentrated. One need look no further than the broad efforts of the Koch network and other activist conservative organizations to shape the media and produce research amenable to their ideological goals to see these sorts of attempts at work (Mayer 2016, Skocpol and Hertel-Fernandez forthcoming).

Finally, psychological status quo bias could contribute to a self-reinforcing feedback connection between income inequality and public opinion. This refers to a psychological process in which people's preferences are anchored by observed reality. One version of status quo bias is system justification, in which people essentially convince themselves that the world in which they live is acceptable because they assume that there are good reasons for the current state of affairs. It is the "it is what it is" attitude taken to the extreme.

Versions of this argument have become prevalent in behavioral economics and political psychology, and the idea of system justification is also connected to the concept of false consciousness that is common in sociological understandings of political behavior. Jost, Banaji, and Nosek (2004) provide an excellent overview of the theory and evidence surrounding system justification, and several of the core hypotheses of system justification apply in the context of opinion responses to inequality. If distributional outcomes are part of the observed status quo, people tend to rationalize the current situation (Kay, Jimenez, and Jost 2002). These rationalizations for the status quo seem to be particularly prevalent among disadvantaged groups (Haines and Jost 2000). Even the poor, for instance, show favoritism toward the rich in a variety of settings. Samuelson and Zeckhauser (1988) provide a wide range of circumstances in which status quo bias generates less than optimal decision making and produces substantial deviation from rational choices.

If status quo bias and system justification affect how people react to economic inequality, this could help explain how mass preferences can contribute to an inequality trap. It would work like this. Inequality moves upward because of any combination of economic, structural, and political factors. People notice the higher level of inequality but do not really see it as a problem because they adjust their preferences to align with the current situation. Some detailed experimental analysis of the system justification argument with respect to attitudes toward inequality shows that people are strongly affected by status quo bias when evaluating income distributions and expressing preferences for redistributive interventions (Trump 2013).

In summary, it is clear that there are competing theoretical claims about how public opinion might respond to changes in inequality. The traditional thermostatic model of opinion in concert with classic political economy models imply that opinion will become more progressive and favorable toward redistributive policies that would ameliorate inequality as inequality rises. On the other hand, several possible factors could undermine the thermostatic link between inequality and public opinion. In fact, some research points to the possibility that rising inequality could actually generate the opposite of a thermostatic opinion response to inequality, with opinion shifting in a conservative direction as inequality rises thereby reinforcing inequality even if government responds effectively to public preferences.

A Look at New Macro-Level Evidence

The discussion above points to the possibility that connections between economic inequality and public opinion are not self-correcting, as in a thermostatic system that prevents economic inequality from moving too far in one direction or the other. In one scenario, inequality and public opinion are simply independent of one another—the public does not pay sufficient attention or connect economic inequality to public policy in ways that allow for the kind of thermostatic relationship that exists in other domains of the political economy. In another scenario, there is a feedback loop between economic inequality and public opinion, but the feedback loop is self-reinforcing rather than self-correcting. Under this scenario rightward shifts in public opinion generate policy changes that increase inequality, and increased inequality generates additional future rightward shifts in opinion that prevent egalitarian policy changes.

Previous work has begun to examine the effect of income inequality on public opinion. Some of the evidence points to self-reinforcing feedback between public opinion and the income distribution. In an analysis of annual income and opinion data from 1952 to 2006, Peter Enns and I (Kelly and Enns 2010) examined how liberalism in the American public's domestic policy attitudes respond to changes in economic inequality. Using the Gini coefficient as a measure of inequality (which, you will recall, emphasizes inequality in the middle of the income distribution) we found that an increase in inequality is associated with future shifts away from progressive policy attitudes. Luttig (2013) finds similar results using a different measure of inequality and analyzing a shorter time period. These results point toward the sort of self-reinforcing connection between inequality and public opinion that could contribute to an inequality trap.[6]

I extend these analyses in at least three important ways here. First, I account for the possibility of feedback between public opinion and economic inequality. Existing work examines only the effect of income inequality on public opinion, and the statistical techniques utilized in this previous work explicitly assume that causation is going in only one direction. The very idea of a self-reinforcing link between inequality and public opinion raises the possibility of a bidirectional relationship. The approach used here relaxes that assumption. Second, I extend the time series analyzed forward by eight years, from 2006 to 2014. This provides an ability to account for Obama's first term and part of his second term and increases the number of years analyzed by nearly 15 percent. Third, I utilize a measure of inequality that focuses on the top of the income distribution. Most previous studies use measures of inequality that focus on the middle of the income distribution. The theoretical framework outlined in chapter 2 is focused on the distribution of power, particularly how rising inequality can place increasing power in the hands of those at the very top of the income distribution. This argues for a measure focused on the extent to which those at the very top pull away from others economically. I use the income share of the top 0.01 percent.[7]

To measure public opinion, I utilize domestic public mood, which was charted above.[8] Mood has several important benefits and a handful of potential problems worthy of discussion. Public mood is a highly aggregated time series measure of public opinion. It combines preferences across dozens of issue domains and hundreds of thousands of individual survey responses, capturing the general sentiment of public opinion on matters of domestic policy. As I have coded it, increasing values of public mood indicate increasing conservatism of public opinion.

The aggregate time series nature of public mood has two key benefits in the context of this analysis. First, aggregating public opinion increases the signal-to-noise ratio in the measure. Whereas individual measures of public opinion are highly variable and often move at random, aggregating public opinion across individuals produces a more stable and meaningful signal (Stimson 1999). To the extent that elected officials respond to public opinion, it appears they are most likely to respond to the general contours of public sentiment rather than unique preferences on a single issue (Stimson 2004). Second, considering opinion collectively across a wide variety of issues guards against excluding attitudes toward policies that have distributional consequences. Previous research has shown that government can shape distributional outcomes through a variety of policy mechanisms, not just the explicit redistribution of taxes and transfers (Hacker and Pierson 2010, Kelly 2009, B. Page and Simmons 2000). As Kenworthy and McCall (2008) argue, it is a mistake to examine only attitudes toward programs that explicitly redistribute income across economic groups. By including attitudes in essentially every domestic policy domain, public mood insures that programs that redistribute income as well as those that shape economic opportunity are considered.

This second benefit of public mood also has its drawbacks. While it is useful to look at public opinion broadly construed to get a sense of how the general ideological preferences of citizens respond to changes in inequality, lumping all opinions together prevents examination of more specific attitudes. Survey coverage of attitudes toward redistributive programs and programs focused on economic opportunity is simply insufficient to allow for an analysis of annual change over any significant length of time. Micro-level data does, however, allow for an examination of attitudes toward redistribution as well as programs that both redistribute income and shape the market in ways that affect economic opportunity at less regular intervals. Because of this, I also analyze micro-level public opinion data in the section to follow. By utilizing a combination of aggregate time series and micro-level data, I attempt to discern the extent to which each type of analysis (with its particular weaknesses and strengths) paints a similar picture with regard to economic inequality and public opinion.

The first results that I report are based on an analysis of annual data, with the two key variables being top income shares and public mood conservatism as described above. The temporal nature of the data allows me to examine the timing of changes in both public opinion and income inequality. This provides the opportunity to consider causation flowing in either or both directions between these two key variables. And, of course, we are not limited to examining only opinion and inequality. In fact, the models I discuss below include other variables that might indirectly link opinion to inequality. That is, if public opinion shapes distributional outcomes, the effect is not likely direct. Instead, at least some of the effect of opinion might happen because shifts in opinion first lead to changes in election and policy outcomes that then affect inequality.[9] We can sort those kinds of issues out to some extent with temporal data. The fact that we can observe variation over time also helps to avoid the potential for spurious correlation. While there is no way to overcome the inherently associational nature of data on observed public opinion and inequality, our confidence in results can be raised by the fact that each variable is modeled as a function of its own previous values and *lagged* values of the other variables in the system. Any variables that explain the current value of the outcome also likely explain previous values. So by controlling for prior values of the outcome, any important variables excluded from the analysis are in large part accounted for.

Figure 3.2 provides a visual depiction of the public opinion–economic inequality feedback loop.[10] Essentially, these charts show how the path of one variable would change if there was a hypothetical, standard deviation increase in the value of another variable. The results show some evidence of an opinion-inequality feedback loop that is consistent with an inequality trap. Figure 3.2a simulates what happens to top income shares when public opinion shifts to the right. The results are noisy and never reach statistical significance, which is consistent with a high degree of slippage between changes in general public opinion and an economic outcome like income inequality. But there is the hint of a positive relationship in which conservative public opinion translates into higher levels of inequality than would otherwise exist. Figure 3.2b shows how opinion responds to rising

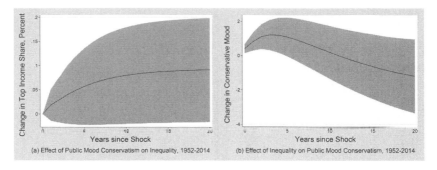

(a) Effect of Public Mood Conservatism on Inequality, 1952-2014   (b) Effect of Inequality on Public Mood Conservatism, 1952-2014

3.2. Is there a reciprocal relationship between inequality and public opinion?
Source: Author's calculations from annual data, 1952 to 2014.
Note: Charts plot orthogonalized cumulative impulse response functions based on a vector autoregression including top 0.01 percent income share and public mood conservatism. Models also include the top capital gains tax rate, top income tax rate, financial deregulation, and congressional partisanship. The plot represents the predicted effect of a standard deviation shift in one variable on the other variable over a twenty-year period.

inequality. Here again the results are less than clear. In the first several years after an increase in inequality, opinion responds by becoming more conservative, but this effect goes away over time.

The results here, then, are consistent with the traditional form of a trap in which rising inequality fails to produce a political response to undo it. First of all, the effects of public opinion on distributional outcomes are highly uncertain. There is a good possibility that shifts to the right in public opinion eventually translate into policy changes that produce more inequality. The results here point in that direction, and other studies focused solely on that question have found evidence of such a relationship. But we know that the effects of public opinion on outcomes are highly contingent and that the policy-making process in the United States can muddle the effects of mass preferences on outcomes (Achen and Bartels 2016, B. Page and Gilens 2017). All this is to say that even when people want more equal outcomes, the political process makes it challenging for them to get what they want.

But the evidence here also suggests that what they want does not change in a self-correcting way to rising inequality. Over the long term there is little effect of inequality on mass preferences. And in the short term the public seems to respond by slightly *increasing* its preference for conservative policies in the face of rising inequality. That is a self-reinforcing pattern as opposed to a self-correcting one. While it is important to point out that at any given time there is widespread support for a variety of redistributive policies (B. Page and Jacobs 2009), the signal of public support for such policies does not get stronger when inequality is higher. This makes it unlikely that mass preferences will create a backlash to rising inequality sufficient to generate real policy change. In the time series evidence presented here, there is no evidence that the public provides a braking mechanism in the face of rising inequality. But this aggregate analysis leaves many questions unanswered. In the next portion of the analysis I explore what is happening underneath the aggregate time series variation analyzed to this point by examining micro-level variation in public opinion.

Shifting from the Public to People

In the analysis to this point I have been focused on change over time at the aggregate level. The question has been how the public as a whole responds to change in inequality and how those changes in aggregate opinion filter through the political system to influence inequality. We have seen evidence that points toward the possibility of self-reinforcing feedback between inequality and public opinion. While the effect of opinion on inequality is too uncertain to say with clarity that conservative opinion pushes inequality higher, that appears to be the general direction of the relationship. The evidence is somewhat clearer that opinion becomes more conservative in response to rising inequality. But this response is small and impermanent.

The benefit of the aggregate approach to this point is that it enables a direct examination of how opinion and inequality respond to one another over time—it captures the possibility of a self-reinforcing *relationship* fairly directly. And focusing on aggregated public opinion across multiple issue domains ensures that the opinion response is not isolated to one domain and captures attitudes related to both redistribution and economic opportunity. But public mood also captures attitudes toward much more than redistribution and economic opportunity. This could contribute to the noisy estimates and the sensitivity to model specification present in the analysis above.

I now shift gears to look at individual-level attitudes. This individual-level analysis goes beyond the aggregate time series approach in several ways. First, it allows an analysis of attitudes specific to redistribution. Second, it provides the possibility of examining attitudes toward specific policy options that fall under the category of either redistribution or market conditioning/economic opportunity. Generally speaking, this approach allows us to see whether individual-level attitudes change in a manner consistent with the pattern of self-reinforcement, with the focus now on how attitudes change as the context of income concentration in which a person is situated at the national- and/or state-level context changes. The individual-level analysis also allows me to explore some of the mechanisms of self-reinforcement posited above by seeing how the context of income concentration shapes distributional attitudes for different types of people. In the next sections I first analyze general attitudes toward redistribution and then move toward even more specific attitudes toward federal policy proposals that have consequences for the distribution of income.

Individual Attitudes toward Redistribution in General

Between 1978 and 2014, the General Social Survey included an item about individual attitudes toward government redistribution on twenty-two nationally representative surveys. In this item, respondents are presented with the option of placing themselves on a scale in which 1 means that the government ought to reduce the income differences between rich and poor and 7 means that the government should not concern itself with reducing income differences. I have recoded the responses so that scores can range from 0 to 6 with higher scores indicating more support for redistribution. Since the question was asked repeatedly over multiple years, we can consider how variation in national-level inequality is associated with these individual responses in support of redistribution. That is, there is a national-level context of inequality, and we want to know whether support for redistribution is higher or lower when this national-level context of inequality changes, all while controlling for individual-level characteristics.[11] The core question I'm interested in is whether people report different perspectives on government redistribution as national-level inequality changes.[12]

In an initial analysis I focus on how individual attitudes toward redistribution change under differing levels of income concentration. The dependent variable is support for redistribution.[13] The key explanatory variable is national-level inequality in the year of the survey, measured as the share of income going to the top 0.01 percent. I include individual-level controls for income, sex, race/ethnicity, age, and education.[14] The model also includes an interaction term between income and inequality, which allows us to see how the effect of income inequality varies among the rich and the poor.[15]

Examining how the effect of inequality on attitudes toward redistribution changes across individuals with different incomes is important here as a first step in differentiating between the four potential explanations of a self-reinforcing link between inequality and opinion discussed earlier in the chapter. If changing trust in government drives any self-reinforcing feedback effects, then it is unlikely that people at differing income levels would respond differently to increasing inequality since trust in government has largely shifted in tandem across income groups.[16] The same is true of the status quo bias explanation. If it is simply the case that people adjust their acceptance of inequality upward as inequality increases, this should happen across income groups. As well, if a self-reinforcing pattern of opinion and income concentration is generated by elite manipulation of mass opinion, we would expect to see a decline in support for redistribution among both the rich and the poor. The rich would become less supportive of redistribution as inequality rises for self-interested reasons and then convince those in the rest of the income distribution to support their preferred position. Under any of these explanations, rising inequality should predict lower support for redistribution across income groups.

But one of the four mechanisms predicts a different pattern. If ethno-nationalism and/or racist sentiment drives a self-reinforcing connection between inequality and public opinion, the rich and the poor would likely respond differently. Recall that as scarcity becomes a more prominent concern, the psychological response tends to be increased fear of others, a tendency toward out-group bias, and unwillingness to provide resources to others. As inequality increases, scarcity is not necessarily an increasing concern for those at the top of the income distribution. Quite the opposite, in fact. As the rich pull away from the rest, their relative economic position becomes more secure. But for those at the middle and, especially, the bottom, rising income concentration represents a decline in relative economic position and could reasonably trigger a focus on scarcity. This means that those toward the bottom of the income distribution would be more likely than those at the top to respond to rising inequality with less support for redistribution.

The key result is in figure 3.3a. The line in this chart shows the marginal effect of a unit-increase in top income shares on support for redistribution as income increases (along with confidence intervals). Recall that the central question of this analysis is whether people report different preferences for redistribution as inequality rises. In this chart, the answer to that question is yes where the confidence interval does not overlap the zero point identified by the solid horizontal line. If the estimate is negative, that means higher inequality is associated with less support for redistribution while positive values indicate that higher inequality is associated with more support for redistribution. The extreme left portion of the chart shows the effect of inequality on redistribution attitudes among the poorest respondents while the right of the chart shows the same effect for the richest respondents.[17] The results here suggest that attitudes toward redistribution are shaped by

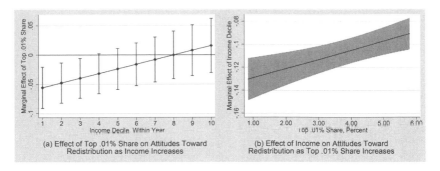

(a) Effect of Top .01% Share on Attitudes Toward
Redistribution as Income Increases

(b) Effect of Income on Attitudes Toward
Redistribution as Top .01% Share Increases

3.3. Attitudes toward redistribution and rising inequality.
Source: Author's calculations from GSS data.
Note: Charts plot the predicted marginal effect of an increase in inequality on support
for redistribution for those with differing levels of family income. Calculations based on
a multilevel logit model including national-level top 0.01 percent income share at time
of survey, race/ethnicity, sex, age, education, and income along with income interacted
with inequality.

the context of income inequality among a subset of low-income Americans.
Higher inequality is associated with less support for redistribution (the estimated effect is negative), but only in the left portion of the chart, which
reports the effect among lower-income individuals. The attitudes of middle-
income Americans are not affected to a statistically significant degree by
inequality, and the richest Americans, if anything, are more supportive of
redistribution as inequality is higher. This pattern is consistent with the predictions of the response-to-scarcity mechanism discussed above, and it is
also consistent with the modest aggregate effects of inequality on opinion
in the earlier time series analysis.

It would be tempting to conclude from these results that rich people
are more supportive of redistribution than the poor, at least as inequality
reaches high levels. But that would be a misinterpretation of the evidence.
It is important to remember that this first chart is reporting the marginal
effect of inequality on attitudes toward redistribution. The fact that the line
is higher among the rich than the poor does not necessarily mean their support for redistribution is higher, but that they are less affected by changes
in inequality than the poor. What we have seen so far is simply that the
self-reinforcing relationship between economic inequality and opinion diminishes as we examine individuals with higher income. This result says
nothing about the effect of income, providing information only about the
effect of inequality as income rises. Figure 3.3b shows clearly that the effect
of higher income is always to reduce support for redistribution regardless

of the level of inequality. There, the marginal effect of income is plotted across all observed levels of inequality. The effect is always negative, with higher income associated with less support for redistribution. The effect of income on reducing support for redistribution is not as strong, however, as inequality increases.

These results are consistent with the time series results reported above. There we saw a small but significant shift toward the right in response to an increase in income concentration. Here we see that focusing on individual attitudes toward redistribution produces a similar pattern. In contexts of higher inequality, some people at the bottom of the income distribution become less supportive of redistribution. The obvious question is why a self-reinforcing response to inequality is most prevalent among the poor. The fact that we see this pattern undermines some potential explanations of a self-reinforcing opinion response to inequality. As discussed above, if status quo bias, trust in government, or elite manipulation are at work, it is unlikely that this self-reinforcing pattern would only be present among the poor.[18] But this pattern is consistent with racial attitudes as a driving force.

To explore the role of racial attitudes explicitly, I start with the model above but add an index of racial bias as well as an interaction between this index and top income shares.[19] This will allow me to assess how the effect of income inequality on attitudes varies for people with differing racial attitudes. We will also be able to see whether the income effect identified above is still present when considered alongside racial attitudes.[20]

Figure 3.4 shows the key results. These charts demonstrate the importance of racial attitudes in shaping attitudes toward redistribution. The left chart shows that those who are more racially biased respond to rising inequality differently than those who are not as biased. While these estimates are quite uncertain, the most biased respondents are the only ones who respond to rising inequality with less support for redistribution. Notably, in results not shown here, the strong moderating effect of income on the effect of rising inequality identified previously is completely eliminated once racial attitudes are accounted for, suggesting that racism is the true driver behind the results to this point. In figure 3.4b we see the effect of racial bias on attitudes toward redistribution as the level of inequality increases. No matter the level of inequality, racism is associated with less support for redistribution. But rising inequality enhances this effect.

The results above reveal an intriguing pattern of individual attitudes toward the general idea of government redistribution. Most interestingly,

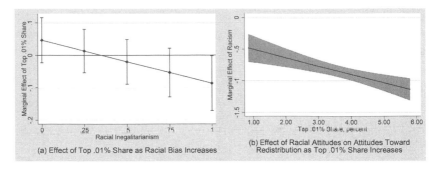

3.4. Racial bias, attitudes toward redistribution, and rising inequality.
Source: Author's calculations from GSS data.
Note: Left chart plots the predicted marginal effect of an increase in inequality on support for redistribution for those with differing levels of racial bias. Right chart plots the predicted marginal effect of an increase in racial bias on support for redistribution for those in increasingly unequal economic contexts. Calculations based on a multilevel logit model including national-level top 0.01 percent income share at time of survey, sex, age, education, racial bias, and income along with income and racial bias interacted with inequality.

there is evidence that rising inequality is associated with less support for redistribution among those toward the bottom of the income distribution. This also means that the preferences of the rich and the poor converge to some extent as inequality increases, which is an interesting finding that will have implications for our discussion of the role of polarization in America's inequality trap in chapter 6. We have also seen that this pattern across income groups can be explained by racial attitudes. Simply stated, those who are more racially biased respond quite differently to rising inequality than those with less racial bias. The self-reinforcing response to rising inequality is isolated to those with the highest levels of racial bias.

This individual-level evidence, of course, does not completely nail down causation. One potential critique is that inequality rises when sentiment becomes more conservative, so the association we observe is not really a response of preferences to rising inequality but a response of inequality to less support for redistribution. There are a couple of reasons not to be overly concerned about this issue. First, the aggregate analysis discussed earlier shows that any effect of public opinion on distributional outcomes takes several years to materialize, so it is unlikely that current attitudes are driving current levels of inequality. Second, when the models here are re-estimated with a control for party identification, the results do not change appreciably. So if attitudes toward redistribution are part of a more general attitudinal shift, statistically holding partisanship constant should go a long way toward ameliorating these concerns.

Individual Attitudes toward Concrete Policies

The individual-level analysis above provides some useful insights in addition to the earlier aggregate-level findings. But the analysis is still incomplete in at least two ways. First, the variation in inequality analyzed above is purely temporal. So it may not be all that surprising that the results corroborate the finding that portions of the population respond to rising inequality by reducing support for redistribution. That is, in both the time series analysis and the individual analysis to this point, inequality varies only over time. Ideally, we would see similar patterns of correlation between attitudes and income concentration when inequality varies across cross-sectional geographic units as opposed to purely over time at the national level. Much larger cross-sectional samples are needed to examine geographic variation in inequality as opposed to temporal variation at the national level. Second, we have been able to analyze questions about general attitudes only toward redistribution. We must turn to a different data source to see whether the patterns noted above for general attitudes are also present for more specific policy attitudes.

For several years, the Cooperative Congressional Election Study (CCES) has collected data on extremely large samples of the American public. Using CCES data, we can analyze large enough samples at the state level to generate reasonable inferences. The state is a useful geographic context within which to consider the effects of inequality. While national-level inequality is important, it is also clear that states have their own political culture and people commonly compare and contrast themselves with people living in other parts of their state (Cramer 2016). This provides an opportunity to determine whether the relationships identified above for the national level extend to geographic variation across the important, yet smaller, political units defined by the American states. The CCES also asks about several policy proposals each year, with these questions referencing specific pieces of legislation voted on in Congress. Below, I utilize data from the 2006 CCES, which asked respondents about their position on a capital gains tax cut as well as the minimum wage.[21] The 2006 CCES includes responses from more than thirty-six thousand respondents, with at least seventy-five respondents from each state.

I start in figure 3.5a with an analysis of attitudes toward the capital gains cut.[22] One of the key features of this policy is that it is explicitly redistributional, and it largely falls on those with high incomes. The underlying model includes a dependent variable coded 1 if the respondent opposes the tax cut and 0 if they support the tax cut. So probability of opposition indicates a pro-redistribution position since capital gains taxes are paid by those with substantial wealth and income. Other individual-level variables included in the model are age, race/ethnicity, sex, education, and income.[23] I include top 1 percent income share at the state level as a contextual variable. I also, as with the GSS analysis above, include an interaction between individual-level income and context-level inequality to present a more nuanced picture of how inequality and income jointly influence attitudes toward redistributive public policy. The results here corroborate the previous analysis. As state-level inequality increases, support for redistribution declines among poorer respondents. Variation in inequality at the state level, however, has little to no effect on those with high income. We also see here, again, that the poor are more likely to support redistribution than the rich but that the attitude gap between those at the bottom and those at the top of the income distribution actually narrows as inequality increases.

The next set of results in figure 3.5b examines support for increasing the minimum wage, using an identical modeling strategy and set of controls.[24] Examining the minimum wage allows me to examine an attitude that is less focused on explicit redistribution than it is ensuring opportunity for low-wage workers. As well, while the capital gains tax focuses on limiting the incomes of those at the top, the minimum wage is focused on increasing incomes at the bottom. We see a somewhat different pattern here. In this case, the poor become *modestly less supportive* of the minimum wage as state-level inequality increases. The rich, however, become *much more supportive* of a minimum wage hike as inequality increases. Together, the effects on the rich and the poor largely cancel out, meaning that in this policy area we do not see clear evidence of a self-reinforcing link between inequality and policy attitudes. Essentially, the rich and poor become indistinguishable on

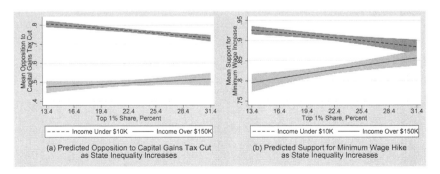

3.5. Support for minimum wage increase among the rich and poor as inequality increases. *Source*: Author's calculations from CCES data.

support for the minimum wage at the highest levels of inequality, and the decline in support among the poor as inequality increases is canceled out by a shift in the opposite direction by the rich.

Conclusions

The analysis in this chapter began with an examination of over sixty years of data that hinted at a pattern of self-reinforcement between economic inequality and public opinion. As inequality increases, public opinion becomes somewhat more conservative, which may produce policy outcomes that maintain high levels of inequality. I then moved to an analysis of individual-level attitudes more specific to redistribution. Using more than a dozen national samples, I presented evidence that suggested a conservative response to rising levels of inequality that is present primarily among the poor. If anything, the rich become more supportive of redistribution as inequality rises while the poor go in the opposite direction, with the shift of poor Americans dominating the aggregate opinion shift.

We saw similar patterns when I shifted to analyzing a very large single cross-section where specific policy attitudes were the outcome of interest. There, however, we saw that there is not a uniform self-reinforcing response to rising inequality across all policy domains. Patterns among the rich and the poor were consistent no matter the outcome analyzed, but when analyzing attitudes toward the minimum wage there was no discernible aggregate shift away from support for the minimum wage as inequality increased.

Additional analysis suggested that racial attitudes are the primary driver of these patterns. People who are more racially biased respond quite differently to rising inequality than those with more egalitarian racial attitudes. It is only those with a high degree of racial bias who respond to rising inequality in a self-reinforcing manner. And once racial attitudes are accounted for, the differential responses to rising inequality across income groups are no longer present.

None of the analyses in this chapter considered separately, it should be noted, can completely identify the causal effect of inequality on public opinion. But, taken together, the variety of approaches all point in the same general direction. Whether we looked at aggregate movement over time on highly aggregated measures of public opinion or micro-level variation in attitudes toward specific policies, there was some evidence of a self-reinforcing link between inequality and public opinion. The evidence is consistent with the conclusion that public preferences and the ways that people respond to changing inequality contribute to America's inequality trap.

So how central a role does public opinion play in perpetuating an inequality trap? I would call mass preferences a coconspirator rather than a primary culprit. Opinion is at least a coconspirator because there isn't a clear thermostatic response to rising inequality. If the public sent a decidedly stronger signal in support of egalitarian policy in the face of rising inequality, opinion would be off the hook as a contributor to the inequality trap. Without a strong opinion signal in support of redistribution as inequality rises, though, mass preferences at the very least make it easier for high levels of inequality to be maintained once they are in place. And to the extent that there is an opinion response to rising inequality, it appears that support for redistributive policies actually declines among at least a subset of the population.

That said, there is good reason not to assign too much blame to public opinion. First of all, there is generally a high degree of support for redistributive programs in the American public. If the majority of Americans got what they wanted on redistribution and policies promoting economic opportunity, we would have at least a somewhat more egalitarian economy. For a variety of reasons, some of which I return to in chapters 5 and 6, policy outcomes are often not aligned with broad mass preferences. In the end, the effects of public opinion on distributional outcomes are modest and diffuse, and this argues against public opinion as a key linchpin in the spiral of inequality.

Secondly, self-reinforcing opinion responses to rising inequality are fairly limited and uncertain. Public opinion does not appear to help much in terms of escaping the inequality trap, but it also does not respond in a way that is likely to push rising inequality even higher. It is only among a poorer and frankly more racist segment of society that preferences respond in a self-reinforcing way as inequality rises. And the aggregate response is relatively small and impermanent.

Finally, there is some potential for the opinion response to rising inequality to become different as time goes along. There are some signs that opinion may begin to respond in a self-correcting way to income concentration in the future. Chief among these signs is experimental work showing that presenting people with clear evidence regarding inequality, priming them to be concerned about inequality, and helping them connect disparities in economic outcomes to disparities in economic opportunities can lead to increased support for egalitarian policies (McCall, Burk, Laperrière, and Richeson 2017). Most studies examining responses to inequality in the real world, however, suggest that the conditions present in these experimental settings are not the norm.[25] But this could change if progressive policy makers begin to discuss economic inequality in different terms and conservative politicians reduce their reliance on racial animus as a political strategy.

The bottom line here is that the way the public responds to rising inequality plays at least some small role in perpetuating America's inequality trap. You will need to read on to learn about some of the more central culprits. Next up is election outcomes.

FOUR

Elections and the Inequality Trap

Elections have consequences. That's what we hear over and over again when new leaders take office. It's a statement designed to remind opponents that they lost and that they have a responsibility to acquiesce to the will of the people as expressed in the latest election. The "will of the people" is, of course, a complicated idea. The notion that winning an election represents a popular endorsement of every policy position taken by a candidate in an election is obviously wrong (Achen and Bartels 2016). Voters have many things in their minds when they vote, and policy preferences are often not at the forefront. Even for those who are voting on policy grounds, the calculus is complex when there are but a few candidates, none of whom match one's policy preferences perfectly. And ranking candidates based on their relative policy desirability may produce different rankings on different policies. All these calculations are summarized in a simple, categorical voting decision.

But in some ways it doesn't really matter whether voters are sending a policy signal with their selections in the voting booth. What matters is how elected officials behave in light of the latest election outcome. If a political party gains or expands its legislative majority or attains control of the executive branch, that matters. And there are times when election results are broadly viewed as a policy mandate for newly elected leaders (Grossback, Peterson, and Stimson 2006). Regardless of whether the public is capable of sending a true policy message via an election, it is no doubt true that elections have consequences. When different elected leaders with different policy preferences take power, they generally use that power to pursue their preferred policy outcomes. This is perhaps seen most clearly during a presidential transition, in which the new president takes large numbers of executive actions to both roll back actions of the previous administration and do what is possible through executive action (both symbolic and substantive) to shift outcomes in a new direction. The legislative process is obviously much more convoluted and requires a great deal of compromise, and I'll talk about this fact more in the next two chapters, but even in the legislative realm it is clear that changes happen when the balance of power shifts. Those who say that all politicians are basically the same and decry the two parties as presenting a false choice are just wrong. Strong progressives and conservatives alike can legitimately critique their preferred parties for lacking ideological purity, but there should be no question that election outcomes make a difference for how society functions, the outcomes that are pursued, the strategies for pursing them, and the results produced.

Over the past fifteen years, scholars from a variety of disciplines have been exploring the question of whether elections have consequences for the income gap between the rich and the poor. At least since the New Deal, Democrats have been seen as the more propoor, proworker party while Republicans have tended to be more supportive of the interests of business and those with high incomes. This pattern, of course, is far from perfect. But for most of the twentieth century it is not difficult to craft a narrative in which we would expect to see income gaps rise under Republicans and decline under Democrats. To be sure, the recent path of inequality points to the conclusion that the distribution of income is not *fully* controllable by public policy. Economic and demographic conditions matter powerfully, and inequality has risen for decades regardless of party control of national policy-making institutions.

But several analyses that examine the effects of election outcomes and income inequality have shown that inequality tends to rise more when Republicans have more power and less when Democrats are in charge. While inequality cannot be fully controlled through the political process, the consequences of elections do appear to extend to distributional outcomes. There is certainly still debate about the details of the political underpinnings of inequality, but we have substantial evidence that which party gains power in policy-making institutions and the content of the policies they enact affect the dynamics of economic inequality over time (Bartels 2008, Kelly 2009, Volscho and Kelly 2012).

The question I turn to in this chapter, though, is not whether election outcomes affect inequality but whether inequality feeds back into politics by shaping election outcomes. Elections, in this chapter, are another possible pathway for inequality to shape politics in either a self-reinforcing or self-correcting pattern. In the previous chapter the focus was on public opinion. As I will discuss below, many of the same factors that connect opinion and inequality might generate a similar feedback effect between inequality and election outcomes. By shifting the focus to election outcomes and voting behavior I ascertain whether the attitudinal patterns discussed earlier also reveal themselves in political behavior.

Mechanisms of Self-Reinforcement through Electoral Outcomes

In the last chapter we saw at least some evidence pointing to a self-reinforcing relationship between economic inequality and public opinion. The same factors that contribute to a nonthermostatic opinion response to rising inequality could also be observed in election outcomes if the attitudinal patterns uncovered previously translate into political behavior in the voting booth. To the extent that rising inequality is associated with an increase in conservative preferences that then increase support for Republican candidates, we would see a pattern of self-reinforcement through the pathway of election outcomes. But there are several mechanisms in addition to opinion to consider when voting behavior and elections are of interest. Beyond the various ways that inequality can shape elections through public opinion, I discuss turnout effects, gerrymandering, and geographic sorting below.

The Broken Opinion Thermostat

The thermostatic model that was the theoretical focus for much of the discussion in the previous chapter is one aspect of a broader system-level theory of American politics explicated most fully in *The Macro Polity* (Erikson, Mac-Kuen, and Stimson 2002). In this model, public opinion translates systematically into voting behavior and election outcomes, which produce policy outcomes that become objects of evaluation for the mass public thereby evolving into new inputs for the overall system. Shifts to the left in public opinion produce enhanced power for Democrats in policy-making institutions. Democratic power in national politics produces more left-leaning policies that, in the context of inequality, reduce income concentration.[1]

It does not seem to be the case that distributional outcomes feed back on public opinion in the self-correcting manner represented by a thermostat. And if the remaining parts of the macropolitics model are operative, the opinion response we saw in the last chapter could quite readily contribute to a broader set of self-reinforcing connections between inequality and American politics. If a move toward the right in the public mood produces election outcomes more favorable to Republicans, then the rightward shift in opinion as a response to rising inequality among some citizens that we saw previously would undermine support for Democratic politicians and make egalitarian policy shifts less likely. In other words, the self-reinforcing connection between inequality and opinion could feed forward in the system to election outcomes.

Therefore, the same potential underpinnings for the connection between inequality and opinion could apply to elections. In the context of opinion, I mentioned ethnonationalistic/group-biased responses to scarcity, trust in government, elite domination, and status quo bias as potential explanations for the self-reinforcing pattern. I argued that the fact that the attitudes of the rich and the poor often respond in very different ways to rising inequality points toward group-biased responses to scarcity as the most likely explanation. That racial attitudes were such an important moderator of the self-reinforcing opinion response to rising inequality further supports this conclusion. The focus in this chapter is how these four mechanisms might play a role in shaping *electoral* responses to rising inequality.

Turnout

Attitudes seem to respond to inequality in a self-reinforcing manner. But how does political behavior change as inequality rises and falls? Recent research has discussed the possibility that the decision to vote is tied to the ebb and flow of economic inequality. Some of this work relies on cross-national evidence, while other work focuses on variation over time and across geography in the American states. This is potentially important if we are concerned about how election outcomes respond to changes in income concentration. If upward shifts in income concentration generate a more upper-class-biased electorate, this could create an additional path through which inequality shapes election outcomes since there is evidence that the class composition of the electorate has an effect on who is elected, what policies are pursued, and how distributional outcomes shift (Franko, Kelly, and Witko 2016). One can also see the possibility here of a feedback loop between inequality and election outcomes with turnout as an intervening variable closing the feedback loop.[2]

One of the clearest expositions of the inequality-turnout connection comes from Frederick Solt (2008, 2010). Solt discusses three theories of economic inequality and political participation, with varying predictions about the nature of the relationship. The first is relative power theory (Goodin and Dryzek 1980). From this perspective, the electoral participation of both rich and poor citizens should decline with rising inequality, but this effect is larger for the poor than the rich. This theory is rooted in the view that economic and political power are intertwined. If money translates into political

power broadly construed, those with more income will have disproportion-
ate effects on the issue agenda and in defining the scope of political conflict
(Goodin and Dryzek 1980, Solt 2008). As inequality rises, under this view,
the ability (intentional or not) of the rich to prevent discussion of issues
on which there is a class divide increases as well (Schattschneider 1960).
As issues that are important to those lower in the income distribution are
deemphasized in political debate, their incentives to vote will decline. To a
lesser extent, the payoff for voting would also be diminished for the rich as
issues that evidence class cleavages are moved to the periphery of politics.
This theory is closely connected to the elite domination theory of public
opinion mentioned earlier.

A second theory of inequality and turnout is conflict theory (H. Brady
2004). Conflict theory predicts *increased* turnout as opposed to decreased
turnout in response to rising inequality. The well-known political economy
model of Meltzer and Richard (1981), which I have referenced before, starts
with the very simple supposition that policy preferences are connected to
one's position in the income distribution. While this pattern is far from
perfect, there is overwhelming evidence that this is true in the United States.
Specifically with regard to distributional preferences, the poor are much
more supportive of redistribution than the rich. Conflict theory posits that
as inequality increases the preferences of the rich and the poor will diverge.
Most importantly, as preferences diverge, political conflict should increase,
and the perceived benefits of voting should increase across the income distribution. But if inequality is lower, there should be greater political consensus, which reduces the payoffs for participation in elections.[3]

The third relevant theory on this point is resource theory (H. Brady,
Verba, and Schlozman 1995). Resource theory predicts that inequality will
have quite different effects on turnout for those at different points in the
income distribution. At its core, resource theory argues that the likelihood of
electoral participation is driven by the resources available to an individual.
A person will take on the costs of participation if they are able to afford
them. While individuals can obtain relevant resources for participation in
a variety of contexts, those with less income are less able to participate in
politics than those with higher income. As the income gap increases, then,
participatory gaps are predicted to rise as well. As the relative resources of
the poor decline, their participation is expected to decline as well. But for
the rich, the effect is just the opposite, with increasing inequality enhancing
participation. It is important to note, however, that voting is the type of participation least likely to be affected by the availability of economic resources.

Each of these theories has quite different implications for the turnout effects of rising inequality. To understand these divergent implications it is key to understand that it is *relative* participation that is relevant for understanding the feedback effects of inequality via this pathway. Previous research points to class bias in voter turnout, or the degree to which electoral participation is associated with income, as an explanation of distributional outcomes (Franko, Kelly, and Witko 2016). Turnout gaps between the rich and the poor produce less egalitarian state-level policies that serve to increase income inequality (Franko, Kelly, and Witko 2016, Leighley and Nagler 2007). The resource model, then, predicts a self-reinforcing connection between inequality and turnout patterns. Inequality rises; this drives up the turnout of the rich and reduces the turnout of the poor, widening class bias in turnout, which then reinforces inequality. Relative power theory also predicts a self-reinforcing pattern between inequality and turnout since the electoral participation of the poor is reduced more than that of the rich as inequality rises. But the self-reinforcing effects are not nearly as strong in this framework as the resource framework. Finally, conflict theory essentially predicts no self-reinforcing pattern of inequality and electoral participation. Using cross-national analysis of survey data, Solt (2008) finds a pattern most consistent with the relative power perspective. Electoral participation declines dramatically for the poorest respondents when inequality increases and has a negative effect on all but the richest respondents. He finds similar effects in an analysis of state-level variation in turnout (Solt 2010) as well as campaign contributions (Ritter and Solt 2019).

Levine's (2015) work suggests much the same pattern with a different underlying theoretical mechanism and relying on a different analytical approach. He uses an experimental approach and focuses on types of participation other than voting to show that many of the economic challenges that have contributed to rising inequality are demobilizing. But rather than focus on strategic calculations or economic incentives, he points to the rhetoric surrounding economic insecurity as the culprit in undermining participation. Reminding people that their situation is economically precarious makes them less likely to support political causes and participate in politics. In sum, rising inequality could produce changes in turnout patterns that disadvantage Democratic candidates thereby furthering a pattern of self-reinforcing inequality. At the same time, however, this work highlights the possibility that forms of participation other than voting are likely most sensitive to resource constraints and priming of scarcity considerations. So it is far from clear that any self-reinforcing pattern of inequality and election outcomes is driven by turnout responses to rising inequality. I will explore this possibility more directly below.

Political Geography and Partisan Gerrymandering

Another set of factors that could produce inequality-reinforcing electoral outcomes relates to political geography and partisan gerrymandering. One of the favorite targets of progressive reformers is the redistricting process. The argument goes something like this. Republicans win state legislatures. Those legislatures then take charge of the redistricting process and draw lines that make it increasingly hard for Democrats to win state legislatures and the US House. If redistricting were taken out of the hands of politicians who draw lines for political purposes and were shifted to nonpartisan entities charged with drawing districts based on nonpolitical criteria, this problem could be overcome and electoral competition could be restored.

There is an attraction to this argument. If partisan gerrymandering has increased with rising inequality, this gerrymandering has systematically disadvantaged Democrats, and reforms could undermine partisan gerrymandering and restore electoral parity, it provides a clear policy recommendation for undermining one source of self-reinforcing inequality. And the evidence for the power of partisan gerrymandering is, on its face, pretty powerful. House seats are increasingly safe. Much of the electoral competition in the House has shifted from general elections to primaries, with politicians fearing the loss of their job as much or more because of a primary challenge than losing to an opponent from the other party. These strategic incentives would pull members of both parties away from the general election center toward more extreme activist segments of their primary-participating, ideologically extreme party voters. One of the most popular presentations of this argument is provided in the elegantly titled book by Daley (2016). McGann, Smith, Latner, and Keena (2016) provide a less elegant title but more rigorous presentation of this argument, complete with careful social scientific analysis.

The problem is that there is quite a lot of evidence that partisan gerrymandering does not play a *decisive* role in any systemic advantages currently accruing to Republicans in legislative races. One way to think about a systematic partisan tilt in legislative races is to compare the seat share won by a party to the vote share in an election. If a party gets a greater proportion of seats than votes, that suggests something about the electoral institutions is giving them a systematic advantage. Looking at recent results from US House elections points to an advantage for Republicans. In 2016, Republicans received less than 50 percent of votes cast in House races but received over 55 percent of the seats. A similar pattern held in 2014 and 2012 as well. Since Republicans took control of several state legislatures prior to the 2010 redistricting cycle, this would seem to point to partisan gerrymandering as a source of this Republican "seat bonus" in the US House.

However, this Republican "bonus" has been around for several election cycles and was in place prior to the latest round of redistricting. While some of this bonus could be explained by previous partisan gerrymandering, there are a few pieces of evidence that undermine gerrymandering as the explanation. First, drilling down into the state data shows that the Republican seat bonus exists about as often in states where Democratic legislatures or non-partisan entities conducted the latest redistricting as in states where Republicans controlled the redistricting process. Second, states with large urban populations were more likely than those with larger rural populations to have a Republican seat bonus.

This evidence is largely consistent with an argument made by Chen and Rodden (2013), who suggest that while partisan gerrymandering may be a partial explanation for a systemic Republican advantage in Congress, the more important explanation is rooted in political geography. Looking at any recent electoral map in red and blue makes it clear that Democratic voters are clustered around urban centers while Republicans are spread out over a much wider geographical area. This geographic sorting, which has increasingly been the object of scholarly attention (Bishop 2009, Reardon and Bischoff 2011, Sharkey 2013), helps to explain how Democrats could be disadvantaged in ways that go beyond partisan gerrymandering. The clustering of Democratic voters in high-density urban centers makes it difficult to draw competitive electoral districts. Since Democrats are clustered in high-density areas, Republican voters are more likely to have an efficient distribution of voters. Landslide victories in legislative races may make for safe seats, but winning by too much creates wasted votes. That is, you don't need to win with a 60 percent margin—you only need 50 percent plus 1. Any extra votes could be allocated to a different district in order to maximize overall seat share in a legislature.

Democratic voters, simply stated, are distributed in a wildly inefficient way. It would, in fact, take a great deal of intentional effort to undo the Republican advantages created by geographic sorting through redistricting. Urban areas would have to be sliced and diced and lumped together with much larger low-density areas. Such districts could be competitive and create a more level playing field in some senses, but the districts would also violate many of the districting criteria that reformers often discuss, such as geographic, economic, and social contiguity. The focus on geographic sorting also generates a plausible expectation that the Democratic electoral disadvantage goes beyond the House of Representatives. If political gerrymandering is the heart of the problem, the electoral effects should be restricted to the House. If the issue is really geographic sorting, then effects are more likely to be seen in the Senate and the electoral college.

Whether the explanation for an increasing Democratic disadvantage in legislative elections is rooted in gerrymandering or geographic sorting, it provides a potential pathway for a self-reinforcing relationship between inequality and elections. The key question is whether the Republican advantage has increased over time, and there is some evidence that patterns of geographic sorting are partially explained by rising inequality (Reardon and Bischoff 2011). So part of the goal of this chapter is to explore whether political geography and/or political gerrymandering have contributed to self-reinforcing feedback between inequality and elections.

Do Elections Contribute to an Inequality Trap?

The above discussion suggests several questions related to potential feedback between economic inequality and election outcomes in the United States. The first question I focus on is whether, in fact, election outcomes and economic inequality are connected in a self-reinforcing system as in figure 4.1. The best way to gain leverage on this initial question is to examine how economic inequality and election outcomes have unfolded over time. There is quite a lot of existing evidence that election outcomes shape distributional outcomes, with Democratic victories associated with less inequality than Republican victories. But to my knowledge none of these previous tests allowed for the possibility of feedback from inequality to elections. The analysis that follows allows assessment of the nature of any feedback processes between inequality and election outcomes in either direction.

The results reported below rely on an analysis of annual data on economic inequality and partisan power in national political institutions from 1913 to 2014. I examine connections between inequality and partisan power

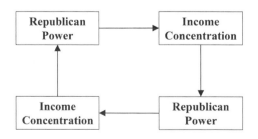

4.1. A self-reinforcing pattern of elections and inequality.

in the House, Senate, and presidency in three separate analyses.[4] As in much of the analysis to this point, inequality is measured as the share of income (including capital gains) flowing to the top 0.01 percent of tax units from the World Inequality Database (http://wid.world). Partisan power in the presidency is measured with a dichotomous indicator that equals 1 when the president is a Democrat and 0 otherwise. For the House and the Senate, I separately measure for each chamber the percentage of seats held by Democrats.[5] The goal is as parsimonious a model as possible while including variables that could provide indirect linkages between the two primary variables in each model.

By examining changes over time in income concentration and election outcomes, I can utilize information about the timing of movement to learn about the nature of feedback between inequality and partisan power. Essentially, these models allow me to answer two key questions. When inequality increases at one point in time, does partisan power change at later points in time while controlling for the current and past balance of partisan power? And when the balance of partisan power shifts, does inequality change at future points in time while accounting for current and past levels of inequality? In each set of results there are two charts. One reports the effect of a shift toward the Democratic Party (from Republican to Democratic control of the presidency or an increase in seat share in the House or Senate) on top income shares. The other reports the effect of an increase in top income share on Democratic power. So that we can see when effects are present, the effects of the increase are calculated over a twenty-year time horizon in each set of analyses.[6] Importantly, these charts account for feedback effects between inequality and politics. So the charts take account of the fact that a shift in partisan power at a particular point in time could lead to additional changes in the future due to feedback from inequality. This is the key reason why we see such large effects in some of the analyses below.

I start with the results for the House in figure 4.2. The left chart shows how inequality responds to a standard deviation increase in Democratic seat share in the House. Over the entire twenty-year time horizon, the presence of Democratic legislators in the House reduces top income shares. When more Democrats are elected in the lower chamber of Congress, inequality becomes lower than when Republican are elected. And those effects happen over a lengthy period of time. The right chart shows the reverse effect—the response of Democratic seat share to an increase in inequality. When inequality rises, there is a substantial drop in Democratic seat share. I will return in a moment to more on the scale of this effect.

What do these results have to say about the nature of feedback between

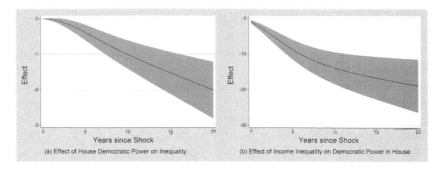

(a) Effect of House Democratic Power on Inequality   (b) Effect of Income Inequality on Democratic Power in House

4.2. Is there a reciprocal relationship between inequality and House elections?
Source: Author's calculations from annual data, 1913 to 2014.
Note: Charts plot orthogonalized cumulative impulse response functions based on a vector autoregression including top 0.01 percent income share and the percentage of Democratic seats in the House of Representatives. Models also include union strength, financial deregulation, and the top capital gains tax rate. The plot represents the predicted effect of a standard deviation shift in one variable on the other variable over a twenty-year period.

inequality and election outcomes? Simply stated, inequality and House elections evidence temporal association that is consistent with an inequality-reinforcing feedback loop. When Democrats are elected to the House, inequality is lower than it would otherwise be with greater Republican power. But if Republicans gain power, inequality is higher than it would otherwise be. As inequality rises, the representation of Democrats in the House is reduced. This reduction in Democratic power is associated with future increases in inequality, thereby closing the self-reinforcing feedback loop.

When analyzing House elections, evidence for inequality-reinforcing feedback is strong. But does this pattern extend to Senate and presidential election outcomes? It is important to come to grips with this question, first, to determine how extensive the inequality-election feedback loop is. But this question is also important because it sheds light on the extent to which partisan gerrymandering might play a role in supporting this feedback loop. Of House, Senate, and presidential elections, only the House is elected in geographic districts that are drawn via an ongoing political process. State lines are fixed, so the geographic constituency of Senators is fixed as well. Since presidential elections are determined by electoral votes assigned by state, the situation for presidential elections is similar to the Senate. If political gerrymandering is part of the equation here, we should see much weaker results for Senate and presidential elections. And if political gerrymandering is the sole force generating a self-reinforcing inequality-election feedback cycle, then the effects observed for the House should be completely nonexistent in Senate and presidential elections.

Figure 4.3 shows the results for an analysis identical to the one reported above for the House, but now with Senate and presidential election outcomes considered respectively. Figures 4.3a and 4.3b show the results for the Senate. The left chart shows the effect of Democratic seat share in the Senate on top income shares, and the right chart shows the reverse effect. As with the House, the results for the Senate are consistent with a pattern of self-reinforcing inequality. Democratic power in the Senate reduces inequality and increased inequality reduces Democratic seat share in the Senate. Figures 4.3c and 4.3d show the results for presidential elections. Again, the results are similar to those for the House and Senate, though the results are much noisier for the president, which is not surprising given that party power changes less often in the White House than in Congress.[7]

Increasing Democratic power tends to reduce inequality, and Republicans do better electorally as inequality rises. But is the magnitude of the feedback effect similar across all three institutions? Making comparisons across

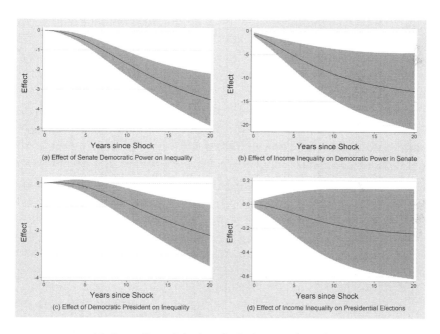

4.3. Inequality and elections for the Senate and presidency.
Source: Author's calculations from annual data, 1913 to 2014.
Note: Charts plot orthogonalized cumulative impulse response functions based on VARs. Models include the percentage of Democratic seats in the Senate or Democratic control of presidency along with top 0.01 percent income share. Models also include union strength, financial deregulation, and the top capital gains tax rate. The plot represents the predicted effect of a standard deviation shift in one variable on the other variable over a twenty-year period.

the three sets of results sheds light on the extent to which partisan gerrymandering may be to blame for the trap-like pattern of self-reinforcement
we see in these results. It is fairly straightforward to look back and see that
the feedback effects are strongest in the House, followed by the Senate, and
then the presidency. The key is to examine how partisan power responds
to rising inequality. When inequality increases by a standard deviation, the
cumulative effect is a 20 percent reduction in seat share in the House, a
12 percent reduction in seat share in the Senate, and statistically insignificant reduction in the probability of a Democratic president.[8]

A couple of key points can be drawn from these results. First, the results
suggest that something more than political gerrymandering is driving the
feedback loop. There may be many other good arguments for removing redistricting from partisan legislatures, and the fact that the feedback effect
here is largest in the House and smallest for the president does point to at
least some partisan gerrymandering effects. But the fact that we observe this
feedback effect in both House and Senate elections suggests that there is
more going on here than just political gerrymandering. Geographic sorting
in tandem with institutions that fail to allocate representation proportional
to votes is likely a big part of the story. While the consistency of results across
both legislative chambers suggests that the sorting effect is not restricted
to the congressional district level, sorting could be happening at both the
district and the state levels in ways that contribute to the patterns observed
here. Second, it is useful to note previous results finding that election outcomes affect the distribution of income are reproduced here, even when
the modeling strategy used accounts for two-way causation. Across both
legislative chambers as well as the presidency, we see partisan effects on
income inequality.[9]

The Micro Underpinnings of Inequality-Reinforcing Elections

Analysis of aggregate time series is very helpful in determining whether self-
reinforcing feedback between inequality and politics is present. In fact, I
think it is the key evidence in this part of the inequality trap. But such analysis does little to explain why such a pattern exists. In the previous chapter, I identified four micro-level processes that might generate changes in
public opinion that could also undermine the ability of Democrats to win
elections. Four potential explanations for such patterns were introduced:
(1) ethnonationalism and general in-group bias in response to relative deprivation, (2) declining trust, in which people who have become less trusting of government respond to rising inequality with increasing skepticism

of policies to reduce the gap between the rich and the poor, (3) elite domination in which increasing economic stratification provides economic elites with the power to shape the political context in a way that undermines linkages between objective interests and the expressed preferences of those lower in the income distribution, and (4) status quo bias, whereby people simply become accustomed to the status quo and essentially support whatever level of inequality happens to be present at the current time.

In the earlier analysis of opinion I was essentially able to rule out status quo bias as an explanation of the aggregate patterns we saw. The rich and the poor would both respond similarly to rising inequality if this were the explanation. The results showed very different responses based on income, with the poor becoming less supportive of redistribution and the rich becoming more supportive as inequality grows. In the analysis of voting behavior in this chapter I will explore in more detail the potential role of trust and elite dominance as well as extend the analysis of racial identity to voting behavior.

In addition to these explanations for opinion responses to rising inequality, I discussed earlier in this chapter the potential turnout effects of rising inequality. If rising inequality depresses turnout, particularly among the poor, rising inequality could lead to compositional changes in the electorate that would systematically advantage Republicans. I will analyze individual-level turnout in this chapter to assess whether rising inequality has changed electoral participation in a way that helps to support the patterns of self-reinforcing feedback between inequality and election outcomes that we have seen above.

For the remainder of the analysis in this chapter, I will be assessing individual-level variation. Instead of asking how some phenomenon has moved over time using annual time series date, I will ask why some people behave differently than others, using individual-level factors as a core part of the explanation. At the same time, I will consider the context in which people are situated as an additional explanation for their behavior. Similar to the previous chapter, I am interested in how people's behavior changes when they live in a more or less equal economic environment.[10]

A Turnout Effect?

This portion of the analysis begins by examining turnout at the individual level in presidential elections from 1952 to 2012. The data for this analysis come from the American National Election Studies. Respondents are asked whether they voted in the previous November election and are coded 1 if they voted and 0 otherwise.[11] The key explanatory variable is context-level inequality. Here, the context of inequality varies over time at the national level, measured by the top 0.01 percent income share. The goal is to determine whether the likelihood of voting goes up, goes down, or is unaffected by the level of inequality. Along with context-level inequality, I include individual-level measures of income, sex, race and ethnicity, age, and education. The key result is shown in figure 4.4a, which charts the probability of voting on the y-axis as national-level inequality increases on the x-axis. This analysis provides an estimate of how the individual-level probability of voting changes as inequality rises.[12]

The results do not support the hypothesis that turnout has been driven down by rising inequality.[13] Figure 4.4a shows that the probability of voting is essentially flat across increasing values of income concentration. A clearer test, however, of whether rising inequality might generate turnout effects that serve to reinforce inequality comes from comparing the turnout effects of inequality among high- and low-income citizens. Even if income inequality is generally not associated with the probability of voting, it could be the case that this effect differs for people at varying points in the income distribution. To the extent that we have evidence of turnout patterns shaping distributional outcomes, it is the relative turnout of the rich and the poor that matters (Franko, Kelly, and Witko 2016). To examine this possibility I added an interaction term between individual-level income and context-level inequality, which provides the ability to determine whether the effect of inequality on turnout varies by income. Those results are plotted in figure 4.4b. This chart is identical to the previous one, except that now I plot

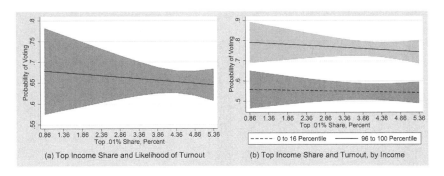

(a) Top Income Share and Likelihood of Turnout   (b) Top Income Share and Turnout, by Income

4.4. Turnout effects of economic inequality.
Source: Author's calculations from ANES data, presidential elections 1952–2012.
Note: Charts plot the predicted probability of self-reported turnout as inequality increases. Calculations based on a multilevel logit model including national-level top 0.01 percent income share at time of election, race/ethnicity, age, education, and income.

predicted probability of turnout for the richest and poorest categories of respondent separately. The results show that, while the rich are more likely than the poor to vote, the turnout gap between the rich and the poor is basically constant regardless of how much income concentration is present. This undermines the idea that the pattern of self-reinforcing election outcomes is produced by the effect of inequality on turnout patterns.

A Voting Behavior Effect?

The next set of results examines voting behavior as the outcome of interest. Here, the dependent variable is the individual-level voting decision, coded 1 for a Democratic House candidate and 0 otherwise.[14] As in the above analysis, the data come from the American National Election Study (1952 to 2012), and the key explanatory variable is context-level inequality measured at the national level with over-time contextual variation. Controls are included for individual-level income, sex, race/ethnicity, age, and education. This analysis allows me to determine whether voters become more or less supportive of Democratic congressional candidates as the context of inequality changes, while holding a variety of demographic characteristics constant.

The results are plotted in figure 4.5, where the probability of voting for a Democratic candidate in the most recent House election is charted on the y-axis and the level of inequality is on the x-axis. As inequality increases, the likelihood of a voter supporting the Democratic candidate declines substantially. In the most equal contexts, the predicted probability of voting for a Democrat is nearly .60 while that probability drops to around .50 in the most unequal contexts. These results do not include a control for voter partisanship. This is intentional since differing contexts of inequality might shape partisan identification and I want to fully capture the association between inequality and vote choice. But the general pattern here continues to hold even when partisanship is included.[15] An additional potential concern about these results is that support for Democratic candidates has simply trended downward along with inequality as support for Democrats in southern states has declined. In order to account for this possibility I reestimated the model above while including a time trend, and the results continue to support the same conclusion.

These results provide a micro-level foundation for what we saw earlier in the aggregate analysis. As inequality increases, support for Democratic candidates erodes. This is yet again a pattern of self-reinforcing inequality. Here we simply see the pattern play out at the individual level. But the analysis to

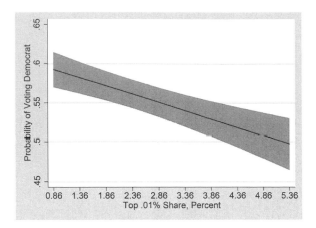

4.5. Individual level voting for Democratic congressional candidates in varying contexts
of inequality.
Source: Author's calculations from ANES data.
Note: Chart plots the predicted probability of support for Democratic House candidate
among those voting in the most recent election as inequality increases. Calculations based
on a multilevel logit model including national-level top 0.01 percent income share at time of
election, race/ethnicity, age, education, and income.

this point still does not help to differentiate between competing theoretical
explanations for why this pattern is present.

Inequality, Declining Trust, and Vote Choice

Using a framework similar to the general analysis of voting behavior and
inequality above, I shift focus here to potential explanations for the general
pattern of declining support for Democrats as inequality increases. One factor that may play a role is trust. As Hetherington (2005) points out, lower
levels of trust in government institutions can undermine support for state
interventions of various types. Since Democrats are generally the party most
likely to support such interventions, it is not a large leap to suggest that low
levels of trust could undermine electoral support for Democratic candidates.

To shed light on this possibility, I again conduct a multilevel analysis
of individual-level voting for House candidates from American National
Election Study (ANES) data.[16] The key explanatory variable is the national
context of inequality, varying over time. In this analysis, in addition to the
controls from the previous set of results, I add a measure of trust in government. This variable is based on responses to a question: "How much of the
time do you think you can trust the government in Washington to do what is
right—just about always, most of the time or only some of the time?" I have

coded the variable so that higher scores indicate higher levels of trust. This measure of trust is also included as an interaction term with context-level inequality. This allows me to determine whether those with different levels of trust in government are affected by inequality in different ways.

If variation in trust is a key factor generating a connection between increasing inequality and declining support for Democrats, these results should reveal a pattern in which the effect of inequality reduces Democratic support more among those with low levels of trust than those with higher levels of trust. I chart the relevant results in figure 4.6. This figure plots the effect that inequality has on support for a Democratic House candidate on the y-axis as trust in government increases along the x-axis.

We see no support for the idea that declining trust drives the connection between inequality and voting behavior. Regardless of one's level of trust in government, the effect of inequality is essentially the same. While the effect of inequality is statistically insignificant for those with the lowest levels of trust, the effect is negative and statistically significant at all other levels of trust. To the extent that we pay attention to the lack of statistical significance for the effect of inequality among those with low trust, the pattern is opposite of expectations. Those with the least trust in government would become less supportive of Democrats as inequality rises if trust were the explanation

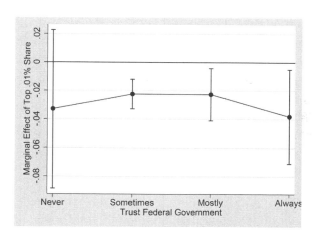

4.6. Marginal effect of inequality on voting behavior as trust increases.
Source: Author's calculations from ANES data.
Note: Charts plot the predicted marginal effect of an increase in inequality on support for Democratic House candidates for those with differing levels of trust in government. Calculations based on a multilevel logit model including national-level top 0.01 percent income share at time of election, race/ethnicity, sex, age, education, and income along with trust in government and trust interacted with inequality.

for the decline in Democratic support as inequality rises.[17] Yet those with the lowest trust are the only group that fails to evidence a statistically significant reduction in support for Democrats as inequality rises. So we need to look elsewhere to explain the overarching pattern.

Inequality, Racial Attitudes, and Vote Choice

In the next portion of the analysis I seek to shed some light on how race may or may not contribute to the self-reinforcing link between economic inequality and voting behavior that we have seen in this chapter. The ANES has asked a variety of questions about racial attitudes over the years, and here I want to conduct an analysis similar to the one above—with voting behavior in House elections as the dependent variable and the national-level context of inequality as the key explanatory variable in a multilevel logit model. But in this analysis I introduce a measure of racial attitudes as well as an interaction term between racial attitudes and economic inequality in order to determine whether the effect of inequality on voting behavior is different for white non-Hispanics with more and less egalitarian racial attitudes.

The specific question I analyze here asks respondents whether the government should help blacks or blacks should help themselves, arrayed on a seven-point scale. I code the variable so that higher values represent less egalitarian racial attitudes. Several other racial attitude items are available in the ANES, and I selected this item because it has been asked on the largest number of surveys, thereby providing the largest possible variation in the context of inequality. There are a couple obvious concerns with this measure. The first is that it explicitly references government policy toward blacks, which might tap into political ideology in concert with racial attitudes. To guard against this possibility, along with controls for ethnicity, age, sex, education, and income, I include a control for self-identified ideology in the results reported below. As a second way to deal with this potential problem I replicated the results below with different measures of racial attitudes that do not reference government policy explicitly. The results remain essentially unchanged.[18]

Figure 4.7 shows two plots that shed light on the question of how the effect of inequality on voting behavior is conditioned by racial attitudes. In the left chart, I show the marginal effect of inequality on support for Democratic House candidates as racial attitudes become less egalitarian. In the right chart, I show the predicted probability of supporting a Democratic candidate for respondents with the most (dashed line) and least (solid line) egalitarian racial attitudes. The results are striking. For those with egalitarian racial attitudes, higher levels of inequality are associated with more

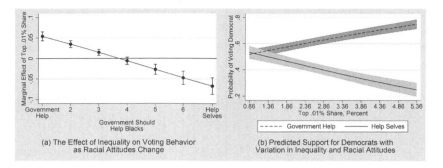

(a) The Effect of Inequality on Voting Behavior as Racial Attitudes Change

(b) Predicted Support for Democrats with Variation in Inequality and Racial Attitudes

4.7. Inequality, racial attitudes, and voting behavior.
Source: Author's calculations from ANES data.
Note: Chart plots the predicted probability of support for Democratic House candidate among those voting in the most recent election as inequality increases. Calculations based on a working-class logit model including national-level top 0.01 percent income share at time of election, age, education, and income. White non-Hispanics only.

support for Democratic candidates. This is the epitome of a *self-correcting* relationship between inequality and voting behavior. But as racial attitudes become less egalitarian, the effect of inequality changes dramatically. Once racial attitudes become moderately inegalitarian, the effect of inequality is reversed, with higher inequality associated with less support for Democratic candidates. This, of course, fits a self-reinforcing pattern.

The chart on the right drives this point home even more starkly. Those with quite different racial attitudes are no different from one another at the lowest levels of inequality. This is evidenced by the fact that the lines for the most and least egalitarian respondents are nearly identical and their confidence intervals overlap on the left side of figure 4.7b. But when inequality is higher, the voting behavior of these two groups diverges dramatically. Those with egalitarian racial attitudes are much more supportive of Democratic candidates than those with inegalitarian racial attitudes when inequality is high.[19] Overall, these results are highly consistent with a theoretical story in which those most predisposed toward racial animus have those attitudes activated in contexts of relative deprivation, thus becoming less supportive of Democratic candidates who are more pro–civil rights and in favor of redistributive social and economic policies.

Inequality and the Trump Vote in 2016

As one final piece of the analysis, I turn to voting decisions in the 2016 presidential election. Donald Trump's victory in 2016 clearly came as a surprise, and there is ongoing debate about the factors that contributed to his electoral success. Here, I will focus on the potential role of economic inequality. One of the narratives that has emerged since Trump's victory is that the economic stagnation of the working class enhanced support for Trump. If this narrative is correct, we would expect to see support for Trump increase in contexts of high economic inequality. In particular, we would expect rising inequality to drive up support for Donald Trump in lower-income states with larger working-class populations and among voters with the lowest levels of education.

Analyzing support for Donald Trump in the 2016 election not only helps to shed light on the current debate over Trump's ascendency to power but also provides the opportunity to see whether the connections between inequality and voting seen above translate into a very different context in a very different analysis. To this point, the results have been based on contextual variation in inequality at the national level over time. By focusing on the 2016 election we can see whether the results are similar when we focus on contextual variation at the state level cross-sectionally. In addition, the results to this point have focused on vote choice in congressional elections. The analysis here provides the opportunity to assess these effects in a presidential election contest. If we see similar patterns as above in an analysis of cross-sectional variation in inequality in a presidential election (and a presidential election, I would note, that many seem to see as historically unique), this would greatly strengthen the conclusion that inequality undermines support for Democratic candidates.

In figure 4.8 I chart the predicted probability of voting for Donald Trump as income concentration in the voter's state increases.[20] Self-reported voting in the presidential election is the dependent variable, coded 1 for Donald Trump and 0 otherwise (nonvoters are excluded). State-level inequality comes from Frank (2009), which calculates top 1 percent income share for each state based on income tax return data similar to the methodology used for the national top income share data used throughout the book. I include individual-level controls for demographic characteristics (sex, education, family income, and age) and partisanship. The individual-level data come from the 2016 Cooperative Congressional Election Study, which includes large numbers of respondents in every state. I also control for state-level median income in order to account for the fact that previous studies find that inequality and income operate very differently in rich and poor states (Gelman, Park, and Shor 2008). These results reveal a pattern quite similar to the one seen in the analysis above. As state-level income inequality increases, support for Donald Trump increases as well.

These results bolster the conclusion that rising inequality undermines

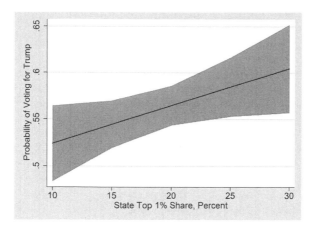

4.8. Predicted likelihood of Trump vote as state income concentration increases.
Source: Author's calculations from CCES data.
Note: Chart plots the predicted probability of support for Donald Trump among those voting
as inequality increases. Calculations based on a multilevel logit model including state-level
top 1 percent income share, race/ethnicity, age, education, income, partisanship, and state
median income.

electoral support for Democrats. The results also appear to be consistent
with the narrative that an economic malaise among the working class that
has been primed by increasing economic inequality contributed to Trump's
victory. To dive into that question a bit more it is helpful to see how the
effect of inequality varies across different types of people as well as in different state economic contexts. Figure 4.9 presents two charts that show
how the effect of state income concentration on Trump support varies as
the median income of the voter's state increases and as the voter's level of
education increases. The underlying models are identical to those above
except that state median income is interacted with state inequality to produce figure 4.9a, and individual level education is interacted with state inequality to produce figure 4.9b. The variation in the effect of inequality on
support for Trump is not consistent with explanations of Trump support
rooted in a disaffected working class. While we saw above that support for
Trump increases as state inequality increases, this pattern is most prevalent
in richer states and among more educated voters. In poor states (on the left
of figure 4.9a), increased inequality is not associated with increased Trump
support. And the least educated voters (on the left side of figure 4.9b) are
actually less likely to support Trump as inequality rises.

The main drawback of the data source I use is that information about
racial attitudes is not collected for the full nationwide sample. Therefore, I

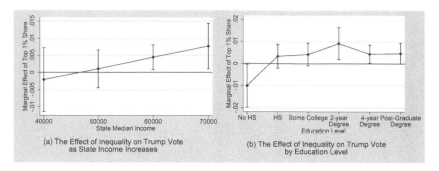

4.9. Inequality and Trump support by state income and individual education.
Source: Author's calculations from CCES data.
Note: Charts plot the predicted marginal effect of an increase in inequality on support for Trump as state median income and individual-level education increases. Calculations based on a multilevel logit model including state-level top 1 percent income share, race/ethnicity, age, education, income, partisanship, and state median income. For the left chart, an interaction between state median income and state inequality is also included. For the right chart the model includes an interaction between state-level income and individual-level education.

cannot assess the role of racial attitudes in these results. And it is important to note that those with the lowest levels of education were, in fact, most likely to vote for Donald Trump despite the fact that they were less likely to vote for Trump when living in states with higher levels of inequality. I suspect that we would see strong effects of racial attitudes that might also condition the effects of inequality in important ways, as we saw above in the analysis where inequality varied over time. More and better data will be required to determine if this conjecture is correct.

Conclusions

To conclude this chapter, I want to draw attention to three takeaways from the analysis so far. First, we have seen patterns in policy attitudes and political behavior that are consistent with an inequality trap in America. When inequality rises, attitudes do not become more progressive and supportive of redistribution, and attitudes may even move in the opposite direction. In addition, electoral outcomes respond to rising inequality in a manner consistent with an inequality trap, with election outcomes shifting in favor of Republicans in the House, Senate, and presidency. The changes in attitudes and behavior that come with rising inequality have the distributional consequence of moving inequality higher yet—a self-reinforcing feedback cycle.

Secondly, we have seen evidence consistent with self-reinforcing inequality using a variety of techniques and data sources. None of the analyses in this chapter and the last are, considered separately, bullet-proof evidence of a self-reinforcing feedback cycle between economic inequality and political attitudes and behavior. But we have seen evidence of such feedback using measures of both public opinion and voting behavior. The pattern is present to at least some extent in both highly aggregated measures of public opinion as well as very specific policy attitudes. Both macro analysis of movement over time and micro analysis leveraging variation in inequality over time and across geography has shown similar patterns. Elections for the House, the Senate, and the president all present similar patterns of response to inequality. Taken together, all this leads to at least a moderate degree of confidence that we are, in fact, observing a pattern of self-reinforcing inequality through political behavior and public opinion.[21]

Finally, the results point to race as an important factor contributing to the observed pattern of inequality-reinforcing shifts in attitudes and behavior as a response to changing inequality. One theory explaining why the public might respond to rising inequality with a conservative shift in attitudes and less support for Democratic candidates is rooted in group-based social identity that is reinforced as scarcity (or relative deprivation) is primed by rising inequality. As inequality rises, poor and middle-class citizens see themselves falling behind economically. This shift in relative economic fortunes undermines their self-image to the extent that this image is rooted in class-based group identity. As the value of class identity to ego support is undermined, identity is likely to shift toward other groups, particularly based on race and nationality, which activates the electoral relevance of racial attitudes. Such a response would only be exacerbated by Republican politicians who have often primed racial divisions in both their rhetoric and their policy prescriptions.

While the analysis conducted here has not definitively tested all the linkages in the above theoretical chain, most notably because of a lack of data on group identity over a sufficient period of time or in a large enough sample to observe both group identity and change in the context of inequality concurrently, the evidence we have is broadly consistent with this theoretical perspective. In particular, the analysis in the previous chapter showed that the attitudes of poor and middle-income individuals are most likely to respond to rising inequality in a self-reinforcing manner. In this chapter, we saw that the self-reinforcing voting response to inequality is wholly dependent on inegalitarian racial attitudes. Inegalitarian racial attitudes are a necessary condition for inequality-reinforcing voting behavior to occur, and economic inequality heightens the electoral significance of racial attitudes. This is an important finding that certainly needs further investigation moving forward, but the results here reinforce once again the idea that race is central to American politics. What's more, economic inequality and race apparently come together in important ways to shape the functioning of US democracy.

To this point the focus has been on political behavior. We have seen evidence that Americans respond to inequality in ways that help to create an inequality trap. In the next two chapters I shift focus to the institutional settings in which policy making occurs. I ask whether and how the behavior of policy makers as well as the functioning of US policy-making institutions change as a result of shifting inequality.

FIVE

Partisan Convergence and
Financial Deregulation

It was January 3, 1995, opening day of the 104th Congress. Newt Gingrich was the new Republican Speaker of the House, taking the gavel from Richard Gephardt after Democrats lost over fifty seats in the 1994 midterm elections. Republicans also took charge of the Senate after gaining ten seats there, giving them control of both chambers of Congress.

Democrats were reeling not only from the electoral loss but also from the inability to achieve their signature legislative goal of health care reform during the two years of unified Democratic control at the beginning of Bill Clinton's presidency. Progressives had many reasons to be concerned. A reversal of partisan fortunes like this one was likely to have at least some policy consequences. The Clinton White House would now be negotiating with the other party instead of with competing Democratic factions. And the ascendance of Newt Gingrich represented a hard shift to the right within the Republican Party. So not only had Republicans gained more power, but Republicans were becoming increasingly resistant to negotiating toward the middle on important economic policy questions.

Republicans had campaigned on their Contract with America. In it they promised middle-class tax cuts, the elimination of deficit spending, cuts to welfare programs, reductions in government regulation, and cuts to capital gains taxes. The contract, of course, represented a campaign messaging device as much or more than a governing document. The broader agenda of the Republican Party was to reduce taxes on businesses and the wealthy, to cut benefits for low-income families, to decrease barriers to international trade, and to continue the trend toward less government regulation of business.

But there was good reason to think the Republican policy agenda would go absolutely nowhere. A Democrat still controlled the White House. And there were a substantial number of moderate Republicans in Congress. Both of these factors made bipartisanship essential for legislative success. So the question was where could Republicans and at least some Democrats find common ground? And, central to the interests of this book, how would these policy changes affect and be affected by economic inequality?

Looking back we can see that a variety of legislation was approved in the period of divided government during Bill Clinton's presidency. Much of it didn't have obvious distributional consequences or had little to do with the economy. But many of the policy accomplishments during this time were inegalitarian—likely to exacerbate existing economic inequality rather than ameliorate it. Major welfare reform legislation that reduced support for low-income families was approved. Telecommunications regulations were scaled back. Medicare cuts were enacted. The North American Free Trade Agreement was negotiated (even before Republicans took over Congress). Capital gains taxes were cut. And the finance sector was deregulated. In other words, there was some degree of partisan convergence on inegalitarian policy options. This chapter explores the phenomenon of isolated inegalitarian policy convergence, with a particular focus on the case of financial deregulation.

The shift in this chapter and the next moves the emphasis from political behavior—public opinion and elections—to institutions and policy making. I will examine, in essence, how the American policy process may or may not perpetuate an inequality trap.

We saw in chapters 3 and 4 how the cycle of inequality is partially rooted in public opinion and elections, which are the bread and butter of political behavior. By examining how US policy making contributes to the inequality trap, the role of political institutions begins to take center stage. Political institutions like political parties and election rules play a role even when connections between inequality and political behavior are the focus. But institutions move to the center of the story once we start to consider the policy-making process. The previous two chapters featured political behavior as the star of the show with political institutions playing a supporting role. For the next two chapters those roles are reversed. Here, institutions will take the lead.

To be clear, Democrats and Republicans had and have major disagreements about policy in a variety of domains. Democrats have long been the party more supportive of redistribution and other forms of egalitarian (or less inegalitarian) economic and social policy. When Republicans gain seats like they did in 1994 the likelihood of inequality-enhancing policy increases. And as we saw in the last chapter, Republicans tend to find more electoral success as inequality rises. The 1994 midterm elections, of course, came on the heels of two decades of steadily rising inequality. Republican gains in 1994 likely should be attributed mostly to the usual cycle of mid-term losses for the president's party combined with a backlash against the party in power when they attempt to shift policy too far to the left or right. But the results from the last chapter suggest that rising levels of inequality may have further enhanced Republican gains. Electoral outcomes and public opinion provide an important backdrop for policy making and a pathway for inequality to shape policy making indirectly through elections and mass policy preferences.

This chapter will show that rising inequality affects the US policy-making process more directly as well. We will see that the shifting electoral fortunes of the parties and (to perhaps some extent) changes in public preferences are only part of the reason inegalitarian partisan convergence can happen. But how America's policy-making institutions aggregate preferences and process input from competing interests also plays a prominent role in the spiral of inequality. I argue that inegalitarian policy convergence can be at least in part explained by a combination of factors, ranging from unequal political voice to differences in the organizing strategies and success of the left and the right, to the rise of a neoliberal Washington consensus on many aspects of economic policy. Importantly, the factors that drive inegalitarian partisan convergence are more likely to be in place as economic inequality rises. The core message is that US institutions contribute to America's inequality trap.

The analysis in this chapter and the next contribute to an expanding body of research on continuity and change in policy making. This chapter, in its exploration of inegalitarian policy convergence, is interested in change. The next chapter, which focuses on status quo bias, examines continuity.

My core argument is that economic inequality plays a role in the nature of policy change and the implications of policy continuity. This argument is in part inspired by historical-institutionalist approaches to the dynamics of policy making and policy feedback. Prior work in this tradition has often focused on how policies serve to reinforce the status quo and generate stability over time (Pierson 2004, Thelen 2004).[1] This line of thinking about how the design and implementation of policy serves to prevent future policy change is central to the analysis in the next chapter. This chapter, however, is interested more in policy change than continuity, and Mahoney and Thelen (2010) in particular redirect historical-institutionalism toward explaining such change.

Their theory of change begins with the idea that public policies have implications for who has power—that policies have power-distributional consequences (Hall 1986, Mahoney and Thelen 2010, Offe and Wiesenthal 1980, Stephens 1979, Yashar 1997). As the distribution of power that is in part driven by feedback from policies to politics changes, opportunity for policy change emerges. This perspective is borne out in several studies of the development of American social and economic policy (A. L. Campbell 2003, A. Jacobs 2010, Mettler 2005, Mettler 2016, Skocpol 1992, Pierson 1993). But, they argue, which policy changes actually happen is jointly determined by the specifics of existing policy design as well as the political context (Mahoney and Thelen 2010, 15). I emphasize that income concentration is both a result of current policy design and an important aspect of the political context (Soss, Hacker, and Mettler 2007). As an aspect of policy design and political context, then, concentration of income is a likely suspect in explaining policy continuity and change. The next chapter shows how high inequality creates the conditions necessary for status quo bias to exacerbate inequality further. This chapter demonstrates that income concentration can make inegalitarian policy change more likely.

Convergence in the Midst of Polarization

It is well known that party polarization is one of the key characteristics of contemporary American politics. There is debate about the extent to which the mass public reflects the polarization of elected leaders, but it is crystal clear that the ideological distance between Democratic and Republican members of Congress is large and has increased dramatically over the past several decades.

The policy stagnation that polarization creates, the more general aspects of the US system that bias outcomes toward the status quo, and how these characteristics of policy making are connected to America's spiral of inequality are the subject of the next chapter. But there is obviously much more to the story of rising inequality than policy inaction. Instead, there have also been a variety of policy *actions* that have contributed to America's rising gap between the rich and the poor: reduced top marginal tax rates, estate tax reform, changes to means-tested welfare programs, and deregulation of the financial services sector. How did an important handful of inegalitarian policy changes happen in the face of dramatically rising inequality within an increasingly polarized system that is biased toward the status quo? Such policy changes always require a great deal of compromise and deal making that can convince reluctant members from opposing parties with divergent preferences to come on board. The tax reform package of 1986 is a classic example. In some cases, though, changes in the political climate provide opportunities for "isolated partisan convergence." In these cases, policy options that were once contentious become less so, and the divide between the parties declines, opening pathways for policy change.

Part of the reason this is possible, of course, is that political parties are not monolithic. Particularly in the American system it is possible for individual legislators to go their own way in defiance of the wishes of party leaders. Political parties are quite disciplined now in the US Congress, with members of both major parties voting unanimously at increasingly high rates. But there often remains a tension between the desires of party leaders and the wishes of local constituencies. Party leaders seek loyalty from members, but in that loyalty at least some members are put in electoral jeopardy because supporting the party alienates important portions of their constituency. It is for this reason that even in the current context of well-disciplined parties individual legislators are routinely permitted (in small numbers) to defect from the party's preferred position in order to avoid electoral risks. And the discipline that has become typical in recent decades has broken down a bit with the rise of the Republican House Freedom Caucus.

For isolated partisan convergence to happen, it is not typically necessary to accomplish a wholesale conversion of an entire political party from one position to another. What is required is generating sufficient disagreement within the minority party to deter party leaders from enforcing strict party discipline in a particular domain. The focus is on the minority party because I take it as essential that the majority party is supportive for a policy change to occur. If there are major divisions within the majority party, then such divisions are more likely to impede policy making, particularly in the House, where the majority exercises such strong agenda control. Think of the scenario in which John Boehner sought to deal with the Freedom Caucus during his tenure as Speaker of the House. Members of the Freedom Caucus were not very distant ideologically from "establishment" Republicans on a variety of issues, but when it came to tactical decisions the Freedom Caucus was much more willing to seek major policy concessions by threatening actions like withholding debt limit increases. More often than not, the division within the Republican majority prevented policy action in the House. So clear support from a majority party is really a necessary condition for legislative action.

Thinking about this within Rohde and Aldrich's (2010) Conditional Party Government framework is helpful. They are interested in explaining the degree to which members of a party are willing to give greater power to their party leaders in Congress. For party leaders to centralize sufficient power to enforce party discipline, two key conditions must be met: ideological heterogeneity within the party must be low, and ideological disagreement with the other party must be high. If these conditions are met, legislators are willing to give up individual power to party leaders because doing so will further their policy goals without excessively undermining their electoral motivations. While general party polarization enhances the likelihood that legislators will hand over substantial power to party leaders, if there are certain policy domains in which legislators from the party are less unified, then leaders will face strategic incentives to not fully utilize the procedural powers granted to them within that domain.

There is little doubt that Democrats are to the left of Republicans on economic issues. Democrats favor a larger welfare state, more progressive taxation, and stronger labor unions than Republicans. And being to the left on economic issues generally translates into favoring more egalitarian outcomes. As party polarization has increased, the ideological gap between the parties on the economic dimension has certainly increased as well. Figure 5.1 makes this point clear. There, the average DW-NOMINATE ideological scores for members of each party in the House and the Senate are charted from 1913 to 2015.

From the 1940s to the early 1970s, the most notable ideological change among congressional parties was a shift to the left among Democrats in the Senate. Their mean DW-NOMINATE score, in which higher scores connote more conservative roll-call voting patterns, declined by 0.28 from −0.031 in 1943 to −0.311 in 1974. Over that same period, Democrats in the House shifted 0.156 points to the left, while Republicans in the House moved very

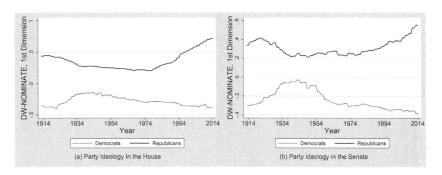

5.1. Party divergence in the House and the Senate, 1913–2015.
Source: Calculated by author based on data from https://voteview.com (Lewis, Poole, Rosenthal, Boche, Rudkin, and Sonnet 2017).
Note: These charts show the average DW-NOMINATE score for Republicans and Democrats in the House and Senate. DW-NOMINATE scores are calculated for individual legislators based on roll-call votes and provide an indication of the conservatism of each legislator. The first dimension of the measure is charted here, which captures an economic dimension of ideology.

slightly to the left and Senate Republicans barely changed at all. Much of the change over this period represents the defection of Democratic legislators in the south to the Republican Party. Since the 1970s, however, Republicans have shifted ideologically much more than Democrats (Bonica, McCarty, Poole, and Rosenthal 2013). House Republicans moved more than 0.5 points to the right (from 0.215 to 0.718), and Senate Republicans moved 0.295 points to the right. Democrats have gone somewhat to the left since the 1970s, but the lion's share of recent increased polarization is due to an extreme shift to the right among Republicans. In fact, Republicans are now substantially more ideologically extreme than they have been over the past one hundred years.

Part of the explanation for Democrats resisting pulls to the extreme left while Republicans have shifted to the extreme right can be connected to the relative power of competing factions and interests within each party. While actors such as the Koch network and the Tea Party have played increasingly prominent roles in the Republican Party, the Democratic coalition has been quite diverse, including civil rights groups, labor unions, women's groups, and large centrist movements like the Democratic Leadership Council (Grossmann and Hopkins 2016). In addition, ideologically progressive Democratic donors have been much less able than their counterparts on the right to create an organizational apparatus to coordinate and exercise influence within the party (Skocpol and Hertel-Fernandez forthcoming).

This chapter looks below the aggregate pattern of party ideological divergence to explore how Democrats in particular may have begun to face incentives to shift toward the center in some issue domains as inequality has risen. In particular, I focus on how and why policy making and party divisions on financial deregulation changed between the enactment of Glass-Steagall in the 1930s until its repeal in 1999. I argue that rising inequality was accompanied by a variety of conditions that made inegalitarian policy making in the realm of financial deregulation more likely, thereby reinforcing inequality.[2]

The story of partisan convergence on financial deregulation makes for the perfect next step in the analysis of America's inequality trap. Financial deregulation as a case of isolated partisan convergence in many ways illustrates how the pathways of self-reinforcing inequality analyzed to this point can contribute to inegalitarian policy outcomes. The conditions for partisan convergence, as we will see, are a partial outgrowth of electoral and opinion responses to rising inequality.

The analytical strategy in this chapter represents a bit of a shift. Consistent with previous chapters, the analysis of partisan convergence presented here is based in part on a quantitative analysis of aggregate time series and micro-level cross-sectional data. But the initial part of the analysis examines the history of financial regulation and deregulation in the United States. Essentially, I conduct a detailed case study of financial regulatory policy comprising both a qualitative and a quantitative component. While quite different in many ways, the two types of analysis utilized here both rely on observing politics and policy over time with the shared goal of assessing the extent to which partisan convergence on financial deregulation happened and shedding light on why.

Financial deregulation is one of a handful of potential cases of isolated inegalitarian policy convergence. Trade policy and other components of what is known as the Washington Consensus are other possible candidates. I focus on financial deregulation for two key reasons. First, financial deregulation has a clear and compelling connection to distributional outcomes. So this policy domain is the most likely candidate for inequality-reinforcing feedback. In fact, in terms of policy changes financial deregulation was likely a key culprit in the rise of US inequality. Secondly, partisan convergence on financial regulation seems unlikely at first blush. The general political context during deregulation was one of increasing partisan polarization and policy gridlock. The electoral base of the Democratic Party traditionally comprised working-class, middle-income, poor, and minority groups that would not typically be seen as beneficiaries of financial deregulation.[3] This case study will reveal, however, that inegalitarian policy making can happen even in a context in which partisan convergence seems unlikely. Before turning to the evidence, I discuss in more detail the underpinnings of partisan convergence and how inequality might have increased incentives for such convergence in the domain of financial deregulation.

Economic Inequality and Incentives for Convergence on Financial Deregulation

Building on the discussion above, it is important to note that any areas of partisan convergence in support of inegalitarian policy that emerge are most likely to be driven by the strategic calculations and behavior of Democrats. There is no doubt that the two major American parties are generally polarized and that the ideological distance between and unity within the parties has increased over much of the time period that economic inequality has been on the rise. There also should be little doubt that the conservative policies generally favored by Republicans are much more likely to increase inequality than the more progressive policies generally favored by Democrats since the New Deal (Bartels 2008, Kelly 2009). This means that for inegalitarian policy shifts to occur, either Republicans have to have sufficient power across the policy-making branches to move forward with minimal Democratic support (the 2017 tax cuts are a perfect example), inegalitarian policy shifts have to be tempered by shifts to the left that bring Democrats on board, or a sufficient number of Democrats need to shift away from traditional egalitarian Democratic party preferences and join Republicans in supporting inequality-inducing policy changes.

This last scenario describes isolated inegalitarian party convergence, and since this scenario is driven by changing behavior among Democratic legislators it is useful to focus on their strategic context and behavioral incentives to understand when and how isolated partisan convergence might occur. In particular, I want to consider how a changing context of economic inequality may or may not generate conditions encouraging partisan convergence on inegalitarian policy action within certain policy domains.

To understand the behavior of legislators, it is useful to start by focusing on their goals. And to identify the general goals of members of Congress, the classic works of Mayhew (1974) and Fenno (1978) remain as relevant as ever. Fenno (1978) identified reelection, gaining stature in Washington, and achieving preferred policy outcomes as the three key goals of legislators, and Mayhew (1974) emphasized reelection as the primary goal of the three. It is fairly clear that without winning elections, members of Congress cannot do their jobs, and winning elections requires building and maintaining a coalition of voters who can help a legislator win primary and general elections.

Recent work by Grossmann and Hopkins (2016) argues that Republican and Democratic legislators build these winning coalitions in quite different ways. Republicans tend to focus on an ideological agenda to build winning coalitions while Democrats make group-based appeals in an effort to build diverse coalitions of support. The coalition-building strategy of Democrats versus Republicans likely provides Democrats more leeway in terms of staking out policy positions and also increases the likelihood of disagreement and divisions within the Democratic coalition. Skocpol and Hertel-Fernandez's (forthcoming) detailed analysis contrasting the behavior of liberal donor groups with conservative groups such as the Koch network highlights how these differences can play out. Efforts to organize liberal donors have been plagued by an inability to enforce discipline around a consistent progressive economic agenda, making them largely unsuccessful in comparison with similar efforts on the right.

Alongside this variation between Republicans and Democrats in coalition-building strategies is the inherent need for economic resources to run campaigns, organize voters, support party organization, and generally do the work of politics. While it may not be the case that raising more money and spending more in campaigns can straightforwardly buy votes or election outcomes, it is clear that modern political campaigns require a great deal of money to operate. Money may not determine who wins, but money does seem to be a necessary (but not sufficient) condition for electoral success. Raising money has become one of the core jobs of members of Congress, so much so that freshman Democrats were at one time told to expect to spend four hours a day making calls to solicit contributions (Grim and Siddiqui 2013). Funding for their individual campaigns is important for their own electoral goals, and financially supporting colleagues and various party organizations is an important aspect of gaining stature in Washington (Heberlig 2003). Whether money matters or not for election outcomes, the ability of legislators to bring in money is of great importance.

The importance of fund-raising provides one possible mechanism, among many others, through which economic inequality might change the practice of politics. As inequality rises, the economic resources that politicians must chase in order to fund political operations is by definition increasingly concentrated among those at the top. If legislators rationally distribute their fund-raising efforts, increasing income concentration will mean that they increasingly target high-income donors (Bonica, McCarty, Poole, and Rosenthal 2013, B. Page and Gilens 2017). Of course it needs to be said at this point that not all wealthy donors have identical policy preferences. I will return to this point below. And it is also important to note that Democrats have long received support from large-dollar wealthy donors, some with ties to the finance sector. But rising inequality over time changes the resource landscape in which policy makers seek financial support. The key point is that to the extent income shifts toward the top of the income distribution, legislators face incentives to seek funding from people with increasingly high relative incomes. To the extent that this happens, it becomes easier for Democratic politicians to turn a deaf ear to the needs of the poor in a similar fashion to the way Frymer (2010) argues they have taken black voters for granted.

Individuals, of course, are not the only targets for political fund-raising. Organizations are also important players in the political money game. And the organizational landscape has been changing dramatically while income inequality has been on the rise. Particularly important has been the declining membership and power of private sector labor unions. In the late 1970s nearly 25 percent of workers were union members. By 2015 that number had declined to less than 11 percent. The decline in unions had an important effect on economic inequality, with declining union membership repeatedly identified as one of the key drivers of rising inequality over this period (R. Freeman 1993, Western 1995, Western and Rosenfeld 2011, Volscho and Kelly 2012).

The declining power of unions also has implications for money in politics. Labor unions have been a traditional source of support for Democratic candidates. But as union membership has declined, so has the ability of labor union contributions to keep pace with contributions from other sources. Witko (2013) shows that as union strength declined in terms of membership, the proportion of Democratic campaign contributions coming from labor unions decreased from approximately 60 percent to under 30 percent. At the same time union contributions were declining in importance, money from corporate sources and wealthy individuals was increasing. Figure 5.2 shows the ratio of contributions per federal candidate from non-labor union sources to labor union sources. This ratio is calculated based on Federal Election Commission (FEC) data available from 1979 to the present, and reliable earlier data are not available to my knowledge. When positive, this ratio indicates that more money was coming from non-labor union sources. The more positive the ratio is, the greater the gap between nonunion contributions and contributions from labor. Along with this "union contribution gap ratio" I chart top income shares. We can see that the union gap in contributions increased from 1979 to the present, and that the union contribution gap ratio is positively correlated with rising

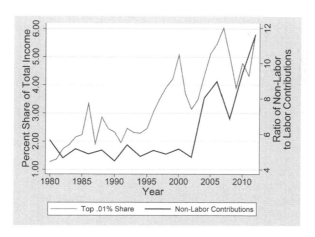

5.2. Campaign contributions from nonlabor sources and top income shares.
Source: Calculated by author based on data from the World Inequality Database and the Federal Election Commission.

inequality. This pattern is very much in line with Schlozman, Verba, and Brady's (2012) finding that the decline in unions is one of the key changes in the interest-group landscape exacerbating unequal voice in American policy making over the past several decades.

Organizations and money matter. Both of these factors changed along with inequality in ways that made inegalitarian partisan convergence more likely. But ideas also matter. At the same time inequality was rising, organizations representing workers were declining, and campaign finance sources were shifting. The way people were thinking about politics and economics shifted as well.

Two related trends seem most central—declining trust in government and an emerging market-focused economic consensus. In chapter 3 I first mentioned Hetherington's (2005) work on the connection between trust in government and policy preferences. He argues that trust in government, which has been declining over much of the period of rising inequality, provides a foundation for accepting government interventions in the economy. When people trust government institutions they are more likely to believe that government can effectively intervene to improve societal conditions, but if society becomes less trusting (as it has over the past several decades) support for such government interventions can be more easily undermined. In a context of declining trust in government, even Democratic politicians who are generally supportive of egalitarian economic interventions may become more easily convinced that such interventions will not work and find it harder to build sufficiently broad political support.

An emerging market-oriented "Washington Consensus" on economic policy further undermined arguments for government economic interventions during the most recent period of rising inequality. Some of the core tenets of the consensus include reducing fiscal deficits, liberalization of trade, and deregulation. The Washington Consensus is most often discussed in the context of international policy, particularly the policy prescriptions imposed on Latin American countries by the World Bank and International Monetary Fund when these countries have sought international aid during past financial crises. But the economic arguments underpinning these ideas also have clear application to domestic policy in the United States. There are certain aspects of the so-called Washington Consensus that were always controversial. But it seems clear that free market solutions to economic and social problems found in the Washington Consensus (and neoliberal thinking more broadly) became more widely accepted from the 1970s on (Krugman 1994) and gained traction especially among Republicans but also among Democratic policy makers (Derthick and Quirk 2001).

Summarizing to this point, several key ingredients have come into place along with rising inequality, providing a pathway for inequality to make partisan convergence in isolated policy domains more likely: (1) the need for financial resources in politics, (2) a Democratic coalitional strategy that embraces ideological flexibility, (3) the enhanced importance of business interests and wealthy individuals in financing campaigns, (4) the decline of labor unions as a counterbalance to corporate interests in Washington, and (5) a shifting landscape of ideas oriented toward free market solutions and consistent with declining trust in government. These conditions make it more likely for Democrats to seek out relationships with and be attentive to the interests of those with money in order to finance their political activities and to be more easily persuaded to adopt free market policies. It is clear, of course, that the partisan convergence these conditions might encourage does not happen on very many issues.

These conditions on their own make partisan convergence possible, but the likelihood of convergence remains low unless a further factor is also present. When wealthy Americans are far to the right of the typical American in their policy preferences, partisan convergence is more likely to occur, with Democratic legislators shifting their policy views closer to Republicans. The five conditions above, then, set the stage for partisan convergence, and the likelihood of partisan convergence is enhanced to the extent that the rich have preferences that are to the ideological right of Americans more generally.

If we examine the limited evidence available about the preferences of very rich Americans, financial deregulation is a good candidate for partisan convergence. While the preferences of the very rich are notoriously difficult to capture given their limited representation in typical sample sizes, several recent data-gathering efforts provide at least suggestive evidence about how the preferences of the ultrarich compare to the public as a whole. B. Page, Bartels, and Seawright (2013) conducted a survey specifically targeting those in the top 1 percent of the income distribution located in the Chicago metropolitan area. In this study, it is clear that the policy preferences of the richest Americans differ in important ways from the broader mass public. In particular, the richest Americans are much more conservative on economic issues than the public as a whole. When it comes to preferences about the regulation of Wall Street, the mass public was more than twice as likely to support increased regulation than those in the top 1 percent Chicago-area sample. Importantly, while B. Page, Bartels, and Seawright (2013) note that wealthy Democrats are substantially to the left of wealthy Republicans, "on economic issues wealthy Democratic respondents tended to be more conservative than Democrats in the general population." This is suggestive of a scenario that would motivate Democratic legislators to converge to some extent with Republicans.

While other surveys have not focused as explicitly on measuring the preferences of the richest Americans, the large samples of the Cooperative Congressional Election Study provide much more information about high-income Americans than typical national surveys. In a report for the Demos organization McElwee, Shaffner, and Rhodes (2016) make it clear that the rich have preferences that are substantially to the right of the public as a whole, and this is particularly the case on economic issues. In that analysis "elite donors," or those contributing more than $1,000 dollars to a campaign, were nineteen percentage points less likely to support the post–economic crisis stimulus package, twenty-four points less likely to support expansion of the State Children's Health Insurance Program, and twenty-six points less likely to support the Dodd-Frank financial regulation legislation. Bonica, McCarty, Poole, and Rosenthal (2013) reach a similar conclusion using very different data that focus more generally on ideological preferences of large-dollar individual donors as opposed to specific policy preferences. Their analysis finds that the richest donors to Democratic candidates are to the right of smaller donors.[4] As they argue, "both Republicans and many Democrats have experienced an ideological shift toward acceptance of a form of free market capitalism which, among other characteristics, offers less support for government provision of transfers, lower marginal tax rates for those with high incomes, and deregulation of a number of industries" (Bonica, McCarty, Poole, and Rosenthal 2013, 104).[5] There is mounting evidence, then, that the wealthy donors that parties increasingly have to court as inequality has risen are to the right of the public on economic issues.

The factors discussed to this point support the idea that Democrats have faced a variety of incentives to move toward Republicans in some areas of economic policy. Which policies actually end up evidencing this convergence depends on both the behavior of Democrats and the agenda set by Republicans. To reiterate a point made earlier, it is highly unlikely even when inegalitarian partisan convergence is taking place that Democrats would be the ones initiating policies to exacerbate inequality. Rather, Republicans initiate the effort and Democrats join (or not). This means that the issues where partisan convergence happens is in part determined by the issues that Republicans decide to prioritize. That Republicans pushed for welfare reform and financial deregulation (among other things) when they needed Democratic support to make these things happen was almost certainly a strategic calculation based on what they thought they could get Democrats to go along with. But the fervor for deregulation within the Republican Party was also the product of a lengthy effort on the part of major donors and libertarian-leaning activists, as has been documented elsewhere (Hacker and Pierson 2010, Skocpol and Hertel-Fernandez forthcoming).

Taken together, the existence of isolated partisan convergence as described above could create another pathway for feedback between economic inequality and financial deregulation. As inequality rises, Democratic legislators may face incentives that push them away from opposing financial deregulation, with deregulatory changes then generating even higher levels of inequality. And this is on top of the pro-Republican electoral effects of inequality that we saw in chapter 4. If feedback of this nature occurs, two key empirical patterns will be present. First, it must be the case that financial deregulation increases inequality. Second, we should see evidence that rising inequality was accompanied by a shift to the right among Democratic legislators. I take up an examination of the empirical evidence on these points next, starting with the question of whether financial deregulation pushed inequality higher. Then I present a combination of qualitative and quantitative evidence regarding how partisan disagreement regarding financial deregulation changed as inequality increased and the economy changed in other important ways.

The Link between Financial Deregulation and Income Inequality

As in previous chapters, I first look for evidence of a specific temporal pattern of feedback between inequality and politics. For a politically fueled spiral of inequality to be present, when some aspect of politics changes that change should be correlated with future changes in inequality. Those changes in inequality, in turn, should further enhance the initial political change thereby producing yet more inequality.[6] In the context of financial deregulation, then, the first question that I address is whether financial deregulation produces higher levels of economic inequality.

A substantial strand of recent research has studied the effect of financial deregulation on income inequality. An initial starting point for this literature is simply noting that inequality in America has been driven higher primarily by rising incomes at the very top of the distribution. There is some degree of sectoral diversity among those inhabiting the top echelons of US income, ranging from performing artists and professional athletes to star attorneys and inventors. But when the focus is at the very, very top, the prevalence of CEOs and those working in the financial sector is striking. Kaplan and Rauh (2010) found that about one-tenth of those in the top 0.01 percent of the income distribution work in finance, while a more comprehensive analysis estimates that nearly one out of every five in the top 0.01 percent are connected to the finance industry (Bakija, Cole, Heim, et al. 2012). Furthermore, increasing incomes at the top of the income distribution have been driven more by capital gains than wages and salaries, which also points to activity in the financial sector as an important driver of rising inequality (Piketty, Saez, and Zucman 2018).

Several studies have provided direct evidence that financial deregulation has pushed income inequality higher. Tomaskovic-Devey and Lin (2011) analyze the connections between financial deregulation and the increasing share of income flowing to the finance sector. Their estimates suggest that as much as $6.6 trillion was shifted to the finance sector since 1980, with banking deregulation explaining a substantial portion of the increase. The increasing share of income flowing to the finance sector is one component of what some scholars have labeled "financialization," and this phenomenon has been identified as an important explanation for rising income inequality in the United States (Lin and Tomaskovic-Devey 2013, Hacker and Pierson 2010, Krippner 2011, Van Arnum and Naples 2013, Witko 2016). Furthermore, feedback relationships between inequality and politics that are the focus of my analysis could change from an upward spiral to a downward spiral if political or economic changes that reduce inequality were to happen.

Examining financial deregulation and economic inequality over time shows a striking correspondence between the two measures. Figure 5.3 charts Philippon and Reshef's (2013) measure of financial deregulation and top 0.01 percent income share.[7] Deregulation was at a high point in the early twentieth century but declined dramatically from the 1930s to the mid-1970s. At that point, momentum for deregulation picked up, increasing substantially since the late 1970s. That pattern, of course, is quite similar to the path of economic inequality over this time period.

Previous work discussed above points to the conclusion that the temporal ebb and flow of deregulation in the finance sector is an important explanation of changes in income inequality over time. But none of these previous studies fully account for potential feedback from inequality into the policy process that generates the regulatory framework for the finance sector. This omission could have both empirical and theoretical implications. If inequality generates political change that makes deregulation more likely, then prior results identifying deregulation as a driver of inequality could have the causal arrow backward or, at the very least, overestimate the effects of deregulation on inequality. And, of course, if inequality increases the likelihood of deregulatory policy making, this suggests another potential

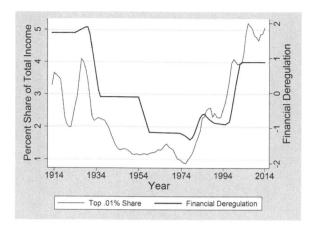

5.3. Income concentration and financial deregulation.
Source: Calculated by author with data from the World Inequality Database and Philippon and Reshef (2013).

mechanism supporting an inequality trap. Above, I discussed how rising inequality might have generated an incentive for Democrats to soften their position on financial deregulation. At this point, I turn to assessing whether one of the core empirical signatures of such a scenario is present—a reciprocal and self-reinforcing connection between financial deregulation and economic inequality.

Have Financial Deregulation and Inequality Reinforced Each Other?

As we just saw, financial deregulation and economic inequality follow a very similar path over time. If it is correct, as I have argued above, that rising inequality contributed to partisan convergence on the issue of financial deregulation and that financial deregulation serves to reinforce inequality, we should observe a reciprocal relationship between these two variables. Specifically, we would expect a positive effect of financial deregulation on inequality and also a positive feedback effect in which increasing inequality generates more deregulation. To test this possible pattern, I again take advantage of over-time variation (from 1913 to 2014) to observe the temporal relationship between financial deregulation and income concentration.[8]

Figure 5.4 shows the results.[9] These charts capture the predicted future effect of a standard deviation shift in one variable on the other variable over time. So the left chart shows what would happen to income inequality

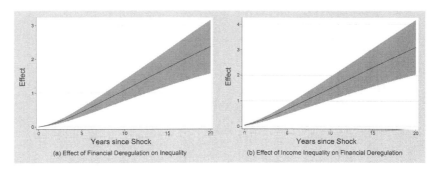

5.4. Is there a reciprocal relationship between inequality and financial deregulation?
Source: Author's calculations from annual data, 1913 to 2014.
Note: Charts plot orthogonalized cumulative impulse response functions based on a vector autoregression including financial deregulation and top 0.01 percent income share. The plot represents the predicted effect of a standard deviation shift in one variable on the other variable over a twenty-year period.

over the next twenty years if financial deregulation increased by a standard deviation. We see the expected positive effect, with increasing deregulation translating into increasing inequality over a long time horizon. The figure on the right plots the reverse effect, showing that an increase in economic inequality generates an increase in deregulation over the course of two decades. These results provide initial evidence that deregulation and economic inequality form a self-reinforcing feedback loop. But is this aggregate pattern due to partisan convergence in the domain of deregulation, or is some other process at work? I turn to that question now.

Deregulatory Convergence in an Era of Rising Partisan Polarization

As an initial strategy for exploring whether and how partisan convergence on financial deregulation may have contributed to the self-reinforcing relationship between deregulation and inequality seen above, I provide a brief history of policy making in the domain of finance sector regulation. My main interest is to explore how partisan coalitions in this domain shifted over time and to identify key actors in this process, focusing in particular on how factors related to rising inequality might have shaped their behavior in this domain.

A large part of the history of finance sector regulation revolves around the Glass-Steagall Act and the various additions and subtractions to it that have occurred over the years. I will use Glass-Steagall and legislative efforts designed to amend it as an organizing structure for discussing the political history of financial regulation and deregulation. Ultimately, of course, Glass-Steagall was effectively repealed in the years after Republicans took over Congress in 1995.

Banking Act of 1933

The starting point is Glass-Steagall. The Banking Act of 1933 was passed by Congress and signed by President Franklin Roosevelt in June 1933. The bill came to be more commonly known as the Glass-Steagall Act because of the primary sponsorship of Senator Carter Glass (D-VA) and Representative Henry Steagall (D-AL). The legislation's stated purpose was to "provide for the safer and more effective use of the assets of banks, to regulate inter-bank control, [and] to prevent the undue diversion of funds into speculative operations."

The perceived need for new regulatory action in the finance sector was driven by the fallout from the stock market crash of 1929 that destroyed substantial wealth and created massive amounts of volatility in the equities market in its aftermath. This volatility in the equities markets posed a threat to the US banking system since losses in equities were inhibiting the ability of banks to lend money and provide a safe place for Americans to keep their financial savings. The reason that volatility in equities markets had implications for more general banking operations was that banks were free to make risky investments in equity positions with the same resources that were part of their commercial banking operations—the "traditional" part of banking involving personal and business loans, savings accounts, and the like. That is, investment banking and commercial banking could be done by the same company with no real separation between the two parts, so losses on the investment banking side had direct implications for the commercial portion of the operation.

For this reason, one of the key provisions of the Glass-Steagall Act was a set of new regulations that prevented the unification of commercial and investment banking operations (Wells 2004). This separation was designed to contain the risk of investment activity and prevent securities investments losses from contaminating the deposit and loan portions of banking activity. Under Glass-Steagall, commercial banks would be very limited in the amount of interaction they could have with securities markets (Preston 1933, Meltzer 2004). Income from securities was capped at 10 percent for commercial banks. Investment banks, on the other hand, would no longer be allowed to deal in savings and loans. As well, there were limitations on how much the leadership of investment and commercial banks could overlap. The same entity was not permitted to own both types of financial

institutions, nor could they share boards of directors. Other important provisions of the law established deposit insurance for deposits in commercial
banks, gave the Federal Reserve much broader oversight of banking activities, limited lending by a bank to its own officers, restricted interest paid on
checking accounts, and allowed branching by national banks within their
home states (Preston 1933).[10]

Glass-Steagall was in large part a crisis response to the Great Depression and its aftermath. Senator Glass had been trying unsuccessfully since
1930 to enact regulations that would allow banks to open branches within
states (to spread risk across larger groups of customers) and to place barriers between commercial and investment banking operations. Prior to the
massive repudiation of Herbert Hoover and his political party in the 1932
election, Hoover was at best a tepid supporter of enhanced regulations and
encouraged the Senate to move slowly on any new attempts to regulate
the banking industry (Perkins 1971, Willis and Chapman 1934). After the
results of the 1932 election were known and the banking crisis of 1933
unfolded, President Hoover dropped his opposition and became a vocal
supporter of Glass's Senate bill to enhance banking regulations. The Senate
bill also faced some opposition from those seeking to protect the interests
of small banks doing business at only one location. While the Glass bill
in the Senate erected barriers between commercial and investment banks,
it also opened up new possibilities for branch banking in which national
banks could open branches in their home state. Senator Huey Long (D-LA)
was unwilling to support Glass's bill until changes were made that reduced
the competition these small banks would face and filibustered the bill until
such changes were made (Kennedy 1973). Eventually, the Glass Senate bill
was passed in January 1933 during the lame duck session of Congress. Support for the bill was bipartisan, with the final vote being 54–9 in favor of
passage. However, the House of Representatives, which would be evenly split
along partisan lines until the new Congress came into session on March 4,
1933, failed to take action on its own companion bill.

Once the Seventy-Third Congress began its session in March 1933, the
results of the 1932 election were fully in force. America's policy-making institutions became dominated by Democrats, with FDR in the White House,
a 58–36 Democratic advantage in the Senate, and a House tilted toward the
Democrats 313–117. In this context, the new regulatory legislation moved
much more quickly. While there was a great deal of wrangling and nego-
tiation regarding the details of deposit insurance and its implementation,
the House (by a vote of 262–19) and the Senate (on a voice vote) both
approved Steagall-sponsored legislation containing the core provisions of

Glass's original Senate bill. A conference committee negotiated remaining differences between the House and Senate version (mainly differences about the extent to which branching would be permitted and how comprehensive deposit insurance would be along with how quickly it would become available), and final legislation was approved overwhelmingly in June 1933 with President Roosevelt signing the legislation quickly.

Like any legislation that is capable of pulling together a winning coalition in Congress, the Banking Act of 1933 was full of compromises. Some legislators would have preferred a more comprehensive bank reform designed to completely unify the regulatory framework applied to state and national banks. Some would have preferred more or less substantial deposit insurance. Some even favored the complete nationalization of banks. The final bill in large part preserved the existing banking system and was, in that sense, conservative. Deposit insurance provided protection to banking consumers but also protected banks from the risks of speculative investments. Separation of investment and commercial banking limited the ability of commercial banks that were protected by deposit insurance to take on risky investments (investment banks received no such protection). It also provided new opportunities for branch banking. The final legislation drew widespread support from both Republicans and Democrats, which was likely due in part to the banking crisis that was unfolding as the bill was being considered.

That said, Glass-Steagall was a Democratic bill. The most serious negotiations over content were between Democratic legislators and a Democratic president. And if we examine the key actors in the legislative process that produced the Banking Act of 1933 we can see that it was clearly a left-leaning bill at the time it was considered. Based on first-dimension DW-NOMINATE scores that essentially place legislators on an economic left-right dimension (Poole and Rosenthal 1997), only seven senators were to the left of Senator Glass (the key sponsor) in the Seventy-Third Congress. Furthermore, Senator Huey Long from Louisiana was the Democrat who provided the clearest opposition to Glass-Steagall when he mounted a filibuster over the branching provision in the bill. He was the most conservative Democratic senator, and just twenty-two Republicans were to his ideological right. Similarly in the House, the primary sponsor, Henry Steagall, was one of the more liberal members of the chamber. His DW-NOMINATE score places him among the top 15 percent most liberal members of the Seventy-Third House. To the extent that there was any serious opposition to the Banking Act of 1933, it came from more ideologically conservative legislators.

Glass-Steagall represented the foundation for financial regulation for much of the twentieth century. As time went along, however, various provisions came under question. Technical modifications were needed on a regular basis, and the politics around financial deregulation shifted in fundamental ways. In order to see how this process unfolded, I briefly discuss some important legislative efforts to modify the regulatory structure set up by the Glass-Steagall Act since its passage in 1933.

Strengthening Glass-Steagall: The Bank Holding Company Act of 1956

The Banking Act of 1933 created a regulatory regime within which bank holding companies in control of a Federal Reserve member bank were included. These regulations, however, failed to address holding companies controlling non–Federal Reserve member banks and other financial entities. As a consequence, a key pillar of Glass-Steagall—the limits on cross-state ownership of banks—was undermined. The ease with which holding companies avoided oversight compelled President Roosevelt to issue a special statement to Congress in 1938 requesting legislation to address the matter. Each successive Congress considered proposals to that end, and these efforts culminated in the Bank Holding Company Act of 1956 (BHCA), which expanded regulatory oversight and strengthened original provisions of the Glass-Steagall Act.

The political environment in the mid-1950s was quite different than the 1930s. In the Eighty-Fourth Congress (1955–57), Democrats had just a one-seat advantage in the Senate (which became a one-seat advantage for Republicans during the course of the Congress) and a nineteen-seat majority in the House, with the presidency held by Republican Dwight D. Eisenhower. The legislative majorities for Democrats were even smaller than they appear considering the fact that a number of Democrats were conservative southerners. However, the political process leading to the BHCA of 1956 was similar in some ways to the one that produced Glass-Steagall.

House Resolution 6227 was the legislative vehicle for the BHCA in the House. Its primary sponsor was Representative Brent Spence (D-KY). It is useful to note right out of the gate that Representative Spence was in the most liberal quintile of the Eighty-Fourth House, and was left of center among members of the Democratic Party. The proposal had a handful of core components: it (1) established criteria for defining a bank holding company, (2) applied federal banking regulations to bank holding companies, (3) granted federal and state regulators authority over bank holding companies, (4) prohibited bank holding companies from making new acquisitions across state lines (this provision was not included in the final legislation), and (5) mandated liquidation of nonbanking assets by bank holding companies. The core purpose of this legislation was to close loopholes in the Glass-Steagall Act that allowed companies owning banks to skirt the regulatory framework established in 1933. Its purpose was "to minimize the danger inherent in concentration of economic power through centralized control of banks."

During House Banking and Currency Committee hearings on February 28, 1955, the chair of the Board of Governors of the Federal Reserve, William McChesney Martin, clearly explained the problems under existing regulation that needed attention:

> [There are] two apparent problems in the bank holding company field. In the first place, there is nothing in present law which restricts the ability of a bank holding company to add to the number of its controlled banks. Consequently, there can well be situations in which a large part of the commercial banking facilities in a large area of the country may be concentrated under the management and control of a single corporation.
>
> In the second place, there is nothing in existing law which prevents the combination under the same control, through the holding company device, of both banking and non-banking enterprises. Obviously, this makes it possible for the credit facilities of a controlled bank to be used for the benefit of the non-banking enterprises controlled by the holding company. Moreover, the ordinary banking business requires a managerial attitude and involves business risks of a kind entirely different from those involved in the banking business. Banks operate largely on their depositors' funds. These funds should be used by banks to finance business enterprises within the limitation imposed by the banking laws and should not be used directly or indirectly for the purpose of engaging in other businesses which are not subject to the safeguards imposed by the banking laws. (https://fraser.stlouisfed.org/title/448/item/7793, 2–3)

The primary opposition to this legislation, not surprisingly, came from bank holding companies. They argued that limitations on their commercial and investment activities amounted to unwarranted meddling by government in a market economy. They suggested that the bill was a thinly veiled attempt at protecting small local banks from competitive pressures that would force them to improve their products and services or go out of business. But the bill's sponsor, Representative Spence, argued during floor debate that "the centralization of banks, of banking interests, is a bad thing for the economy of the Nation" (*Congressional Record*, vol. 101, pt. 6, 8021). He believed the regulatory reforms in this bill would mitigate that problem.

The House bill passed with broad bipartisan support. However, it is clear from the record that the most left-leaning members were the bill's strongest proponents, while opposition generally came from the most conservative Republicans. In the end, HR 6227 passed on a vote of 371–24, with every no vote coming from Republicans.

After the House bill was passed, it was considered in the Senate along with a number of other related bills having their origins in the Senate. To make a long story somewhat shorter, the Senate Banking and Currency Committee held hearings and eventually worked to combine components of several bills, including the original HR 6227. The Senate bill (S 2577) retained all the core components of the legislation approved by the House but modified some portions in relatively minor ways. The most substantive difference between the House and Senate legislation was likely a provision in the Senate bill that permitted acquisition of banking assets across state lines with the approval of regulators. As in the House, nearly all the opposition to the Senate bill came from Republicans, who wanted to allow holding companies more flexibility in the banking sector. Republican opposition was most clearly evidenced in several attempts to amend the legislation in ways that would have loosened restrictions on bank holding companies. In the end, though, the Senate bill was approved by a voice vote, with the House supporting the Senate version as a substantively unchanged version of the bill previously approved in the House. President Eisenhower signed the legislation on May 9, 1956.

The BHCA of 1956, then, marked an important expansion and extension of the Glass-Steagall framework. In a general sense, it was an expansion of federal regulation in the finance sector. After the passage of the BHCA, changes to the regulation of finance were largely technical and essentially maintained the status quo. However, it would not be long until the general consensus around the Glass-Steagall framework would begin to break down. In the next section I discuss expanding legislative and regulatory efforts to weaken the structure that existed after passage of the BHCA.

Financial Deregulation in Fits and Starts

From the passage of the 1956 BHCA until the late 1960s, all was essentially quiet on the financial deregulation front. But with Nixon's election in 1968 a shift began to occur. Nixon convened a Commission on Financial Structure and Regulation in 1970, which came to be known as the Hunt Commission, named after the commission's chair, Reed Oliver Hunt. Hunt was the former CEO of Crown Zellerbach, a large paper manufacturing company headquartered in San Francisco. The charge of the committee was "to review and study the structure, operation, and regulation of the private financial institutions in the United States for the purpose of formulating recommendations which would improve the functioning of the private financial system" (Nixon 1970, 191). Ultimately, the commission recommended a broad array of deregulatory policy changes. Suggested reforms included eliminating limits on the interest rates banks could pay to consumers, removing distinctions between commercial banks and certain aspects of investment banking, permitting more branch banking within and across state lines, and allowing interest-bearing checking accounts.

The Hunt Commission Report released in 1971 laid out an agenda for deregulation of the financial sector. But many of these ideas were deeply controversial at the time. Nevertheless, nearly all the ideas presented in the report worked their way into legislative proposals. Through the 1970s and into the 1980s there was very little legislative movement on financial deregulation. There were three key reasons for this. First, Democrats were generally skeptical of financial deregulation in this period and maintained control of at least one legislative chamber. In particular, Democratic chairs of the relevant congressional committees created insurmountable obstacles to legislative momentum. Second, the financial sector was divided on exactly what deregulatory changes should occur. For instance, expanded branching opportunities were opposed by portions of the banking industry comprising independent banks, and securities companies and insurance firms remained opposed to the unification of commercial and investment banking activities well into the 1990s (Suarez and Kolodny 2011). And third, the general consensus even among Republicans was that strong regulation of the finance sector was necessary to keep financial institutions from undertaking risky activities that might endanger the broader economy. The hard-right conservative movement within the Republican Party had not yet taken form.

Even as early as 1980, however, proponents of financial deregulation were winning at least some legislative victories. The Depository Institutions Deregulation and Monetary Control Act of 1980 and the Garn–St. Germain Depository Institutions Act of 1982 nudged the status quo toward less regulation of the finance industry. These bills eliminated deposit interest rate ceilings, reduced base capital requirements, and lifted prohibitions on savings and loan investments in construction and real estate markets. Both of these bills were largely driven by the economic environment of the late 1970s, in which interest rates were extremely high but banks were limited in how much interest they could pay depositors. This hurt the ability of banks to compete for customers, and there was widespread consensus across party lines that eliminating these restrictions was essential in the economic environment of the day. These bills also, however, expanded the regulatory authority of the Federal Reserve, bringing all banks under their purview and extending reserve requirements to all such banks. Given that just 40 percent of commercial banks were part of the Federal Reserve system in 1980, this was a major extension of regulatory oversight (McNeill and Rechter 1980).

There were also changes in the bureaucratic sphere that moved the dial toward financial deregulation. The regulatory structure put in place by Glass-Steagall and the Bank Holding Company Act of 1956 provided some discretion for regulators in applying the statutory provisions. As time went along, flexibility for regulators was enhanced. In the 1980s through the mid-1990s regulators in the Federal Reserve increasingly provided exceptions to the general rules outlined in Glass-Steagall and the BHCA. For example, the Fed allowed specific commercial banks to expand their investments in mortgage-backed securities and short-term unsecured commercial loans and in 1996 essentially reinterpreted provisions of Glass-Steagall to provide for less separation between commercial and investment banking activities (Suarez and Kolodny 2011).

The legislative floodgates on financial deregulation began to fully open with passage of the Riegle-Neal Interstate Branching and Efficiency Act of 1994. This bill nearly eliminated restrictions on opening bank branches across state lines. By 1994, many states had already made changes to state laws that made it possible for out-of-state holding companies to acquire banks within the state. This created a patchwork system of regulation and aspects of federal regulation were applied very unevenly across states. The Riegle-Neal Act was sponsored by two Democrats, Stephen Neal (D-NC) in the House and Donald Riegle (D-MI) in the Senate. There was bipartisan support for this shift in regulatory policy, with the primary point of contention being over whether companies applying to acquire an out-of-state branch would have to submit to a Community Reinvestment Act review prior to approval (which encourages banks to meet the needs of low- and moderate-income neighborhoods). This legislation removed a substantial aspect of the Glass-Steagall regulatory framework. But this change had become relatively noncontroversial by the mid-1990s. This was a harbinger of larger changes to come—complete repeal of Glass-Steagall.

The Repeal of Glass-Steagall in 1999

The nail in the coffin of a core aspect of the regulatory framework put in place by the Banking Act of 1933 and the Bank Holding Company Act of 1956 was finally achieved under Republican control of Congress with passage of the Financial Services Modernization Act (FSMA) in 1999. The key provisions of the FSMA eliminated the statutory restriction on companies conducting business in both commercial and investment banking.

Part of the downfall of the Glass-Steagall structure was simply that the benefits of regulation were coming under question from thought leaders and policy experts. One core argument in favor of eliminating the firewall between commercial and investment banking was simply that other countries did not have such barriers. United States banks and investment companies were facing restrictions on their activities that similar companies in other countries did not, arguably placing them at a competitive disadvantage. As well, it is clear that regulations can often serve the interests of the regulated industry more than the interests of consumers. Proponents of deregulation in the telecommunications and transport sectors were able to argue effectively that consumers were not well served by the regulatory structures in place and that deregulation would benefit broad sectors of society while limiting most costs to privileged elites in the regulated industries themselves (Derthick and Quirk 2001). Such arguments, along with a political context of declining trust in government generally, helped to change the intellectual environment to one more broadly skeptical of government regulation of commercial economic activity.

On the Republican side in particular there were clearly naked ideological motivations at play as well. Based on their general orientation toward reductions of government economic intervention, Republicans had included a plank supporting repeal of a slew of financial regulations in their party platforms since 1980 (Suarez and Kolodny 2011). From the early 1970s on, an increasingly important group of Republican policy makers were stridently opposed to market regulation of nearly any form, believing that markets were best equipped to police themselves and that excessive government regulation was reducing innovation and economic growth.

The Democrats were also changing, though more slowly. Whereas throughout the 1970s and 1980s nearly every Democratic legislator in Congress was opposed to loosening regulations in the financial sector, by the 1990s that was not necessarily the case. The Democratic Leadership Council (DLC) formed in 1985 with the explicit goal of moving the Democratic Party to the ideological right. Ronald Reagan's success led some Democrats to believe that they had drifted too far to the left, and that they needed to change in order to compete successfully in national elections. Bill Clinton, as a former chair of the DLC, was explicit in his desire to connect the Democratic Party to the business sector and sought to move the party toward the ideological center, particularly on economic issues. Clinton's electoral success in 1992 was viewed by many as a vindication of the DLC's strategy of moving to the right. While there were still many Democrats in the 1990s who were skeptical of financial deregulation, President Clinton was quite open to the idea, as were many of his copartisans in Congress.

With the Republican takeover of the House in 1995 as well as certain retirements and committee chair changes, the staunchly proregulation Democrats who had previously provided a bulwark against erosion of financial regulation were no longer present. This created a clear path for Republicans who had long sought major financial deregulation to push forward on the legislative front.

The FSMA was originally introduced in the Senate by Phil Gramm (R-TX), who it is worth noting was to the ideological right of all but nine other senators in the 105th Congress. Just as the original regulatory structure in the finance sector was a Democratic invention that drew plenty of Republican support in an era of financial crisis (and declining inequality), the dismantling of that structure was a Republican project that was, as we will see, supported by many Democrats in a time of economic prosperity (and rising inequality). There was much more to the FSMA than repealing the prohibition against companies to combine banking, securities, and insurance functions; but that was the core of the bill. And it had immediate impact, in that Citigroup, a company combining these functions into a "megabank," was formed just days before the FSMA was approved, on the assumption that the FSMA's regulatory framework would indeed come to fruition.

Republicans were overwhelmingly supportive of the FSMA. But Democrats were divided. More traditional liberals were quite skeptical of rolling back regulations preventing the creation of giant financial services corporations. But a new brand of Democrat, perhaps best exemplified by President Clinton, were open to increasingly popular neoliberal arguments in the economic realm. As President Clinton indicated in his signing statement for the FSMA, he viewed the bill as a victory for both free markets and consumer protection. And Clinton was far from the only Democrat to support the FSMA. Democrats did extract some concessions regarding consumer protections and regulatory oversight of bank holding companies, and in the end only 16 percent of Democrats in the Senate and 25 percent of Democrats in the House opposed final passage of the FSMA. Clearly, the consensus had shifted on financial deregulation between the 1950s and the passage of the FSMA. After the 2007 financial crisis, of course, Democrats returned to a greater interest in developing effective and stabilizing financial regulations. But even the substantial reforms enacted in the Dodd-Frank legislation are much more free market oriented than the old, some would say antiquated, framework of Glass-Steagall.[11] And we are beginning to see some of the same patterns from the 1990s emerge again in efforts to roll back Dodd-Frank. Republicans in Congress are once again sponsoring bills to deregulate the financial sector, and several Democrats are signing on to the effort by co-sponsoring key legislation (Rappeport 2018).

Quantitative Evidence of the Convergence Hypothesis

Tracing the key legislative changes to regulation of the finance sector provides substantial evidence of partisan convergence. Democrats were the primary drivers of early efforts to regulate the finance sector. And from the 1930s until the 1980s it appears that Democrats were the defenders of that regulatory structure against increasing Republican efforts to ease regulations. Now I want to turn to a different kind of evidence for partisan convergence by analyzing annual time series data from 1913 to 2014.[12] The first question I examine is whether the effect of partisan power in national policy-making institutions on financial deregulation changed over this period. If we see partisan effects on financial deregulation early in the period and diminished partisan effects later in the period, this would be additional evidence of partisan convergence in this domain.

The dependent variable is *financial deregulation*. This annual measure is the same one that was used earlier in the chapter based on Philippon and Reshef (2012). It represents an index of financial deregulation combining separation of commercial and investment banks, interest rate ceilings, and separation of banks and insurance companies.[13] This variable is scaled so that higher values indicate less regulation of the finance sector. The explanatory variables are dichotomous indicators of Democratic control of the presidency, Senate, and House, each coded 1 when Democrats are in control and 0 otherwise.[14]

I start by estimating a simple model in which movement over time in deregulation and party control of policy-making institutions are observed. The question this analysis answers is whether changes in party control of policy-making institutions correspond to income inequality changes.[15]

Figure 5.5 plots the key results from this model. We see a statistically significant negative effect of Democratic control of the Senate on financial deregulation. The effect of a Democratic president is also likely negative but just misses statistical significance.[16] However, party control of the House has no effect over the full period.[17] This result is interesting, possibly suggesting that there were never policy differences between the two parties in the House. However, I am inclined to think based on the historical analysis above that the null result in the House is driven by the fact that the Senate played a more central role than the House in the policy-making process related to financial regulation and deregulation.

The next question is whether the partisan effects above changed over time, consistent with the argument of partisan convergence. If partisan convergence happened as the legislative history of financial deregulation suggests, the partisan effects seen above (in the Senate and presidency) should diminish beginning sometime around the late 1970s. I examine this possibility by reestimating the model above (dropping the House because of its lack of statistical significance in the original model) for years up to 1982 and years after 1982.[18]

In figure 5.6 I chart the partisan effects before and after 1982. In each chart there are two dots along with confidence intervals. The left dot in each chart presents the effect of Democratic control before 1982, while the right dot shows the post-1982 effect. There is evidence that the parties converged in the Senate on matters of financial deregulation post-1982. Prior to 1982, the effect of Democratic control of the Senate on financial deregulation was negative and strongly statistically significant. But after 1982, this effect diminishes to zero. For the president, however, the effect of Democratic control before and after 1982 is clearly not different. It may be that the limited number of years with Democratic presidents after 1982 helps explain why we see no difference here. These results also suggest that to the extent

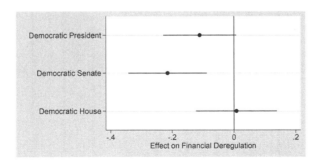

5.5. The effect of partisan control of policy institutions on deregulation, 1913–2014.
Source: Author's calculations from annual data, 1913 to 2014.
Note: Each dot represents the estimated effect of annual change in each explanatory variable on annual change in financial deregulation. The lines around the dots show a 95 percent confidence interval.

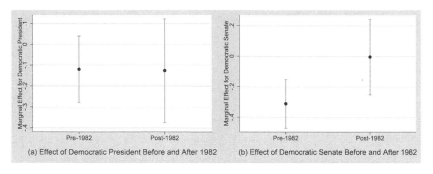

5.6. The effect of partisanship on financial deregulatory policy before and after 1982.
Source: Author's calculations from annual data, 1913 to 2014.
Note: Each dot represents the estimated effect of annual change in each explanatory variable on annual change in financial deregulation. The lines around the dots show a 95 percent confidence interval.

partisan convergence occurred on financial deregulation, the key convergence happened in the Senate, which bolsters the more detailed evidence of partisan convergence that the historical discussion above revealed.

Explaining the Convergence

Reviewing the history of legislative action on financial regulation and deregulation as well as a quantitative analysis of time series data both point to partisan convergence in this domain. The Democratic Party, at least to some extent, shifted toward the traditional conservative position in opposition to government regulation. But what was driving this convergence?

Rising inequality may have been a contributing factor. The timing seems right. After supporting an increasingly strong regulatory framework in the financial sector from the Great Depression through the 1960s, Democratic commitment to financial regulation began to falter just as inequality was beginning to rise. By the time financial deregulation was fully accomplished, inequality had been rising for about two decades, and income concentration had increased dramatically from its low point in the mid-1970s.

The evidence from chapters 3 and 4 can help to explain how inequality could have softened support for financial regulation. Support for egalitarian policy, particularly egalitarian policies that limit the incomes of those at the top, declines among some citizens as inequality increases. This pattern is present primarily among the poor and those with racist attitudes. While there is scant evidence on preferences specific to financial deregulation, if attitudes toward financial deregulation fit into this broader pattern, a key portion of the Democratic Party base may have become less supportive of financial regulation as inequality was increasing from the 1970s to the 1990s. This would have reduced some of the electoral incentives of Democrats to remain defenders of the existing regulatory framework in the finance sector. To the extent that there is evidence on attitudes toward regulation, substantial majorities are likely to be in favor. But even if there is majority support, if this majority has become smaller over time it gives politicians some signal that they have room to maneuver. If such opinion shifts were occurring, they would only have been compounded by the Republican electoral victories of the mid-1990s and the more general shift toward free market thinking among intellectual elites. It is quite clear that the increasing power of Republicans in Congress played an important role in getting the deregulatory ball rolling in Congress.

But it is unlikely that the Democratic shift toward financial deregulation was primarily a response to shifting opinion or electoral outcomes. It is highly likely that the increasing power of the wealthy, who overwhelmingly support neoliberal promarket reforms, and the increasing unity of the financial sector in favor of deregulation played a central role. The power of the wealthy, and the lack of counterbalancing role of labor unions (which is really the only major type of organization that represents middle-class interests), increased in tandem with inequality (Hacker and Pierson 2010, B. Page and Gilens 2017, Schlozman, Verba, and Brady 2012). While it takes little power to stop policy making from happening, rising inequality may have contributed in important ways to the stars aligning for inegalitarian policy change in the regulation of finance.

We have already seen preliminary evidence for the role of income concentration in feeding financial deregulation. Above, we saw that economic inequality and financial deregulation form a positive feedback loop in which increasing inequality generates financial deregulation that begets more economic inequality. And I discussed above how rising inequality might generate incentives, particularly for Democrats, to shift to the right in the domain of financial deregulation. If economic inequality helped to create the conditions necessary for partisan convergence, then the effect of partisanship in the Senate (where convergence was most clearly seen in the analysis above) should be moderated by rising inequality. In this section of the analysis I explore that possibility.

However, there are several other factors related to economic inequality that might also play a role in partisan convergence, and I want to explore those as well. Stagnating wages in the middle and bottom of the income distribution coupled with rising wages for the highly skilled since 1970 created a situation in which the middle class was left behind economically. One potential, if unsustainable, solution to this problem was credit.[19] If credit could more easily be extended to middle- and lower-income families, they could maintain increasing standards of living in the face of declining or stagnating wages. The regulatory environment of the late 1970s, however, made substantial growth in credit to low- and middle-income individuals difficult. The basic trajectory of stagnating middle incomes, increased demand for credit, and the deregulatory response has been documented elsewhere (Gorton 2012, Heathcote, Perri, and Violante 2010, Krippner 2011, Kumhof, Rancière, and Winant 2015, Treeck 2014). This increased demand for credit among low- and middle-income individuals could explain greater support for deregulation among Democrats. While financial deregulation might have previously been seen as a benefit only to the wealthy, the economic context of the 1980s made it possible for Democrats to reinterpret financial deregulation as essential to the short-term well-being of their core constituents. Some Democratic policy makers made this argument fairly explicit. During the House debate of FSMA of 1999, Cynthia McKinney (D-GA) touted its potential benefits to middle- and lower-income Americans: "When banks offer securities, insurance, and other financial services directly and through affiliates, they will bring a new level of convenience and choice to customers from every economic bracket from Decatur, Georgia to Watts, Los Angeles" (US House Committee on Banking and Financial Services 1997). If credit expansion is part of the explanation for partisan convergence, then we should observe smaller partisan effects on deregulation as credit increases.

A second potential explanation of partisan convergence is campaign finance. It is not controversial to assume that donors from the financial sector are more supportive of financial deregulation than average citizens (Gilens and Page 2014, B. Page, Bartels, and Seawright 2013, Schlozman, Verba, and Brady 2012). There is also evidence that politicians are more attentive to their donors than regular constituents (Kalla and Broockman 2016). But scholars of interest groups have rarely found explicit connections between money in politics and policy outcomes (Ansolabehere, Figueiredo, and Snyder 2003). Therefore, if an increasing share of campaign funds have come from the financial sector, it is possible that politicians would become more open to deregulation. If, in particular, Democratic campaign funding sources shifted toward the financial sector this could provide a compelling explanation for partisan convergence. If this explanation is correct, we should observe smaller partisan effects on deregulation as more campaign funds come from the finance sector.

A third potential explanation of partisan convergence on financial deregulation is a shift in the interest system. Labor unions, which were once a strong voice for workers, have declined in membership and become increasingly representative of public sector professionals rather than the traditional working class. As labor unions have declined, corporate interest groups have proliferated, weakening the voice for middle-class interests at the same time that upper-class interests grew stronger. Since labor unions were historically a key source of campaign funding and votes for Democratic politicians, their decline could have especially important implications for the electoral calculus of Democrats. One likely implication of declining support from labor for Democrats is a reduced incentive for Democratic policy makers to support regulatory policies that protect the working class. If this explanation for partisan convergence is correct, we should observe reduced partisan effects on deregulation as the strength of unions decreases.

Finally, a fourth potential explanation for partisan convergence is globalization. In a globalized economy, domestic policy makers could face pressures to deregulate because of increasing international competition. As exposure to international competition increases, a corporate sector that faces regulation can credibly argue that they are placed at a competitive disadvantage relative to competitors based in countries with less regulation. Globalization, in a sense, can reduce the ideological dimensions of the debate over deregulation and shift the discussion in a more technocratic direction. The effects of globalization might also be seen as a reasonable proxy for the effect of ideas, as exemplified by the growing agreement around promarket ideology summarized in the Washington Consensus. If this mechanism is at work, we would expect legislators in contexts that are more highly exposed to the global economy to be more supportive of deregulation. Since Republicans in the United States have long been ideologically predisposed toward limiting regulation, globalization is most likely to have effects on the policy preferences of Democrats, pushing them to converge with Republicans on financial deregulation.

To test for the moderating effects of economic inequality as well as these four related explanations for partisan convergence, I estimate a series of models very similar to the one above designed to capture the effect of Democratic Senate partisanship on financial deregulation. And just as above I am interested in how the effect of partisanship changes over time. Previously, I was focused on whether the partisan effect was different before and after a particular point in time. Now I am interested in whether the partisan effect depends on the values of the conditioning factors discussed above.[20] That is, does the effect of partisanship change as these conditioning factors move higher or lower over time?

Figure 5.7 presents the results. Each figure charts the effect of party control of the Senate on financial deregulation as the level of a second variable changes. For example, figure 5.7a, shows that the effect of Senate party control is negative and significant at low levels of inequality. But as we move from left to right in the chart and the level of inequality moves higher, the effect of party control dissipates. By the time inequality reaches its highest observed levels, the effect of party control is essentially zero. This result is consistent with the idea that inequality has created incentives for the Democratic Party to converge with Republicans in the domain of financial deregulation. Democratic control of the Senate mattered when inequality was low, but when inequality rises this partisan effect goes away.

There is support for two of the four additional explanations of partisan convergence in the Senate. In figure 5.7b we see some evidence that the effect of partisanship was minimized as credit expanded. When total loans per capita increase, the effect of a shift from Republican to Democratic control of the Senate reducing financial deregulation vanishes. This supports the idea that as the potential credit benefits afforded by deregulation broadened, Democratic opposition to deregulation diminished. The moderating effect of trade openness (figure 5.7d) is also in line with expectations. Here we see that when trade openness is low, Democratic strength reduces deregulation. However, when trade openness is higher, the effect of Democratic partisanship is eliminated.

In figure 5.7c we see only suggestive evidence that campaign finance played a role in partisan convergence. While there is not a large shift in partisan effects as finance sector funding for Democrats increased and the observed effects are not significant across the entire range of the campaign finance variable, the direction of the shift is consistent with the idea that campaign finance contributed to partisan convergence. While the results for campaign finance are certainly not strong, they are suggestive. And it is worth noting that availability of campaign finance data severely restricts the time frame for this portion of the analysis. In fact, the campaign finance results are based on data from only 1980 onward, which is the period in which there were no partisan effects of note to begin with. That there is any pattern at all here is therefore notable. Finally, the evidence related to the role of unions in partisan convergence is contrary to expectations. There is essentially no change in partisan effects across levels of union strength. The decline of unions, then, did not drive partisan convergence on deregulation

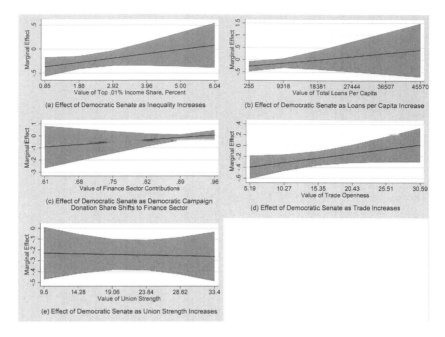

5.7. The conditional effect of partisanship on financial deregulation.
Source: Author's calculations from annual data.
Note: Each line represents the estimated effect of annual change from Republican to Democratic control of the Senate. The estimated effect is allowed to vary depending on the value of the variable on the x-axis (bottom). Each point on the line then provides an estimate of the effect of Senate control at a particular value on the x-axis of the conditioning variable. The shaded area around the lines show a 95 percent confidence interval.

in the Senate. What this suggests is that despite their general decline, unions have remained an important voice within the Democratic Party. However, the decline of unions has been important in the politics of economic inequality in numerous other ways.

Conclusions

This chapter has focused on the possibility that partisan convergence in certain policy domains could have been fueled by rising inequality. I looked in detail at how this process worked in the domain of financial deregulation. In the case of financial deregulation, the partisan convergence that appears to have happened generated consensus around an inegalitarian policy. There may be other policy areas where this could have happened as well. Trade in particular comes to mind (though the distributional effects of trade are unclear) as well as other policies connected to what has become known as the

Washington Consensus. Future research might consider more systematically whether the basic framework outlined here could be applied other examples of inegalitarian policy making.

Using a combination of qualitative and quantitative evidence this chapter produced two core conclusions. First, we saw evidence that financial deregulation and economic inequality are part of a self-reinforcing feedback loop. This finding was the initial step of the analysis, which pointed to why partisan convergence on financial deregulation could be an interesting component of the overarching idea of an inequality trap to which we keep returning.

Next, I discussed the history of financial regulation and deregulation. The early efforts at regulating the financial industry in the wake of the Great Depression were driven by Democrats, and it was difficult for Republicans to muster much resistance in the context of an economic crisis. As time went along, however, Republicans became much more antagonistic toward government regulation of the economy, and financial deregulation entered the policy agenda. Nevertheless, the original regulatory framework created by the Glass-Steagall Act and later expanded by the Bank Holding Company Act of 1956 withstood increasing challenges until the early 1980s. Democratic opposition to deregulation appears to be a key reason why deregulation did not begin to happen in the legislative sphere sooner. But, slowly, the position of Democrats began to shift. While a core group of staunch liberals maintained support for traditional regulation of the finance sector, a new and more moderate group of Democrats warmed to the idea of financial deregulation. When some of the core aspects of the traditional regulatory framework were repealed, most Democrats supported (or at least failed to strongly oppose) the measures. Partisan convergence came onto the scene just after inequality began to precipitously rise.

To provide additional evidence on the question of partisan convergence and its potential causes, I examined time series data over a more than one-hundred-year period. The central finding was that the best evidence for partisan convergence is in the Senate, where there was a notable negative effect of Democratic control until sometime around the early 1980s, when the partisan effect essentially disappeared. In seeking to explain this convergence, I considered economic inequality as well as a handful of other explanations that could be connected to inequality. The results for economic inequality were clear. As inequality increases, the effect of Senate partisanship on financial deregulation evaporates, which is evidence in support of rising inequality reproducing itself through partisan convergence in the domain of regulatory policy. Two other factors, increasing demand for credit and trade openness, both of which could be linked to rising inequality, also had the effect of decreasing partisan differences on deregulation in the Senate.

We saw in this chapter that part of the reason inequality is as high as it is today is deregulation in the finance sector. In the next chapter we will see that once inequality is high, the status quo bias inherent in the US policy-making system becomes particularly problematic for efforts to reduce inequality. In the realm of financial deregulation, policy action was taken that increased the gap between the rich and the poor. Now I turn to what may be more the norm of contemporary American policy making—policy inaction. We will see that such inaction can also contribute to the feedback loop of inequality in the United States.

SIX

Polarization and Policy Stagnation

The 2008 election marked a hopeful moment for progressives. In the wake of the country's largest economic crisis since the Great Depression, Democrats were able to secure unified control of national policy-making institutions for the first time since the early 1990s. Nancy Pelosi would remain Speaker of the House and enjoy an increased majority in the newly elected Congress. Democrats gained firmer control in the Senate, expanding their share in that chamber to as many as fifty-eight seats during the 111th Congress. And, of course, Barack Obama was elected president. Obama, a former community organizer and the first African American to hold the office, was seen as a true progressive. Unified control of government with Obama at the helm would surely produce a wave of egalitarian policy making.

Obama had big plans. He seemed to realize that various forms of inequality had become a major concern, and he wanted to do something about it. He promised universal health care, immigration reform, help for homeowners facing foreclosure, tax increases on the wealthy, and new financial regulations among other things. And some of these ideas were enacted, to at least some extent, under unified Democratic control. The Affordable Care Act dramatically increased access to health insurance, although it did not provide universal coverage and included benefits for wealthy health industry companies and medical providers to ensure their support. Those at the top of the income ladder experienced some tax increases, but not to the extent candidate Obama promised.

Unified Democratic control would not survive the first midterm election of the Obama era. Republicans regained control of the House after the 2010 elections. While that outcome was likely due partially to the predictable pattern of opposition gains in midterm elections, we also saw in chapter 4 that high levels of inequality help Republican congressional candidates. Only so much could be accomplished in just two years of unified Democratic control, certainly not enough to reverse more than thirty years of steadily increasing income concentration. And even with unified control, many compromises had to be made to secure sufficient votes. Once Republicans took control of the House, legislative accomplishments became even more difficult to secure, and Obama had to resort to the more tenuous and impermanent process of executive action in order to make any advances on his progressive agenda.

Progressives in 2008 were rightly hopeful. But they were downplaying one of the first lessons students learn about the US Constitution in civics class—that there are substantial safeguards to prevent tyranny of the majority. The Constitution was constructed to guard against concerns that an untempered and unenlightened majority of the masses could wreak havoc on their fellow citizens using the power of the state, so the founders made sure the democratic system they were creating was not purely democratic. The president would be indirectly elected by a group of elites selected by voters, and suffrage was narrowly constrained compared to modern democracies. Senators were to be elected not by the people but by state legislatures. Only the House would be directly elected by voters.[1]

The system was designed in a way that quick action would be difficult. For legislative action to happen, both chambers of the legislature and the president would have to agree. The American legislative process would require a great deal of consensus to move forward. Moreover, the full power of the state would not be completely controlled by a single actor. Instead, the executive and legislative functions were split, and the judiciary asserted its ability to interpret the law as well as negate legislative and executive actions that were inconsistent with the Constitution. And, of course, the American system is federal, with states as well as the national government playing an important role in governing, further fragmenting state power and limiting governing autonomy.

All this adds up to a system that is inherently conservative—not in the right-left sense of the term but rather in its bias toward the status quo. The American system is not one designed to delight those who would seek to take swift and dramatic action to solve social problems using the power of the state. Action happens, of course, but the process is typically slow and places a high priority on protecting the interests of electoral losers. A great deal of power must be amassed over a lengthy period of time to achieve significant change via the American policy-making process.

This chapter explores how status quo bias in the American policy process can contribute to an inequality trap. As we recall the distinction between a traditional inequality trap and a black hole or doom loop type trap introduced in chapter 2, we see the potential role of status quo bias is more in line with a traditional trap. If status quo bias contributes to an inequality trap, it would work something like this: inequality rises, triggers the relevance of status quo bias in the American system, which then makes it harder to produce the egalitarian policy changes that would reduce inequality. Allow me to elaborate.

The core question here, as in chapter 5, is how America's policy-making institutions and the actors situated within those institutions deal with rising inequality. In focusing on the policy-making process, this chapter builds substantively on the analysis from the previous chapter. There, we saw evidence that rising inequality can facilitate inegalitarian policy making. Thus, rising inequality can help overcome the status quo bias of the American policy process, specifically for a subset of policies that further increase economic inequality. In this chapter we will see that the distributional consequences of status quo bias change as inequality increases. When inequality is low, status quo bias has no effect on income concentration. But when inequality is high, the distributional effects of the policy stagnation resulting from status quo bias tends to be inegalitarian in its consequences. To some extent, the emphasis in this chapter is the institutional setting of the United States and the ways elements of constitutional design such as separation of powers and bicameralism shape the policy response to changing levels of inequality. But the chapter also explores how elite behavior within these institutions is shaped by inequality.

I start with two observations: that the US system generates a strong bias toward the status quo and that increasing partisan polarization is one of the defining characteristics of American politics over the past two decades. I discuss how recent scholarship has sought to tie polarization and status quo bias to distributional outcomes, and I seek to test the degree to which policy stagnation driven by increasing polarization has both contributed to and responded to variation in inequality over time. The evidence presented in this chapter shows that status quo bias in American policy making is yet another mechanism contributing to America's inequality trap.

Conditional Status Quo Bias and the Inequality Trap

Observers of American politics are well familiar with many of the factors that make policy action difficult in the US system. Separated powers along with a bicameral legislature generate multiple veto points. Where veto points abound, policy making is more difficult because actors in a wider range of institutions must come to agreement before policy change can occur (D. Brady and Volden 1998, Krehbiel 1998). Unlike a parliamentary system, where decisions taken by the government are sufficient to enact change, in the United States a majority (or supermajority) in two separate chambers of the legislature as well as the president must come to agreement in order to produce dramatic policy change through the lawmaking process. Having control of even just the House of Representatives presents a political party with the ability, under some conditions, to dramatically influence the policy-making process, particularly by shaping which status quo policies are protected and which policies are part of the policy change agenda (Cox and McCubbins 2005, Finocchiaro and Rohde 2008, Krehbiel 1998, Richman 2011). Enhancing the difficulty of achieving policy action is the fact that actors in the House, Senate, and presidency are serving divergent constituencies—the president with a national constituency, senators elected by states, and members of the House from much smaller districts within states. Finally, the comparative lack of party discipline (relative to many parliamentary systems) and numerous access points for influence in the US policy-making system provide interest groups a high degree of leverage, especially to stymie legislation contrary to their goals (Gilens 2012, Hacker and Pierson 2010, Schlozman, Verba, and Brady 2012).

Within this system of separated powers, the Senate has unique characteristics that further heighten bias toward the status quo (Binder 2003, Wawro and Schickler 2006). Most generally, the Senate is designed to protect the rights of the minority party and even of individual members. In the modern Senate, requiring sixty votes to pass legislation has become quite common. This, of course, is due to the often-discussed presence of the filibuster. There are also numerous other rules and norms in the Senate designed to protect the rights of individual members, including holds on nominations, open procedures for amending legislation on the floor, and the common need for unanimous consent in order to move forward on Senate business. All this makes policy change difficult and often places Senate (in)action at the core of the US policy process.

Three broad scenarios can arise from the stagnation that often characterizes the US policy-making process. The first is *policy drift* (Hacker 2005) or deferred maintenance (Mettler 2016), in which economic or societal conditions shift in a way that modifies the effects of a policy that has remained unchanged. A very simple example of policy drift is the minimum wage. As inflation occurs, the real value of the minimum wage declines. Without enacting a change in the minimum wage, or indexing its value to inflation, the income floor for workers defined by the minimum wage will naturally fall over time. Second, *policy sclerosis* can occur when new circumstances emerge but remain unaddressed because of policy inaction. A useful example along these lines is the increasing income returns to education (Goldin and Katz 2008). While the economy has changed in ways that increased the relative value of education in the marketplace, policy changes to mitigate the distributional consequences of this economic shift have not materialized. Third, existing policies are sometimes *stretched* to problems they were not designed to address. For example, the Clean Air Act was originally designed to reduce airborne contaminants. The target was reducing the release of chemicals that caused negative public health consequences. While the law has been amended and expanded several times since its initial passage in 1963, lawmakers have not been able to agree on reforms that would explicitly confront the growing threat of greenhouse gases. This left the Obama administration no recourse but to craft administrative rules to address problems the law was not really designed to tackle. In each of these three scenarios of policy drift, sclerosis, and stretching, policy inaction has important implications for social and economic outcomes, often with consequences relevant to income concentration.

Policies created in decades past, of course, cannot possibly anticipate every new technological or economic innovation that would make aspects of a law inefficient, inapplicable, or insufficient. Old policy frameworks must be updated to confront new situations effectively. Completely new policies must be created to cope with new policy problems, and old policies sometimes need to be repealed in order to align with current views about the appropriate breadth and purpose of the state (Mettler 2016). But the legislature often cannot make all the updates required to bring policy in line with current needs. Sometimes inaction is simply due to the scope of work that would be required to avoid drift or sclerosis across a broad set of policies. Sometimes it is due to intentional neglect by those whose ideological preferences or economic interests profit from the status quo. And sometimes policy inaction is the result of an inability to reach consensus due to ideological polarization within policy-making institutions that require consensus for policy change to occur.

This bias toward inaction in US policy making is the foundation of what I call conditional status quo bias (CSQB), which is a fancy label for a fairly simple argument about how status quo bias is connected to income concentration (Enns, Kelly, Morgan, Volscho, and Witko 2014). The argument is that status quo bias is a predictor of rising inequality, but only when certain conditions are present, with the most relevant condition being high levels of inequality. Think of it this way: There are lots of reasons that inequality might rise or fall. And many of those explanations for inequality are largely independent of public policy. But public policy affects income concentration (Bartels 2008, Kelly 2009, Hacker and Pierson 2010). When inequality is low, status quo bias favors the maintenance of low inequality because policy intervention would be required to raise inequality, while inaction maintains the status quo. But when inequality is high, it takes policy action to *reduce inequality*. This means overcoming status quo bias. This suggests that the effect of status quo bias on inequality will be different depending on the existing level of inequality. When inequality is relatively low, bias toward the status quo favors maintenance of this equilibrium. But when inequality is relatively high, the effect of status quo bias is just the opposite, constraining the policy action needed to reduce inequality. This expectation is only enhanced by the likelihood that the existing political environment in a low-inequality scenario is likely more egalitarian to begin with than the environment in a high-inequality scenario.

CSQB adds nuance to our understanding of the relationship between institutional structure and inequality. Essentially, this framework suggests that the effects of policy-making rules and institutions change depending on the preexisting level of inequality. If inequality is low and economic conditions are not pushing inequality higher, bias toward the status quo policy framework is unlikely to produce rising inequality. Although stagnation in certain policy areas may have the potential to increase inequality over time regardless of the existing gap between the rich and the poor (Hacker and Pierson 2010), major policy change is likely unnecessary to keep inequality relatively low when economic conditions are not widening inequality. On the other hand, when inequality increases, this is precisely the time serious policy action is needed to halt or reverse the trend. In this situation, status quo bias would enable substantial increases in inequality. This leads to the prediction that status quo bias will induce more and more inequality as the existing level of inequality increases. CSQB, then, contributes to an inequality trap.

This argument builds on work by Hacker and Pierson (2010), as well as McCarty, Poole, and Rosenthal (2006), which examines the connection between partisan polarization, policy stagnation, and economic inequality. Hacker and Pierson (2010) convincingly argue that policy stagnation has contributed to rising inequality in the United States. They show, for instance, that failure to update finance sector regulations (even before the Glass-Steagall framework was repealed) encouraged the use of risky financial instruments, generating massive economic rewards for those at the top while also injecting new risks into the financial system that contributed to the 2007 crisis. McCarty, Poole, and Rosenthal's (2006) focus is on polarization, but they make a parallel argument—economic inequality will rise as policy stagnation, specifically induced by party polarization, increases. The argument of CSQB is similar, but instead of positing a consistent inequality-inducing effect of policy stagnation, I argue that the effect of policy stagnation is highly dependent on the existing level of inequality. Policy stagnation is more inequality inducing when inequality is already high under the CSQB framework but would not be expected to have parallel effects if inequality were low. Another distinction between CSQB and this earlier work is related to the nature of feedback between economic inequality and status quo bias. Hacker and Pierson (2010) appear to anticipate that high levels of inequality could strengthen the connection between policy stagnation and rising inequality. But they do not explicitly analyze this possibility. Instead, they focus on the fact that policy stagnation intensified as the power of moneyed interests increased alongside economic inequality, not the changing implications of status quo bias at differing levels of inequality. McCarty, Poole, and Rosenthal (2006) take a similar view, arguing that inequality and polarization are dance partners, with polarization producing more inequality and inequality producing more polarization. CSQB does not require direct feedback from polarization to inequality. Rather, inequality reinforces itself via status quo bias by changing the nature of the relationship between policy stagnation and inequality, not affecting policy stagnation or polarization directly.

CSQB marks a way to think about how *enduring* institutions can explain varying levels of inequality. This perspective argues that the practical relevance of status quo bias in institutional design is shaped by variations in political-economic circumstances. Consider veto points. Although the number of checks on policy making has not changed in the post–World War II era, the relevance of these veto points has varied over time. If the House, Senate, and president are all in agreement, the fact that there are so many veto players is less relevant than when these players are at odds (Krehbiel 1998). If the veto players argument explains rising inequality, then there should be a positive association between preference divergence across the veto points and income inequality. But if the CSQB argument is correct, the effect of preference divergence on inequality should become stronger and more positive as the gap between the rich and the poor increases.

We can also think about how changing political circumstances shape the implications of the Senate's institutional eccentricities. First, if Stepan and Linz (2012) are correct that the Senate has more explicit power than the House, any partisan or ideological effects (discussed below) should be magnified in the Senate. Second, given the important role of the filibuster in the Senate, if policy stagnation exacerbates inequality, then as the ideological distance between the median senator and the senator needed to overcome a filibuster (the "filibuster pivot") increases, inequality should increase as well.[2] In addition, the conditional component of CSQB predicts that the inequality-inducing effect of preference divergence within the Senate should grow as inequality increases.

In the analysis below, I focus on examining how economic inequality, polarization, and policy stagnation are related to one another using a variety of evidence. I start by seeking to determine whether there is a straightforward feedback relationship between inequality and polarization, which would support McCarty, Poole, and Rosenthal's (2006) view. I also examine evidence of the more complex relationships anticipated by CSQB and motivated by Hacker and Pierson's (2010) arguments about policy drift and winner-take-all politics. I find some support for both views, but the evidence for CSQB is stronger. The results here, as in the previous chapters, point to an inequality trap in America. But the mechanism now is policy stagnation.

Do Polarization and Inequality Reinforce Each Other?

I start with an analysis designed to examine a straightforward version of feedback between party polarization and income concentration. While McCarty, Poole, and Rosenthal (2006) present a variety of evidence that they interpret as supportive of a bidirectional relationship between polarization and economic inequality, at no point do they directly test the hypothesis of a positive feedback relationship between polarization and inequality. If party polarization contributes to a self-reinforcing pattern of economic inequality in the way they hypothesize, the most straightforward evidence of this would be a positive effect of polarization on inequality and also a reciprocal positive effect of polarization on inequality.

Figure 6.1 simply charts two measures of party polarization along with top income shares. Polarization is calculated separately for the House and the Senate, with polarization being the ideological distance between the median Democrat and median Republican in each chamber, based on their roll-call votes.[3] The patterns observed here are strong visual evidence consistent with a pattern of self-reinforcing inequality. Polarization and top income shares track each other very closely over time, and this observed pattern is the key piece of evidence that McCarty, Poole, and Rosenthal (2006) present in support of their argument that inequality and polarization

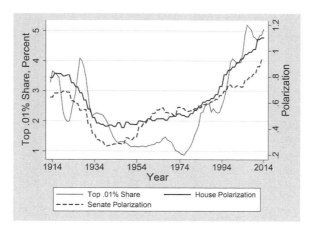

6.1. Income concentration and party polarization in Congress, 1913–2014.
Source: Calculated by author with data from the World Inequality Database and Lewis, Poole, Rosenthal, Boche, Rudkin, and Sonnet (2017).
Note: Top 0.01 percent share is plotted as a five-year moving average.

are part of an ongoing "dance" in which each partner follows the other over time.

This type of visual analysis is a useful first step, but it is far from iron-clad evidence of self-reinforcement. The pattern observed above is consistent with any of three conclusions: that more polarization produces more inequality, that more inequality produces more polarization, or that the relationship goes both ways. The same type of analysis that I have used in previous chapters as a test of self-reinforcing feedback can provide more systematic evidence to identify which direction this relationship goes. Since we have access to annual data over a long period of time (1913–2014) for both polarization and income concentration, we can utilize information about the timing of changes in each variable to figure out whether one is the "first mover." If polarization pushes inequality higher, then an increased level of polarization at one point in time should correspond with higher future values of inequality while accounting for past levels of inequality. If inequality pushes polarization higher, we should see the same pattern in reverse, with current increases in inequality predicting future increases in polarization.

I estimate a model capable of answering these questions and report the results in figure 6.2. The top two charts show how the level of inequality is affected by temporally prior shifts in polarization in the House and the Senate separately. The bottom two charts depict the effect of past shifts in inequality on House and Senate polarization.[4] We do not see evidence of

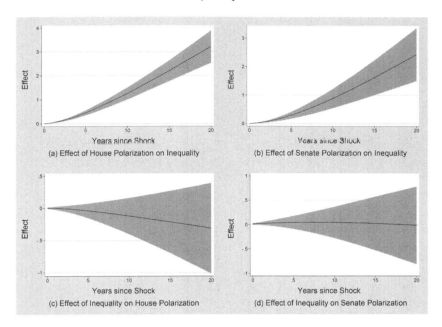

6.2. Is there a reciprocal relationship between inequality and polarization?
Source: Author's calculations from annual data, 1913 to 2014.
Note: The plot represents the predicted effect of a standard deviation shift in one variable on the other variable over a twenty-year period using orthogonalized cumulative impulse response functions based on two vector autoregressions including top 0.01 percent income share, either House or Senate party polarization, and a measure of legislative policy stagnation (J. Grant and Kelly 2008).

direct feedback in these results. An increase in polarization increases top income shares substantially over a long period of time. But the relationship does not go the other way. The bottom charts show that an increase in inequality has no statistically significant effect on polarization in either the House or Senate, and to the extent that there is any indication of a relationship it leans negative rather than positive. This is opposite of what would be expected if straightforward feedback effects were present.[5]

Inequality and Micro-Level Polarization in Congress

The macro-level time series data do not reveal the pattern of relationships between income inequality and party polarization that would be present in a straightforward self-reinforcing feedback loop between polarization and inequality. I now want to go beyond the aggregate analysis above and examine evidence at the micro level, focusing on cross-sectional variation among members of Congress (MCs) to see if additional evidence might point to different conclusions about the role that party polarization plays in an American inequality trap.

Here I examine the roll-call voting behavior of individual MCs. Roll-call voting, of course, serves as the foundation for the aggregate measures of polarization examined above. However, these aggregate measures could obscure important variation across individual MCs. Another way to conceptualize party polarization is to think of it as the effect that membership in one political party as opposed to the other has on roll-call voting. Using this strategy, we can think of roll-call voting behavior as the dependent variable and partisanship as the independent variable. The estimated effect of party is an indicator of party polarization. The question, then, is whether the effect of partisanship on legislative voting behavior is affected by income inequality.

I attempt to answer that question by estimating a model of legislator-level ideology.[6] The dependent variable is the legislator's ideological position (DW-NOMINATE), where higher scores indicate more conservative roll-call voting behavior. The key independent variable is the MCs party, scored 1 for Republicans and 0 for others. Along with this individual-level variable I include a variable that captures change in top 0.01 percent income share between the current and previous Congress (measured in the first year of the Congress). I interact this context level variable with individual-level partisanship as a way to test whether the effect of partisanship changes when the level of inequality is increasing.[7] Perhaps the easiest way to understand this model is to think of it as a series of cross-sectional models estimated repeatedly at different time points. If rising inequality contributes to increased polarization, we would expect the effect of partisanship on ideology to be stronger in cross-sections (Congresses) with increasing inequality than in cross-sections with decreasing inequality.

The key results are charted in figure 6.3. There, I plot the predicted effect of partisanship on ideology in different inequality contexts. The left portion of the chart shows the effect of partisanship when inequality is decreasing while the right side of the chart plots the effect of partisanship when inequality is increasing. The results show that there is no real change in the effect of partisanship on legislative voting behavior as inequality rises. The effect of Republican partisanship always pushes legislators toward conservative voting behavior, and this effect appears to become only marginally stronger when inequality is increasing. These results undermine the argument that rising inequality increases party polarization. Consistent with the previous time series results, this analysis provides further evidence that the

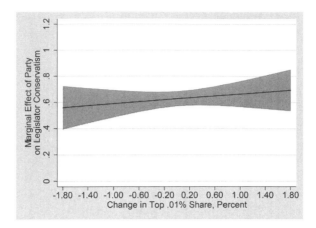

6.3. The constant effect of party as inequality rises.
Source: Author's calculations from biannual data, 1913 to 2014.
Note: Chart plots the marginal effect (with 95 percent confidence interval) of legislator partisanship on legislator ideology in the House within a Congress as inequality is increasing or decreasing. Values on the left end of the chart show the effect of partisanship when inequality is declining while values on the right end of the chart show the effect of partisanship when inequality is increasing. Results are from a multilevel model with legislators nested within Congresses.

relationship between inequality and polarization only goes one way—from polarization to inequality.

Testing Conditional Status Quo Bias and Self-Reinforcing Inequality

Thus far we have seen evidence bolstering the claim that polarization is an important explanation for rising inequality. But we have not found evidence that there is feedback from inequality to polarization. Inequality does move higher when polarization increases, but higher inequality does not affect polarization. Figure 6.4a provides a visual depiction of what we can conclude from the analysis to this point. Since party polarization is a particularly relevant precursor to policy stagnation in a system biased toward the status quo, this evidence is consistent with the conclusion that status quo bias is not part of a straightforward feedback loop with income concentration.

If we were to stop here, the conclusion would be that status quo bias does not contribute in a meaningful way to an American inequality trap. However, I have elaborated a more nuanced *conditional* status quo bias framework in which rising inequality would feed back into the political system not by directly increasing polarization and status quo bias but by *changing* the effects of polarization and status quo bias on future levels of income concentration. This type of pattern is visualized in figure 6.4b. Here, income concentration does not directly affect status quo bias but instead changes the relationship between status quo bias and distributional outcomes. If status quo bias has a more inequality-inducing effect when inequality is high, this pattern would result in a particular form of feedback that would nevertheless produce a spiral of inequality. This, in fact, is the core prediction of CSQB.

To test the extent to which inequality might reinforce itself by changing the relationship between policy stagnation and distributional outcomes, I examine movement over time in economic inequality along with a variety of variables connected to status quo bias, while controlling for other potential explanations of inequality. The key aspect of the analysis is an effort to determine whether the effect of status quo bias changes when inequality rises or falls. For CSQB to contribute to self-reinforcing inequality, we would expect to see the inequality-inducing effects of status quo bias increase as inequality rises.

The dependent variable in this portion of the analysis is the annual share of aggregate pretax, pretransfer income held by the top 1 percent from 1940 to 2006.[8] I consider four variables to assess different facets of status quo bias. First, I include a measure of the ideological distance between the filibuster pivot and the Senate median.[9]

Using these scores for the Senate, I identify the filibuster pivot, which as mentioned earlier is the ideological score of the senator whose vote is required to end a filibuster. For each year I identify the relevant senator by arranging the Senate from left to right in ideological space. When Democrats are in the majority, the filibuster pivot is the senator who is more conservative than fifty-nine other Senators. When Republicans are in power, the

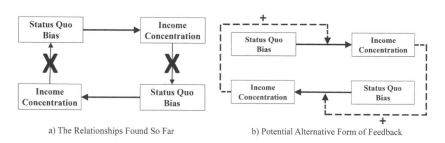

a) The Relationships Found So Far   b) Potential Alternative Form of Feedback

6.4. The evidence so far that the conditional status quo bias form of feedback between polarization and income inequality.

filibuster pivot is the senator more liberal than fifty-nine others.[10] As the distance between the median and filibuster pivot widens, the relevance of the Senate's unique institutional rules concerning cloture increases, and bias toward the status quo in policy making should increase as well. If CSQB is at work, this variable should generate larger increases in inequality when the level of income concentration is higher.

The second measure of status quo bias is designed to capture changes in the relevance of multiple veto points.[11] I calculate the distance between the House median and Senate median, between the House median and president, between the Senate median and president, and between the Senate median and filibuster pivot. I then take the absolute value of the largest distance as an indicator of maximum preference divergence across the main policy-making actors (maximum preference distance). As preference divergence increases, the presence of multiple veto points becomes more problematic for policy making, thereby increasing status quo bias. Again, the effect of this variable should be more inequality inducing as income concentration increases if the arguments of CSQB are correct.

Third, I include the ideological distance between the median member of the majority and minority parties in the House to account for general partisan polarization (House party polarization). The expectation of CSQB is that polarization will increase inequality only when inequality is sufficiently high.

Finally, I include a measure that explicitly captures the amount of policy produced by Congress. This measure, which was originally developed by J. Grant and Kelly (2008), is based on a combination of important and general lawmaking (congressional policy product). It measures overall legislative production during each Congress and taps the idea of policy stagnation. I have coded this variable so that higher values mean more policy stagnation (rather than more policy action as in the original version). Of the four status quo bias variables, this is the most direct measure of the status quo bias concept, since it explicitly captures how much policy is being produced. If the effect of status quo bias is conditioned by inequality, then policy stagnation should increase inequality most when income concentration is high.

To test the conditional hypothesis—that the effects of institutionalized status quo bias are more inequality inducing when existing levels of inequality are high—these measures are interacted with prior levels of inequality. These interaction terms allow a direct test of the hypothesis that rising inequality (whether caused by economic factors, political factors, or both) will be more likely to persist under conditions of greater status quo bias.

Analyzing Conditional Status Quo Bias

I estimate a time series model to analyze movement over time in the variables discussed above.[12] I focus on the core substantive results, which relate to how the effect of status quo bias variables on distributional outcomes changes as the level of income concentration rises. Figure 6.5 presents the marginal effects of each of the four status quo bias variables at all observed values of top income share.[13] Each portion of the chart, then, plots the effect of a status quo bias variable on the y-axis with the level of inequality varying on the x-axis.

Figure 6.5a presents the results for the effect of filibuster pivot distance on inequality. The distance between the median senator and the senator needed to break a filibuster generally has a positive effect on inequality. That is, as the senator representing the filibuster pivot increasingly differs from the chamber as a whole, inequality tends to increase. This is consistent with a general theory of status quo bias and economic inequality. But this effect is not the same at all levels of inequality. For the lowest values of inequality, in fact, this effect is not distinguishable from zero. But as inequality increases, the effect of the filibuster pivot distance increases dramatically. That the inequality-inducing effect of the filibuster pivot distance increases as inequality rises is consistent with the idea of *conditional* status quo bias discussed above. This result is also consistent with a self-reinforcing connection between inequality and status quo bias. As status quo bias increases, inequality generally increases as well. And as inequality increases, the inegalitarian effects of status quo bias are further amplified.

The results for legislative policy production are also consistent with CSQB. When congressional policy production is more stagnant, inequality typically increases. Again, this would be the result predicted by a straightforward theory linking status quo bias to inequality—the status quo allows inequality to increase while policy action generally reduces inequality.[14] But we see in figure 6.5b that the effect of policy stagnation becomes stronger as inequality increases, just as with the filibuster pivot distance. When inequality is high, stagnation increases income concentration more than when inequality is low. This means that legislative *inaction* is especially likely to enhance inequality as inequality rises, which is consistent with the prediction of CSQB as well as self-reinforcing inequality.

The results for interinstitutional ideological distance (figure 6.5c) are not nearly as clear as the results for the first two variables connected to status quo bias, but again the *pattern* is consistent with the predictions of CSQB. While never statistically significant, the estimated effect of the dis-

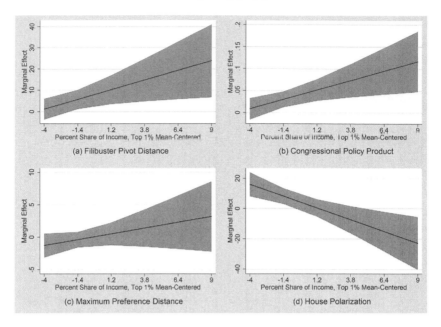

6.5. Effect of status quo bias at observed levels of top income share.
Source: Author's calculations.
Note: Chart plots the marginal effect (with 95 percent confidence interval) of each variable at increasing values of inequality.

tance between the House, Senate, and president is sloped upward, as we would expect if preference divergence across the policy-making institutions of American government produced a bigger gap between the rich and the poor as inequality increases.

Finally, figure 6.5d drives home the point that it is not really general polarization that generates a self-reinforcing link between inequality and America's status quo–inducing institutions. In fact, it appears from these results that polarization actually *increases* inequality when inequality is low and *decreases* inequality when inequality is high. This is not at all consistent with the argument that polarization is a central factor creating self-reinforcing inequality. Once more specific factors connected to status quo bias are also accounted for, the effect of polarization is not relevant to understanding self-reinforcing feedback between inequality and American politics. Rather, the evidence here makes clear that it is the specific institutional context of the United States that contributes to America's inequality trap.

Conclusions

America's institutions are biased toward the status quo. This is in part due to concern over the potential for the majority to use unobstructed policy change to tyrannize the minority, and in part to a desire for serious deliberation accompanied by broad consensus before changing directions. But it is important to point out clearly that the status quo bias inherent in US institutions also seems to benefit the rich. When conditions for status quo bias are present, and when little legislative accomplishment occurs, inequality tends to rise. This is not a completely new story, of course. Several scholars have pointed to the potential distributional consequences of status quo bias in the American political system.

The analysis here confirms results from previous studies that point to increasing polarization and policy stagnation as key explanations of the rise in inequality (McCarty, Poole, and Rosenthal 2006, Hacker and Pierson 2010). The theme of this book, though, is how economic inequality shapes politics in inequality-reinforcing ways. In looking for evidence of such feedback, I found little support for the idea that inequality increases polarization or policy stagnation more generally in the US system.

Instead of direct feedback, I emphasized a theory of conditional status quo bias. This theory suggests that factors connected to status quo bias might respond in more nuanced ways to increasing inequality. Rather than expecting status quo bias to increase directly in response to rising inequality, the CSQB argument is that inequality and status quo bias interact in more complex ways that change the nature of the relationship between status quo bias and inequality. Specifically, status quo bias becomes a greater force for inequality as inequality rises. The feedback that happens under this view is self-reinforcing, but the self-reinforcement comes by changing the nature of relationships within the political system rather than changing the political inputs themselves.

The evidence supports this view. As inequality rises, the distributional consequences of status quo bias become inegalitarian. These results point to the conclusion that status quo bias, certain forms of polarization, and policy stagnation all contribute to America's inequality trap. Inequality feeds back into the policy-making process by changing the implications of status quo bias. Simply stated, the bias toward policy inaction in the American system becomes more inequality inducing as inequality increases. The rich increasingly benefit from America's institutional design as they pull away from everyone else economically.

So if we think about the dramatic rise in inequality that has happened since the 1970s, status quo bias has contributed to the pattern. But the effects are nuanced. When inequality was at its lowest point, it is unlikely that status quo bias played a substantial role in changing the trajectory of inequality toward greater income concentration. Recall that when inequality is low, policy stagnation has no effect on inequality one way or the other (see figure 6.5b). Instead, other factors (possibly exogenous to policy) changed the direction of inequality. But once inequality began to increase, the self-reinforcement that occurs via conditional status quo bias kicked in. The higher inequality moved, the more relevant status quo bias became. And when status quo bias becomes a relevant predictor of inequality, it tends to push inequality higher. So once the momentum of inequality shifted in an inegalitarian direction, America's policy-making institutions helped to keep inequality moving that way.

SEVEN

Can We Escape the Trap?

The concentration of income in the United States is at or near unprecedented levels. The very rich have pulled away from basically everyone else, and those at the very top seem to inhabit a more distinct world than ever before. On one level, this amazing divergence of economic fortunes has obvious consequences—a world of private jets, exclusive clubs, high fashion, and yachts is a world apart from even the most comfortable suburban middle-class American lifestyle. And there are a variety of economic and social consequences of the current divergence between the rich and the rest—hoarding of educational opportunity, declining and diverging life expectancies, and a breakdown of social cohesion to name but a few.

The core argument of this book, however, is that there are other even more pernicious effects of extreme economic inequality that ripple through America's political system. The United States has often been viewed as a shining example of pluralistic democracy, in which no one group or coalition of groups remains on top for very long (Dahl 1967). Today's winners become tomorrow's losers, and the relative power of competing groups shifts back and forth without becoming entrenched in the hands of any one group.

But that pluralist ideal seems far from the actual practice of contemporary American democracy. Economic elites, while certainly not the exact same people and families from one era to the next, appear to have effectively insulated themselves from challengers. The rich keep on gaining relative to everyone else, virtually uninterrupted by even the most tumultuous economic calamities.

This is no mere accident of the market's invisible hand. The creation and maintenance of extraordinarily unequal outcomes is at least in part a product of political power. Who governs and which policies are enacted play a role in determining who wins, who loses, and what the final score is in America's economy. Those at the top of the economic heap have benefited from policy choices that helped them achieve and maintain their relative economic status. The economic winners keep winning by increasing margins, and politics largely determines the rules of the game.

Economic inequality and politics are connected in ways that can generate an inequality trap: the political consequences of rising inequality make future reductions in inequality less likely. An inequality trap helps explain the long-run patterns in economic inequality over the past one hundred years, and the evidence makes clear how several aspects of politics respond to rising inequality in an often inegalitarian fashion. These inequality-reinforcing political responses are rooted in the intertwining of economic and political power and are also supported by common social-psychological processes.

Chapter 3 examined connections between public opinion and economic inequality. While debate about the degree to which the rich disproportionately shape the policy process continues (Bhatti and Erikson 2011, Enns 2015, Gilens 2012, Gilens and Page 2014, B. Page and Gilens 2017, Wlezien and Soroka 2011), the collective public does have some ability to exercise influence over policy outcomes (Erikson, MacKuen, and Stimson 2002). When opinion shifts toward the left, more egalitarian policies and outcomes are achieved, and the opposite happens when the public moves toward the right (Kelly 2009). This means that the public has the potential to serve as a brake on rising inequality, and extant scholarship might make it easy to assume that public opinion acts as a braking mechanism, stopping income concentration from reaching extreme values. That is, when inequality gets high enough, the public says "enough" and shifts in favor of egalitarian policies that would push inequality lower. No matter how much the policy-making process might be tilted toward the rich, public opinion could be the ultimate safety valve. But that is not what happens. Instead, in contexts of high inequality substantial subsets of people become less supportive of egalitarian policies than they are when inequality is lower.[1] Moreover, it's not the rich that reduce support for egalitarian policies as inequality rises— it's the poor. So rather than putting the brakes on rising inequality, if anything, the preferences of the public help rising inequality along.

I presented evidence in chapter 4 that election outcomes also respond to rising inequality in a way that tends to sustain and even exacerbate income concentration. As inequality has risen, Republicans have become more likely to win House and Senate races as well as the presidency. That is not a recipe for reducing inequality since the policies preferred by Republicans—like lower taxes on the rich, less generous social programs, and market-oriented deregulation—are exactly the kinds of policies that help to concentrate income in the hands of the superrich. Part of the reason Republicans have been electorally advantaged by rising inequality may be connected to the public opinion response to inequality discussed above. But much of the advantage is rooted in the way Democratic voters have become more and more inefficiently distributed across states and districts as inequality has risen. Democrats waste a lot of votes in the context of our winner-take-all system because Democratic voters are clustered in high-density locales. And partisan gerrymanders enacted by Republican state legislatures only add to the Democratic disadvantage.[2]

In chapter 5 it became clear that the policy-making process contributes to America's inequality trap through the types of new policies it fosters. There, we saw that as inequality increased, consensus in support of inegalitarian policy change, in the form of financial deregulation, became easier to achieve. Due in part to the ascendance of Republicans in Congress and to changing electoral incentives for Democrats in a context of rising inequality, efforts to deregulate the finance sector overcame the system's status quo bias by the mid-1990s. These efforts had inegalitarian consequences for the concentration of income.

Chapter 6 implicated a fourth characteristic of American democracy as a conspirator in the inequality trap. There, I discussed how status quo bias in a context of rising inequality enables inequality to continue expanding unchecked. Policy making in any system is not easy, but the US system has multiple veto points, which means that making new policy is particularly challenging. Moreover, the Senate's particular institutional rules and norms raise the policy-making bar further. Because of the now routine use of the filibuster, it often takes more than a simple majority to win in the Senate. Even senators acting alone have substantial resources to derail policy making through individual action.

When income inequality is low, status quo bias in US policy making has little influence on future levels of income concentration. But when inequality is high, the distributional importance of status quo bias is activated, making future increases in inequality more likely and future reductions less likely. Status quo bias in the US system interacts with economic inequality in a way that reinforces income concentration consistent with the idea of an inequality trap. Because it does not take a whole lot of political power or clout to stop new policy in its tracks, the resources of those who benefit the most from income concentration are (except in fairly rare circumstances) sufficient to prevent major new egalitarian policy initiatives.

The weight of these findings leaves us with a pressing question: is there any way out of America's inequality trap? The evidence suggests that breaking the vicious cycle will not be easy. This chapter seeks to illuminate this central question. I begin this effort by comparing the government response to the 2008 economic crisis and to the Great Depression. Through this discussion I illustrate just how tight the inequality trap's grip is on contemporary US political economy, and I point to strategies for loosening that grip.

A Tale of Two Crises

The onset of the 2008 financial crisis was devastating. Many people in the United States and around the globe were harmed as it unfolded. In terms of income concentration, however, the Great Recession seemed like an opportunity—for the first time in decades, inequality declined slightly in the aftermath of the 2008 meltdown. An interesting thing about a self-reinforcing inequality trap is that the trap dynamics might reverse themselves, reinforcing reductions in inequality if some external shock alters the trend and income gaps begin narrowing. The downward blip in income concentration after 2008 could have been a small opening to get the train of rising inequality moving in the other direction. But that didn't happen. In the discussion below, I suggest that the structure of contemporary inequality (with income extremely concentrated at the very top) and the existence of a variety of countercyclical economic policies conspired to prevent a stronger response to the Great Recession.

On the heels of an economic collapse that occurred with a Republican in the White House, Democrats took control of all three policy-making institutions of American government. This raises an important point. The electoral advantage that rising inequality provides Republicans is not so strong that it completely eliminates the ability of Democrats to gain power on occasion. The ebb and flow of economic outcomes like unemployment, inflation, and economic growth remain the primary drivers of legislative and presidential election outcomes. So even in contexts of high inequality, Democrats can win when the economy is faring poorly and Republicans have pushed policy further to the right than the public wants.

So the 2008 economic crisis was in some ways a perfect storm favoring Democrats, a perfect storm that had the potential to produce an escape from the inequality trap. With unified control of national policy-making institutions, Democrats did take some notable steps toward enacting important egalitarian policy change. The Affordable Care Act expanded insurance access and increased taxes on the rich, with clear egalitarian consequences in the short term through straightforward redistribution and the potential to contribute to a more equal playing field of economic opportunity in the medium to long term. This was an important egalitarian policy accomplishment, and even with unified Democratic control, it very nearly failed. Part of its path to success, in fact, was that it gained the support of entrenched, wealthy groups like hospital associations and doctors. They could see the expansion of health insurance access as good for their bottom line and in line with their economic interests (and, I'm sure, many of them simply see providing care to more patients as a noble thing to do). In other words, the ACA is an egalitarian policy accomplishment, but with plenty of provisions sprinkled in that help the already well-off.

Another significant egalitarian policy change in the aftermath of the Great Recession was the Dodd-Frank financial regulation package. Dodd-Frank was designed to rein in some of the most obvious risk-taking behavior in the financial sector that had been made possible by deregulation in the 1990s. There is little doubt that Dodd-Frank moved the dial back toward a more regulated finance sector. But the implementation of Dodd-Frank was challenging and has remained largely incomplete. Regulatory agencies, for instance, have not taken full advantage of the powers granted them in the legislation. That, combined with a finance-friendly culture at the Federal Reserve and other regulatory institutions, has limited the impact of Dodd-Frank provisions that could most directly combat income concentration (L. Jacobs and King 2016).

What else happened in response to the financial crisis of 2008? Unemployment benefits were extended multiple times to help those displaced by the downturn. Major infrastructure spending flowed via the American Recovery and Reinvestment Act in order to stimulate economic activity. But a major government lifeline (some would say bailout) for large financial institutions and other important American companies was a central element of the policy response. At the same time, notably missing was a serious bailout for homeowners newly underwater on their devalued homes (L. Jacobs and King 2016). One can certainly argue about the wisdom and overall impact of these responses, and the initiatives that were enacted did soften the blow for middle- and lower-income families affected by the economic crisis. But the response to the 2008 crisis was a far cry from the massive policy shifts and government economic intervention implemented in the wake of the Great Depression. Postrecession policy making on behalf of ordinary citizens was largely incremental and limited in scope given the scope of the economic crisis

By contrast, completely new social programs designed to benefit those with the fewest resources were generated as part of the Depression-era New Deal.[3] Here are some of the highlights. Social Security, enacted in 1935, is currently the largest social program in the United States, and it dramatically reduces inequality by providing income to elderly retirees. Jobs programs such as the Civilian Conservation Corps and Civil Works Administration were created to stimulate employment. The Public Works Administration made massive investments in infrastructure, creating bridges, dams, highways, and jobs. The Glass-Steagall Act placed major new restrictions on how financial companies could conduct business, protecting consumers from default. It was a massive policy response to a massive economic problem.

In many ways, the era prior to the Great Depression was consistent with an inequality trap as discussed in this book. And that era, in fact, provides some of the data points included in the previous analyses that provide evidence of an inequality trap. But it seems like the Great Depression kick-started a process that began a long-term reversal of economic inequality. The vicious cycle of an inequality trap appears to have been converted into a virtuous cycle of escape, no doubt augmented by the economic and social changes spurred by World War II.

The 2008 economic crisis and the much more restrained policy response, on the other hand, was insufficient to knock America loose from its current inequality trap. Perhaps it's just a matter of a major war being added to the mix, but that strikes me as a horrible price to pay to accomplish a reduction in inequality. I also am not convinced that such a set of events would have the same egalitarian effects today as it did in the 1940s. Furthermore, inequality was already on a downward trajectory prior to World War II. So the fact that the most recent economic crisis has shown no evidence of reversing the trajectory of inequality suggests to me that a major war would not undo the inequality trap.

Why was the post-2008 response so much more restrained? Some might argue that the 2008 crisis was just not as large as the Great Depression. While that may be true, the two crises were at least of a similar scale, and the responses simply were not. In fact, part of the reason the 2008 crisis may have been somewhat less dramatic might be explained by the existence of some programs and policies that came into existence following the Great Depression and then were maintained and expanded in the interim. The social insurance programs in existence in 2008 limited the economic damage to American families. Imagine the crisis without Social Security or unemployment insurance or Medicaid. It would have been an even uglier picture. That these programs were already in place may have dampened the need

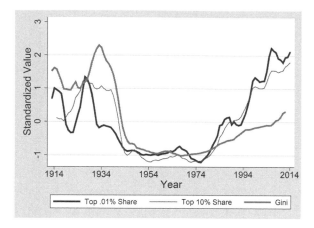

7.1. Examining the "top-heaviness" of income inequality in old and new Gilded Ages.
Source: Author's calculations from World Inequality Database.
Note: Values standardized to mean = 0 and variance= 1, five-year moving average.

for and support of major new initiatives in response to the Great Recession. The policy response to the Great Depression was also likely helped along by lower levels of party polarization than were present after the 2008 crisis.

There is another key difference between the Great Depression and the Great Recession that may be relevant to the divergent policy responses and the postcrisis trajectory of inequality. This difference relates to the underlying details of the income distribution. Figure 7.1 helps illustrate what I mean.

Figure 7.1 shows three different measures of inequality. The first should be familiar at this point—top 0.01 percent income share. This measure captures income concentration at the very top of the income distribution. The second measure expands to the top 10 percent, still capturing income concentration at the top, but defining the top more broadly. Instead of examining the concentration of income among the uberrich (as the top 0.01 percent measure does), looking at the top 10 percent share expands to include the upper middle class. The final measure is the Gini coefficient, which captures how income is distributed across the entire income distribution, from the poorest to the richest. The Gini is particularly sensitive to economic inequality in the middle portion of the income distribution, making the measure much more focused on inequality within the middle and bottom than the top income share measures are. To give a sense of this characteristic of the Gini, the score will change about as much if the gap between the sixtieth and

fortieth percentile doubles as if the gap between the ninety-ninth and fortieth percentile doubles. In the figure, I have converted each of these measures
to a common scale so that they can be more readily compared over time.

The chart tells an interesting story. As we well know by this point, current levels of income concentration at the top are at historical highs. And
the general contours of inequality are similar regardless of measurement
strategy—there is a peak in the 1930s, a low-point in the 1970s, and a steady
increase since.

However, the intensity of these peaks and valleys varies considerably
across measures, depending on whether we focus on inequality in the middle
of the income distribution or income concentration at the top. During the
Great Depression, for instance, the Gini coefficient was at its highest point
ever, while the top 10 percent share and especially the top 0.01 percent were
lower than the Gini and lower than their current levels. Thus inequality in
the middle of the distribution was comparatively more severe than inequality at the top during the Great Depression.[4] The situation is flipped during
the current Gilded Age. Today focusing on the top of the distribution suggests deeper inequality than focusing on the middle. By the end of the time
period charted, top 0.01 percent income shares are the highest of the three
measures, and the Gini is the lowest. As well, the top 0.01 percent income
share is higher now than it ever was in the 1930s, while the Gini has never
reached its previous high-water mark in 1934 despite several decades of
steady increases.

All this is to say that American inequality is now much more a product of
the rich pulling away from the rest than it was during the Great Depression.
Over the past four decades, inequality has gone up no matter how you measure it. But since the 1970s, income divergence has been driven much more
by the top separating themselves from everyone else than it has been by gaps
between people in the middle part of the distribution. This point has also
been made elsewhere (Atkinson, Piketty, and Saez 2011, Hacker and Pierson
2010, Piketty and Saez 2006), but it bears repeating. Early twenty-first century America could be more of a "Gilded Age" than the original.

The fact that inequality in the middle of the distribution was relatively
more important than concentration at the very top during the 1920s when
compared to the early 2000s may shed some light on why the Great Depression produced a downward turning point in inequality and the Great Recession did not. There are obviously other important differences between these
two points in economic history. But these inequality patterns together with
divergent policy responses to the Great Depression and Great Recession raise
the possibility that the self-reinforcing feedback effects of income inequality

and politics may be more entrenched when inequality is concentrated at the top as opposed to more broadly spread throughout the income distribution.

One mechanism that might generate these patterns is that power is more likely to be concentrated in the hands of the rich when inequality primarily concentrates resources at the very top as opposed to being defined by separation in the middle of the distribution. Because the concentration of power is likely to accompany the concentration of resources that occurs when income inequality is driven by the rich pulling away from the rest (as is the case these days), the political and policy process features of the inequality trap would be significantly more magnified by rising inequality at the top than by increasing inequality within the middle of the distribution. Another potential mechanism is that the mass public may respond differently when they see income concentration in the middle as opposed to the top of the distribution, being more likely to react negatively to inequalities they experience when their neighbor gets a new car than those they never see, such as when a hedge fund manager in Manhattan buys a third house. The fact that inequality is concentrated at the top more than ever may help to explain why a major crisis generated an escape from an apparently severe inequality trap in the 1930s while the trap we are in today seems to have remained intact even after the Great Recession. The evidence here is merely suggestive, however, so this dynamic merits attention in future research.

How Escape Might Occur

Inequality in the United States reinforces itself through a variety of political mechanisms, most importantly features of the policy process. We have seen that inegalitarian policy making is more likely to occur as income concentration increases and that bias toward the status quo increasingly benefits the rich as inequality rises. Public opinion and, especially, elections also contribute to the inequality trap. In the face of rising inequality, some Americans—a subset who are generally poorer and more racially resentful—reduce their support for redistributive policies and increase their support for Republicans.

A strategy for escaping the inequality trap must consider these varied aspects of American politics that contribute to self-reinforcing inequality. And we should take seriously the fact that the nature of income concentration is quite a bit different than in earlier periods of high inequality. We cannot simply rely on the next big economic crisis to create an escape path from the inequality trap.

What, then, can be done? There are no easy answers, and many other scholars and political observers have imagined a variety of policy ideas that could be deployed to combat political and economic inequality (see, for example, B. Page and Gilens 2017). Imagining a world different from the one we actually inhabit and identifying the policies that would exist in such a world is probably the easy part. Getting to that world from here is the real challenge. The complexity and breadth of the factors that have created the inequality trap on the one hand make exiting the trap difficult. On the other hand, because there are so many contributing factors, there are many possible ways of attacking the trap. The overall strategy for escaping America's inequality trap will require a combination of political and economic changes that undermine inequality in all its forms. The political changes need to enhance the power of economic nonelites. The economic changes must focus on reducing the gap between rich and poor. To the extent this can be achieved, the current feedback between inequality and politics that I've identified in this book could be thwarted.

Demographic Change as an Escape Path

The mass public plays at least a small role in creating America's inequality trap. By failing to respond to rising inequality with increased demand for redistribution and electing more Republicans, Americans help to keep inequality in place as inequality rises. The analysis of public opinion and voting, however, points to racial resentment as a key ingredient in the response to rising inequality. It is only among those with moderate to high levels of racial resentment that the public response to rising inequality helps to create an inequality trap.

Changing demographics are likely to undermine this dynamic. For many years, political strategists have expected demographic change to fundamentally alter American politics. The expectation has been that Democrats would become more successful and Republicans would have to become more progressive to compete in an electorate becoming less and less white. It is easy to scoff at such expectations given the current political climate. But the importance of demographic change should not be dismissed.

It seems that in the face of changing demographics, Republicans have settled on a short-term strategy designed to heighten racial animosity among white Americans and bring these racial considerations to the forefront in attitude formation and voting behavior. This has often been a winning strategy, in part because of extraordinary levels of economic inequality. Republicans have also been fairly explicit in efforts to extend the life of the majority-white electorate even if the majority-white population is on its way out. While the extent to which nonwhite voter turnout can be suppressed through efforts such as voter ID laws, reducing access to polling places, and purging voter rolls remains the subject of debate among scholars, the intent of these actions as well as current efforts to restrict immigration is fairly transparent. The goal is to keep the electorate as white as possible for as long as possible.

This is working for Republicans right now because the white population remains sufficiently large and racial inegalitarianism can be sufficiently activated among this population in a context of extreme economic inequality. However, even if current levels of economic inequality remain for the foreseeable future and racial animosity among whites can be successfully triggered for political gain, the wheel of demographic change continues to turn. It is unlikely that any policy efforts will be able to prevent the American population (and eventually the electorate) from becoming majority nonwhite.

In the medium to long term, then, relying on a strategy that focuses primarily on attracting the votes of whites will no longer work for Republicans. That suggests future success for Democrats and the need for a change in strategy for Republicans. How this all shakes out is not completely predictable at this point, as it is possible that the party system will be fundamentally altered as these demographic changes continue to play out, but the analysis in this book suggests that demographic trends may disrupt some of the feedback from rising inequality to inegalitarian mass preferences and voting behavior. The racial animosity that seems to be a necessary condition for an anti-redistribution, pro-Republican response to rising inequality is likely to be undermined by changing demographics.

These demographic changes could dramatically reshape the aggregate response to high levels of inequality, in terms of both opinion and voting behavior. Racial animosity toward nonwhites is largely a nonissue for nonwhites. Thus, all the analysis of individual-level attitudes and voting behavior presented earlier in the book focuses on white respondents. But further analysis suggests that the feedback effects of inequality, conditioned by racial attitudes, which we saw among whites are much less likely to be present among nonwhites, so as the population becomes less dominated by whites, the pro-Republican, anti-redistribution response to inequality that happens because of racial animosity is likely to diminish.

In figure 7.2 I reproduce the results from figure 4.7, but here I focus on blacks and Latinos only. In the earlier results we saw that non-Latino whites with racially inegalitarian attitudes are less supportive of Democratic candidates in contexts of high inequality. But when analyzing blacks and Latinos as I do here, we see no such interaction. More importantly, no matter how

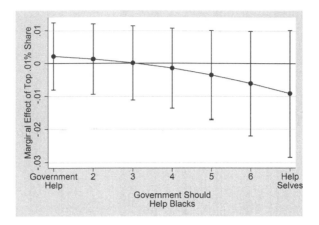

7.2. The response of nonwhites to rising inequality.
Source: Author's calculations from ANES data.
Note: Chart plots the predicted marginal effect on support for Democratic House candidate among those voting in the most recent election as inequality increases. Calculations based on a multilevel logit model including national-level top 0.01 percent income share at time of election, age, education, racial bias, and income along with racial bias interacted with inequality. Only blacks and Hispanics are included in this analysis.

you slice the data, no subset of the black and Latino population becomes less supportive of Democratic candidates for Congress in contexts of higher inequality.

Attacking Racism

Part of the inequality trap described in this book would likely exist with or without the presence of racial animosity in segments of the mass public. But the pro-Republican electoral response to rising inequality appears to be strongly conditioned by the racial attitudes of whites. Undermining racism, racial resentment, implicit bias, and general antipathy toward nonwhites would reduce the hold of the inequality trap as it manifests itself through feedback from inequality to mass attitudes and vote choice.

Undermining various manifestations of racism is no easy task. A substantial body of research has shown that the presence of nonwhite minorities in social settings can generate antipathy toward nonwhites (Abrajano and Hajnal 2017, Enos 2014, Hughey 2014, McDermott and Samson 2005, Taylor 1998). Racial bias is a deeply ingrained psychological force, and even talking about bias with members of the dominant group can trigger unintended backlash effects (DiAngelo 2011).

But I think there is room for hope. Some progress has been made on the problem of racism over the past forty years. Overt racism is still far too common and seems to have made something of a comeback over the past decade, but blatant racism is much less common today than it was decades ago (Mendelberg 2001). Supporting and encouraging strong social norms against racial bias likely has played a role in that progress, as have anti-discrimination policies and social activism for racial equality.

Clearly, though, more progress is needed. One strategy that appears to be successful in undermining racial bias is a particular form of social contact. The mere presence of diverse groups and basic interaction between groups is often not enough to generate intergroup empathy. But positive social interactions, with people from divergent groups working in common toward a goal, is more likely to achieve this positive effect (Brown, Brown, Jackson, Sellers, and Manuel 2003), though perhaps not completely necessary (Pettigrew, Tropp, Wagner, and Christ 2011). One could imagine joint community improvement projects where students from predominantly white schools join forces with students from more diverse schools. This could create a context for the kinds of positive intergroup contact that can undermine negative stereotypes, reduce threat perceptions, and foster empathy. It would likely be useful if these joint projects targeted both majority-nonwhite and majority-white neighborhoods and communities. More diverse and inclusive churches and other community organizations could also foster these types of positive contact experiences in a variety of ways.

Broadening Power—in Politics and the Market

As we saw in chapter 5, when inequality rises it creates windows of opportunity for partisan convergence on inegalitarian policy. Certain aspects of economic and political power must be decoupled if the inegalitarian policy convergence component of the inequality trap is to be undermined. It means enhancing the political power of those in the middle and bottom of the income distribution even in the face of rising inequality.

One key tool of political power for middle- and lower-income Americans is voting. Who votes matters. When turnout is skewed in favor of the rich, inegalitarian policy and the unequal outcomes these policies foster become more likely (Franko, Kelly, and Witko 2016, Leighley and Nagler 2007). Voting has the potential to be a major equalizer in the landscape of political power. Many other forms of political participation and influence require economic resources. But voting does not, at least in theory. But the rich have certain built-in advantages even in voting, in large part due to the many institutional hurdles to voting the United States puts in place.

Making voting easier, if done carefully and with the clear intent of em-powering those with relatively meager economic resources, could reduce the turnout advantage of the rich. Automatic registration would reduce one major hurdle to voting. Holding elections on a national holiday would make participation easier for those who cannot afford to take time away from work. Coordinating the election calendar to increase overlap between national, state, and local elections so that people don't have so many elec-tion days to show up for could also be helpful. Many recent state-level efforts to make voting harder, by making it harder to register, reducing the number of polling places, and requiring photo IDs to vote, are, of course, attempts to move things in the other direction.

Another important mechanism of power for nonelites is organizing, through entities such as labor unions. Labor unions have long been one of the few organized voices for middle-income Americans (Hacker and Pier-son 2010). As is well known, their membership has been declining steadily for decades. Reinvigorating the labor movement would restore an impor-tant voice to the middle class in the policy process. But there is no magic wand that can be waved to generate labor union membership and political clout. Those on the right have taken policy steps to undermine the ability of unions to organize and maintain their membership to be sure, but much of the labor union decline can be attributed to economic factors. That said, rolling back recent efforts to undermine unions would be helpful on this front, and additional policy changes that make it easier for unions to orga-nize as a voice for workers could also be implemented. But in the short term it is unlikely that union decline can be substantially reversed.

This means that other strategies for increasing the voice of workers must be explored. Importantly, the power of workers needs to be enhanced not just in the political process but in the market. Unions provided power in both of these domains, and generally market power and political power are intertwined. Employers currently exercise extraordinary asymmetric power in labor relations. Despite very low levels of unemployment, wages are ris-ing only slowly. Employees find it difficult to shift jobs, and employers often exercise a sort of take-it-or-leave-it approach to hiring, particularly in low-wage, low-skill positions. And in more professional jobs, employers increas-ingly utilize tactics such as no-compete clauses to deter current employees from jumping ship for higher pay. Undermining such practices would en-hance worker power. One promising policy proposal in this vein is Senator Elizabeth Warren's plan to require worker representation on the corporate boards of America's largest corporations. This would provide workers with a seat at the table that was often occupied by labor unions in the past. It would force corporations to take into account the well-being of a broader set of stakeholders than is typical under current corporate structures. It has promise to reconfigure market power in important ways.

But action beyond the typical capital-labor divide might also prove fruitful. Labor unions have been in decline for decades, so placing hope exclusively in the labor movement is likely a mistake. There are a variety of other organizing dimensions that could be activated in an effort to escape the inequality trap. Perhaps most hopeful are current attempts to build a broad movement for social justice, as evidenced through efforts such as Moral Mondays and Black Lives Matter. While there is a strong racial component to these justice movements, as is appropriate and far from unexpected given the long history of racial injustice in the United States, such movements also make strong claims for economic equality. With a great deal of effort to build on these movements, and work to reduce the racial bias that so often deters economically disadvantaged whites from joining in these efforts (see "Attacking Racism" above), these could become powerful and broad-based movements for change. And the changes advocated could undermine the inequality trap in fundamental ways.

Overcoming Status Quo Bias

The main conclusion of chapter 6 was that status quo bias in American policy making contributes to higher inequality when existing levels of inequality are sufficiently high. This suggests that in a context of high inequality, undermining status quo bias could aid in escaping the inequality trap.

There is one primary change that could both reduce status quo bias and be fairly easy to implement quickly—eliminating the filibuster in the Senate. There are obvious objections to such a strategy. After all, eliminating the filibuster could speed the introduction of inegalitarian policy just as easily as it could make egalitarian policy change more likely. This is a legitimate concern, but it appears that obstacles to policy change have historically been much more likely to impede egalitarian policy change than to impede inegalitarian policy making. The best long-run strategy for undermining the inequality trap is to remove or dramatically restrict use of the filibuster.[5] Even so, the American system contains numerous veto points and will remain heavily biased toward policy stagnation. The changes required to undermine other aspects of status quo bias—like reducing the number of legislative chambers or shifting to proportional representation—would be much more difficult to achieve. The Senate can act on its own to narrow the applicability of the filibuster.

Making the Income Gap a Political Priority

Many of the reforms discussed above require political action. Specifically, political action by those in the position to make public policy is required, so those in government will need to act if anything is to change. And the overall message of this book is that these actions are made all the more difficult in the current context of high inequality. So it takes political will on the part of Democratic Party elites (since Republicans policy makers are essentially completely uninterested in undermining economic inequality) to make these things happen. Reducing both political and economic inequality needs to be a core priority of the Democratic Party, and to the extent that success is achieved on this front, further advances will become more feasible.

Egalitarian political change is most difficult when inequality is high. In particular, Democrats are less likely to gain the level of power necessary to produce policy change in the context of extreme income gaps. But Democrats can gain power even when inequality is high, since other dynamics are at work alongside inequality. The key, then, is for Democrats to be ready with a truly egalitarian agenda if and when they are able to regain levers of power. When it comes to the social and economic policies that can reduce income inequality, there is a long list of options that are well known. And the progressive wing of the Democratic Party is currently gaining strength, making egalitarian politics more likely to take a prominent position on the Democratic agenda. This could make escaping the inequality trap more likely.

To be clear, though, many of the reforms needed to fundamentally alter the power structure of American politics requires a sustained reversal of partisan electoral fortunes and a deviation from typical policy-making processes that are unlikely to occur. This means trying to find small places for partisan agreement that move the dial toward egalitarianism. Lindsey and Teles (2017) have a useful roadmap for finding some of those potential areas for bipartisan egalitarianism. In the meantime, a prodemocracy, economically egalitarian social movement such as the one outlined by B. Page and Gilens (2017) is likely a necessary precondition for producing the election outcomes and the ongoing pressure needed to enact reforms sufficient to reverse the inequality trap.

Beyond Politics and Policy

I also think it is important to at least consider how our personal choices affect the opportunities and well-being of others. Those interested in pursuing equality don't have to focus just on policy. Those who are economically advantaged could consider giving up some of that advantage. One place where this could happen is in the realm of primary and secondary education. Doing so would no doubt be a difficult decision, because it is the children of the advantaged who would most be affected. It's good and natural for people to want the absolute best for their kids, but if a system is perpetuating inequality we have to consider whether participating in that system to further our (and our kids') advantage is really the right thing to do.

Those who can afford the best private school in town might consider a public option instead. Those who can buy a house zoned for the best elementary school could make a different choice. Doing this would incentivize the advantaged to be active in local school buildings where kids other than their own might benefit from parent involvement, producing possible spillover effects, generating educational and economic opportunities for a broader array of children and families. Such choices are obviously deeply personal, and I would never want to encourage someone to knowingly harm their children. But it is worth considering whether attending an adequate local public school is actually all that harmful in the long run. Even if an economically advantaged parent is unable or unwilling to send their child to a "troubled" public school, they could at the very least consider participating in the fund-raisers of schools other than their own. Where I live in Knoxville, Tennessee, for instance, there is an annual coupon book sale in which kids sell coupon books and their school keeps (most of) the proceeds. I am sure similar programs exist elsewhere. Instead of supporting a student at a school with lots of affluent families, why not support somebody at one of the less affluent schools? It is a small thing to do, but it could chip away at inequities in economic opportunity that are rooted essentially in opportunity hoarding by the well-off.

Becoming involved in the lives of children (and adults!) is also a potential way to disrupt the practice of opportunity hoarding on a personal level. No matter how good our public schools are and how much less-advantaged parents are able to invest in their children, those at the top of the economy are in highly beneficial social networks. I am not sure what policy intervention could limit those kinds of advantages, but those in more privileged positions could seek to share some of their advantage. Being present in social contexts with people from a variety of economic backgrounds opens up possibilities for this sort of interpersonal opportunity sharing (in public schools, community organizations, progressive activist groups, churches, or local sports leagues, or by playing with the kids at a nearby park). Mentoring or sponsoring people with fewer advantages could also create such opportunities. Once cross-class relationships are built and our social circles bridge divides that often exist between the more advantaged and those with less, we can begin to deconstruct some of the barriers to opportunity that exist for many of our neighbors. Of course this is not easy. It isn't always feasible. And it requires a lot more than writing a check. Social costs and personal costs will likely accrue. But tangible action to share advantage is the antidote to opportunity hoarding. And it is important to note that those in advantaged positions don't bear only costs by connecting with those who lack their advantages. There is mixed, but growing evidence that participation in diverse groups produces better social outcomes along a number of dimensions (Gurin, Nagda, and Lopez 2004, S. Page 2010).

I have no idea whether the actions necessary to create a more egalitarian economic and political system can be achieved, and I admit to having serious doubts. What I do know is that the reality of the American political economy described in this book represents only what has been and is now. As the investment houses are required to say: past performance is not indicative of future results. In the same way, an inequality trap in the past does not guarantee an inequality trap in the future.

Things can change. And my desire is that we are on the cusp of such change. The political engagement inspired by Donald Trump's presidency is real, and it may just be the first step toward escaping America's inequality trap. I hope this book has provided a useful diagnosis of some of the problems currently present in the system. It is well past time to change course.

ACKNOWLEDGMENTS

This book traces its origins to a gathering at Yale University's Institute for Social and Policy Studies in April 2015. There, the institute teamed up with the Washington Center for Equitable Growth to bring together several scholars thinking about various consequences of economic inequality. The discussions that happened there helped to crystallize several ideas that had been swirling around my mind for quite some time relating to a feedback cycle between economic inequality and American politics. One discussion in particular got the ball rolling on this book, when I had an opportunity to share some of my preliminary ideas about how the American political system has responded to rising economic inequality with Larry Jacobs. I am so grateful to Vesla Weaver and Jacob Hacker for including me in that group of scholars, to the Washington Center for Equitable Growth for supporting that gathering, and to all the scholars who attended and contributed so many useful ideas. Particular thanks are owed to Larry Jacobs for listening to my rough ideas at that meeting, encouraging me to develop them further, providing feedback as the manuscript progressed, and being so supportive throughout the writing and publication process.

As the project developed, I accumulated many additional debts of gratitude. I greatly appreciate feedback on various aspects of the book that I received from participants in seminars at the University of Wisconsin Institute for Research on Poverty and Political Science Department, the Texas A&M Political Science Department, the Penn State University Center for American Political Responsiveness, the University of Houston Political Science Department, the Indiana University Political Science Department, the Columbia University Political Science Department and Center for Wealth and Inequality, the Russell Sage Foundation, the University of North Carolina Political Science Department and Center for European Studies, and the

University of Iowa Political Science Department. Many specific people provided useful feedback at these gatherings and other venues where I shared drafts of this work. In particular, I want to thank Michael Berkman, Deirdre Bloome, Jason Casellas, Katharine Donato, Bob Erikson, Tim Hellwig, Alex Hertel-Fernandez, Evelyne Huber, Paul Kellstedt, Justin Kirkland, Herbert Kitschelt, Michal Kurlaender, Suzie Linn, Dave Lowery, Jamila Michener, Dina Okamoto, Alex Pacek, Ben Page, Justin Phillips, Eric Plutzer, Brian Powell, Robert Shapiro, Boris Shor, Fred Solt, John Stephens, Dara Strolovitch, Caroline Tolbert, Linda Tropp, Joe Ura, Andrea Voyer, Richard Wilson, Chris Wlezien, Jerry Wright, and Ling Zhu. The anonymous reviewers of this manuscript also provided unusually constructive and useful input, for which I am appreciative.

I am so grateful for the work of a handful of graduate and undergraduate research assistants and collaborators who worked with me on this project and other projects that were underway while this manuscript was in progress. In particular, Eric Keller provided a great deal of useful input on the project and helped in substantial ways with the analysis of financial deregulation in chapter 5. Portions of that chapter build on the article we coauthored in 2015. Andrew Leming did an amazing amount of background research and reading for the qualitative aspects of the financial deregulation analysis. That he was still an undergraduate while he did this makes it all the more impressive. Gio Pleites-Hernandez has been working with me since the later phases of the project. And Jace Prince worked on a separate project while I was completing this manuscript, and without the time he freed up for me by working on that project, this one would have taken much longer to complete.

My collaborators on specific portions of this project and other parts of our broader research agenda deserve much of the credit for how my thinking has developed on this project over time. Much of chapter 6 is built on the foundation of the *Journal of Politics* article on status quo bias that several of us worked on together and published in 2014. I am so thankful for the brilliant Peter Enns, Bill Franko, Jana Morgan, Thomas Volscho, and Chris Witko. They are all excellent coauthors and partners in the research endeavor. All who are reading this, however, should never seek them out as collaborators as that would cut into the time I have to work with them.

I was incredibly fortunate to spend the 2017 academic year in residence at the Russell Sage Foundation as a Visiting Scholar. The foundation provided me an incredible environment in which to complete this book. The foundation was the most supportive academic community I have ever experienced. The quality of conversation there and the importance of the work others were doing was inspiring. I am forever indebted to the other members of the 2017 Visiting Scholar class and look forward to seeing all their great work come to fruition. The freedom to focus my attention on this manuscript and other related projects while at RSF was an incredible luxury, and I am so grateful to the foundation's trustees and staff for their support of my work. The Carnegie Corporation of New York also supported this work through a Carnegie Fellowship. Support from Carnegie has provided resources that allowed me to spend focused time on this project, and will allow me additional time to conduct follow-up work. The views I express here are, of course, my own and do not necessarily reflect the views of the Russell Sage Foundation or the Carnegie Corporation of New York. I am also grateful to the University of Tennessee and the College of Arts and Sciences for agreeing to provide the time away from teaching that allowed me to complete this book.

The most detailed and intensive feedback I received while working on this manuscript came from a workshop at the University of Tennessee. I am grateful to the Department of Political Science and the Howard Baker Center for Public Policy for providing funding for that workshop. I am especially thankful to the participants—Nick Carnes, Marty Gilens, Adam Levine, Jana Morgan, Elizabeth Rigby, Joe Soss, and several graduate students. They were incredibly gracious in engaging with a manuscript that needed a great deal of work in a way that was encouraging, helpful, critical, and insightful. There is little doubt that I failed in effectively engaging with all their feedback, but there is no doubt that the manuscript became stronger because of their efforts. And the workshop was more than just good work. It was great fun filled with interactions that I wish were more common.

The two people I love most in the world, Jana and Arwen, have been supportive during this project in so many ways. The Jana in this paragraph and the last are one and the same. She is my partner in every aspect of life—spouse, coparent, collaborator, and critic. This project would not have been completed without her. Her generosity in discussing ideas early in the project, providing feedback throughout, and being supportive in so many other ways as the project came to fruition is impossible to overstate. And our delightful daughter, Arwen, helped to make life an amazing and wonderful adventure as I worked on this project. In addition to Knoxville, Tennessee, we spent significant time in Lima, Peru; Quito, Ecuador; and New York City while this project was underway. And her flexibility and joy in the journey at such a young age contributed to making those travels an inspiration rather than a hurdle to overcome in completing this book.

Jana encouraged me and provided the time and space for me to spend a few days away at a writing retreat when I needed to complete the first draft of the manuscript. I ended up working at the Convent of St. Birgitta in Connecticut while Arwen and Jana spent some time with Jana's parents. The time at the convent was amazingly productive. It was a quiet retreat in a beautiful place where I could completely focus. It was exactly what I needed. The nuns there were extraordinarily welcoming, and I participated in many interesting conversations with other guests over meals while there. I am thankful for the time that retreat provided and the hospitality that was extended.

Finally, I appreciate the support of our network of friends around Knoxville and our extended family scattered about elsewhere. It is incredibly valuable to have people to care about and who care about you. I've had numerous conversations with friends and family about this project over the years, and I've learned a great deal from those conversations. More importantly, it has been wonderful to have so many worthwhile distractions throughout the course of this project. I am so thankful to friends and family for providing those distractions and staying connected with me even as I've been engrossed in this work.

CHAPTER ONE

1. Trump has also, of course, taken the nontraditional position of raising tariffs and limiting international trade, but the overall agenda during the Trump presidency to date has not deviated substantially from the probusiness, antiregulation, tax-cutting agenda that has defined Republican policy priorities for several decades. The overall thrust of the agenda does little to combat income concentration and does a fair amount to further exacerbate it.

CHAPTER TWO

1. A self-reinforcing feedback system is also present if a decrease in one component creates further decreases in that component. The key is that the effect of both arrows in the figure have the same sign. Self-reinforcing feedback systems are also known as positive feedback systems, though there is no normative connotation to "positive." Self-reinforcing systems can be good or bad from a normative perspective.

2. As long as the effect of each arrow is opposite signed, there is a self-correcting, or negative, feedback process in place. Again, negative does not have a normative connotation here.

3. Of course other indicators also provide real information about people's lives — unemployment has profound effects on those experiencing it. But compared to economic inequality, I see unemployment and other similar measures as less indicative of deep political-economic structures and power relations.

4. But see J. Campbell (2011) and Kenworthy (2010) for results that question the central role of partisan politics in distributional outcomes.

5. For additional related work see Faricy (2015), Piketty and Saez (2003), Volscho and Kelly (2012), and Western and Rosenfeld (2011).

6. However, this situation arises much less often than would be expected based on objective economic interests (Bhatti and Erikson 2011, Branham, Soroka, and Wlezien 2017, Ellis and Ura 2011, Soroka and Wlezien 2008, Wlezien and Soroka 2011).

7. I do not mean to imply that the class of oligarchs is perfectly fixed in the United States (or any other context). Membership in this elite group changes over time, but in an oligarchic system, those who are at the top at any given time have the capacity to utilize economic power to protect their economic standing.

8. Economic elites, of course, are not a political monolith. There is almost certainly

variation in the policy preferences of those who are in America's economic strato-sphere. But regardless of preference variation, high levels of economic inequality serve the short-term economic interests of the rich, and there should be little doubt that the economic preferences of the wealthy tend to be toward the ideological right.

9. See also Klein (2014).

10. Economic inequality can also be measured with a focus on wealth or consumption as opposed to income. I focus on income because it represents *currently available* economic resources. To the extent that wealth can be used in the service of shaping politics, wealth is generally first converted to income prior to its direct employment. Wealth represents a potential storehouse of political power, but income represents current political power in a more direct way. Consumption does not fit well at all with the type of resource that is politically relevant in the context of an inequality trap.

11. The top-coding issue refers to the fact that, in order to protect the anonymity of citizens responding to the census income survey, those with very high incomes are lumped together into a single category regardless of how high their reported income actually is. Think of it this way. If you happen to select Bill Gates as a respondent to the income survey and he reports his income along with his general geographic location, it's not too hard to guess who the person with the $11.5 billion income in the Seattle area is. That means that all of Bill Gates's other responses to the income survey could be tied to him personally, which is a violation of the strict confidenti-ality protocols required for census data collection. So instead of listing Bill Gates's income as $11.5 billion, the data set released to the public would report his income as some fixed value substantially less than that. These top-code values change over time. Until 1995 all those in the top-coded category were assigned a single value. In 1962, for example, anyone with wages greater than $50,000 was coded as having $50,000 in wages. That top-code value rose in fits and starts to $99,999 in 1985 and by 1995 was $199,998. Beginning in 1995 a more complex replacement value for top-coded incomes was calculated, based on the average earnings for other top-coded individu-als with similar demographic characteristics. In 2010, the top-code replacement value was in the range of $326,000 to $568,000 depending on demographic category. See https://cps.ipums.org/cps/topcodes_tables.shtml for a more detailed discussion of top-coding and how it has changed over time.

12. It is important to acknowledge that the policy response to the Great Depression also played an important role in reducing inequality. The economic crisis of 2008 did not generate the same sort of policy response. I will discuss at various points why the political response to two economic crises in the context of very high inequality was so different. In one, the response seemed to start the country on a path toward self-reinforcing equality. The other largely maintained the status quo of self-reinforcing inequality.

13. I regress the current level of inequality on the level of inequality from the past year.

14. One obvious criticism of this simple analysis is that the results may be driven by trends in the data. To account for this possibility, I also estimated versions of the regression that include linear and/or quadratic trend terms. The pattern of future in-equality rising in response to an increase in inequality remains when controlling for such trends. It cannot be emphasized enough that this simulation assumes no other exogenous interventions after the initial increase in inequality, which helps to put in context the large long-run effects depicted here.

15. At some point, there is a limit to the inequality-inducing feedback effects of rising in-equality. Simple mathematics puts a ceiling on how high top income shares can rise.

There is no expectation that the inequality trap described in this book leads to perfect income concentration in the hands of the superrich. The inequality-reinforcing effects of high inequality do dissipate over time, and eventually the effect moves from pushing inequality higher to simply maintaining extremely high levels of inequality. We see the beginning of this pattern in this chart, since the predicted path of inequality is beginning to level off at the end of the twenty-year period.

16. Recall that in a static trap inequality goes up and stays up but does not necessarily continue higher. A dynamic trap is one in which rising inequality generates additional future increases in inequality.

17. Readers accustomed to the multivariate regression tradition will note that little to none of my analysis makes use of straightforward ordinary least squares regression, which has been the workhorse of quantitative social science for decades. Typical multivariate regression is very useful in a variety of contexts, and all the techniques I apply in the remainder of the book can trace their origins back to basic regression. But basic regression simply cannot cope with the data structures that I analyze or the theoretical framework on which I rely. If the goal were to isolate the effect of one variable on another, basic time series regression with some tweaks to guard against two-way causation would be appropriate. But that is not my goal. Rather, I want to fully account for and capture the feedback effects between politics and inequality. That makes a technique like VAR more appropriate. In my micro-level analyses I rely a great deal on multilevel models. These models are actually quite close cousins to traditional multivariate regression. But getting appropriate estimates of standard errors (essential for reaching accurate inferences) when the data are structured hierarchically (meaning individuals nested within other units like time or geography when that nesting likely leads to correlated errors) requires a shift away from standard OLS.

CHAPTER THREE

1. This is an inherently *aggregate* model. It is certainly not the case that every individual is constantly monitoring what government is doing on every policy topic. The thermostatic model requires only that some people monitor and respond thermostatically while the rest respond randomly.

2. This is an important point to emphasize as it relates to understanding the theoretical implications of the analysis to come below. The thermostatic model that Wlezien (1995) outlines is specifically about how the public's preferred policies (P^* using the model's nomenclature) respond to the current policies produced by government (P). When P moves away from P^*, the public responds by reporting preferences even further in the opposite direction to give a thermostatic signal. Here, I am moving outside of the original thermostatic model by examining the connection not between P^* (preferred policy) and P (policy) but between P^* and the social outcomes influenced by policy. So, to be clear, I am not directly testing the original thermostatic model, and when I reference a "broken thermostat," it is not the thermostat as it exists in prior political science literature but in the modified extension I am describing here.

3. Data come from the 1987 and 2000 General Social Survey, which asked respondents how much an average person in each of the following occupations earned: mason, doctor, bank clerk, shop owner, CEO, skilled worker, farm worker, secretary, bus driver, unskilled worker, member of federal cabinet, lawyer, sales clerk, owner of large factory, and supreme court justice. The ratio is computed by dividing the highest- to the lowest-paid occupation for each respondent and then averaging across all respondents.

4. See also Bartels (2008).
5. This finding is also consistent with experimental results finding that when people are primed to think about inequality, their support for redistributive policies increases (McCall, Burk, Laperrière, and Richeson 2017). However, Wlezien and Soroka (2017) offer a different perspective, arguing that people's redistributive preferences are driven by a combination of existing levels of welfare spending, economic growth, and inequality. They suggest that people do notice all these factors, but each cuts in a different direction. Nonetheless, they also find that opinion responses to inequality are not self-correcting so long as controls for existing policy and general economic conditions are included.
6. More recent studies focused on variation at the subnational level have found evidence of a self-correcting relationship between inequality and attitudes toward redistribution (Franko 2016).
7. The results are fairly similar if the top 1 percent is analyzed.
8. From Stimson (1999) updated from http://stimson.web.unc.edu/data/, accessed January 21, 2016. I have reversed the coding from the base version to make a self-reinforcing pattern more straightforward to observe.
9. Specifically, I estimate a vector autoregression including top 0.01 percent income share, public mood conservatism, top capital gains tax rate, top income tax rate, financial deregulation (a slightly modified version of Philippon and Reshef's (2013) discussed more in chapter 5), and percent Democrats in Congress. The additional variables were chosen because they have been found in prior studies to affect the concentration of income and could be shaped by general shifts in opinion. The Bayesian Information Criterion indicates optimal lag length of one, so one lag of each variable is included in the model. Johansen's (1988) test does not indicate the presence of cointegration, so all nonstationary variables (top income share, top income tax rate, and deregulation) are differenced prior to estimation. More details on the type of model used here are available in online appendix A.
10. The visualization that I focus on is the cumulative orthogonalized impulse response function (COIRF). Importantly, this is the effect that is produced both directly by a change in an explanatory variable as well as indirectly through other system variables as well as feedback between variables in the system. The error bands represent 68 percent confidence intervals as suggested by Sims and Zha (1998). I also considered models with time trends to account for the possibility that results are driven by deterministic trends. Models including trends produces substantively similar results. To construct the COIRFs, I assume the following causal ordering (from endogenous to exogenous): income inequality, capital gains tax, income tax, deregulation, congressional partisanship, public mood. Therefore, policies and partisan power are assumed to intervene between public opinion and income inequality. The main alternative I considered was placing income inequality at the other end of the chain, preceding public mood. The substantive conclusions change little under this alternative.
11. This is accomplished with a multilevel linear regression model in which individuals are embedded within years. Such a model accounts for a data structure in which individual respondents are nested within other units. In this case, the unit they are nested in is years.
12. It could be that inequality at the national level is more or less relevant to people's thinking than inequality at more localized levels. Later in the analysis I will estimate other models that examine variation in inequality at the state level.

13. The variable is EQWLTH from the GSS cumulative file recoded so that higher values indicate support for redistribution on a 0 to 6 scale.
14. Models including partisanship as a control produce similar results.
15. Full model results are available in online appendix C.
16. In the next chapter I more directly analyze the effects of the trust in government explanation in an analysis of voting behavior.
17. I have also considered models that allow the effect to vary nonlinearly across income groups as well as models that measure income in just three categories. The basic pattern presented here holds in those models.
18. With regard to elite manipulation, it could be that we simply are not able to capture the preferences of the actors who would actually be responsible for executing the manipulation of opinion. Such actors may be so high in the income distribution that surveys fail to capture their opinions. So it is possible that the potential manipulators of opinion respond to rising inequality by more strongly opposing redistribution. I cannot rule out that possibility entirely with the data I have access to here.
19. The racial bias index is based on four items included in the GSS in twenty-four surveys from 1977 to 2014 (RACDIF1–4). The items ask respondents why blacks are poorer than whites, and each item asks respondents to state whether they agree or disagree with a particular explanation: discrimination, less ability to learn, lack of educational opportunity, and lack of willpower. I recode each variable dichotomously so that responses blaming blacks rather than society are coded 1 and other responses 0. I then average across the four responses to obtain a measure that ranges from 0 to 1 with higher scores indicating more racial bias.
20. Since the racial attitudes questions were presented only to white respondents, this analysis focuses only on white non-Hispanics.
21. The specific variables are v3075 for the capital gains tax cut and v3072 for the minimum wage item. Items are dichotomous, and I have recoded each item so that 1 is the more redistributive position, that is "opposing" the capital gains cut and "supporting" the minimum wage hike. While gaining the ability to examine cross-sectional variation in the context of inequality as well as more specific issue attitudes, we lose the ability to assess the effects of racial attitudes with this data source, since no questions about racial attitudes were included for the full national sample. However, we will see that the income patterns are similar to those above, which does not undermine the conclusions to this point about racial bias.
22. The analyses here, like those of the GSS data above, rely on a multilevel modeling strategy in which individuals are embedded within states. All the models below were also estimated with inequality varying at the even smaller geographical unit of the congressional district. The patterns were similar but estimated with more uncertainty. Since the dependent variable is dichotomous (support or opposition of a policy change), I estimate a mixed-effects logit model. This strategy allows me to obtain accurate estimates for the effect of both individual level variables and contextual (state) characteristics. It also allows me to determine how economic inequality in the state shapes policy attitudes and/or changes the effects of other individual-level characteristics such as income.
23. A model including both individual-level partisanship and state-level median income produce very similar results. This suggests that the pattern here is not simply driven by different partisan patterns in rich and poor states as in Gelman, Park, and Shor (2008).

24. Again, the results are comparable when adding an individual-level control for partisanship and a contextual-level measure of state median income.

25. See Franko (2016) for a state-level study that does find some increasing support for redistribution as inequality rises.

CHAPTER FOUR

1. Achen and Bartels (2016) present a very different picture of the connection between public policy preferences and election outcomes - largely that they don't exist and are especially irrelevant in very close elections. But the idea that the outcome of elections have important effects on economic and social outcomes is less disputed.

2. There are clearly numerous other types of political participation that provide ways for citizens and organized groups to signal their preferences to elected officials (Baumgartner, Berry, Hojnacki, Kimball, and Leech 2009, Berry 1984, Gilens 2012, Verba, Schlozman, and Brady 1995). Here, however, I am primarily concerned with the outcome of elections as opposed to ongoing communication between the public and politicians. The most direct and relevant participatory effect on election outcomes is voting, so turnout is my focus here.

3. The results on opinion from the last chapter showing that the rich and the poor tend to converge on redistributional preferences as inequality increases raises doubts about the mechanism linking inequality to increased participation in this theory, but the general idea that wide gaps between the rich and the poor could mobilize participation needs to be considered.

4. The results do not differ much if partisan power in all three institutions are included in a single analysis.

5. VAR models are estimated. Along with inequality and election outcomes, these models include union strength, financial deregulation, and the top capital gains tax rate. The results are similar regardless of whether these additional variables are included in the model. The Bayesian Information Criterion indicates optimal lag length of one, so one lag of each variable is included in the model. Johansen's (1988) test indicates the presence of cointegration.

6. Specifically, the charts are orthogonalized cumulative impulse response functions. For the purposes of creating IRFs, the causal ordering assumed is as follows: income concentration, deregulation, capital gains tax, party power, union strength. This set of results is not sensitive to assumptions about causal ordering. Sixty-eight percent error bands are included as suggested by Sims and Zha (1998).

7. If we assume that inequality is the first variable in the causal chain rather than the last, as reported here, the result for presidential elections changes slightly, with a more clear feedback effect uncovered.

8. One might at first blush worry that some of these effects are almost impossibly large. But we need to remember that these are cumulative effects that account for positive feedback between electoral outcomes and inequality over a long period of time. This means that a standard deviation shift in one variable at a specific point in time will actually translate into a much larger shift once feedback effects from election outcomes to inequality are considered. As well, it is important to remember that these charts simulate the effect of a shift in party power or top income shares that continues in perpetuity. The reality is that a shock in one direction is unlikely to persist indefinitely and will often be followed by shocks in the opposite direction. With these caveats in mind, the effects are important primarily in that they show the potential

power of the relationship between politics and inequality, but they are not incredibly large.

9. As in Kenworthy (2010) and Volscho and Kelly (2012) the effects of presidential election outcomes may be slightly smaller than the effects in the legislature. But partisan effects are present on income concentration using the methodology employed here that allows for bidirectional causation.

10. For some of the analysis the economic context is measured at the national level, with the context changing only over time. For other parts of the analysis, the economic context is measured based on geography, with inequality varying at the state level. The type of models I estimate here are known as multilevel models or hierarchical models. These models are appropriate when individuals are embedded in geographic or temporal units, as is the case here.

11. Since the outcome variable in this analysis is dichotomous, I utilize a logit estimator, which is appropriate for a dichotomous dependent variable.

12. The measure of turnout here is based on self-reports, which are biased upward. This explains why the predicted probabilities are so high.

13. Other studies that have incorporated both cross-state and cross-temporal variation have found that turnout is depressed by rising inequality (Solt 2008, Solt 2010), but in the purely temporal analysis here I find no such effects.

14. Again I am estimating a logit model to account for the dichotomous outcome.

15. Several prior studies show that party identifiers can react very differently to the same social conditions (Bolsen, Druckman, and Cook 2014, Enns, Kellstedt, and McAvoy 2012, Jerit and Barabas 2012). So it is worth noting that an interaction term between party identification and inequality, which provides insight on whether Democrats and Republicans respond differently to changing inequality, shows that the effect of inequality does not differ by partisan identification.

16. Here the data run only from 1958 to the present, excluding 1960 and 1962 because of availability of the trust measure.

17. Another way that trust could link inequality to voting behavior is by providing an indirect causal pathway through which inequality affects vote choice. However, the results here also show that there is no independent effect of trust on vote choice, which undermines the possibility that inequality has indirect effects on vote choice via trust.

18. More detailed psychological measures of racial resentment would be useful in this analysis, but utilizing such measures would dramatically limit the time frame that could be analyzed.

19. In order to be sure that this result is not driven by the racial issue evolution that produced regional parties that are more neatly polarized on racial issues than they were prior to the civil rights era, I reproduced these results for respondents from only the north. This helps overcome the possibility that voting for southern Democrats in the House had very different racial implications than voting for northern Democrats in the early years of this analysis (when inequality was also relatively low). This analysis produces similar results to those reported here.

20. This analysis is based on a multilevel logit model.

21. Of course it is not the case that inequality spirals upward forever. Eventually, random economic shocks tend to push inequality in the opposite direction, which could start a new downward cycle of reinforcement. And election outcomes are not completely determined by inequality. Rising inequality places Democrats at a disadvantage, but

other economic factors and general political conditions can still produce important Democratic victories.

CHAPTER FIVE

1. Much of this literature discusses "institutional change." Public policy is only one aspect of a broader category of institutional change, but the historical-institutionalist literature on institutional change is primarily about policy change and continuity.

2. For a related argument focused on the underpinnings of financial deregulation, see Suarez and Kolodny (2011).

3. It is worth noting the Democrats have long received a great deal of financial support from large-dollar donors, including both the financial industry and labor unions (Hacker and Pierson 2010). We will see below that the mix of financial support received by Democrats appears to have contributed to their convergence with Republicans on the issue of financial deregulation.

4. They find that rich Republican donors are also more moderate than less wealthy donors.

5. For similar results based on different data, see Schlozman, Verba, and Brady (2012).

6. To reiterate a point I have tried to make throughout, a spiral of inequality does not have to be upward. In the contemporary context, the spiral has indeed been toward higher inequality, but the very same positive studies that explicitly analyze the effects of financial deregulation on economic inequality have found that deregulation is one of several policy choices that have shaped economic inequality in recent decades (Fortin and Lemieux 1997, Hacker and Pierson 2010, D. Jacobs and Myers 2014, Keller and Kelly 2015).

7. The original measure of deregulation is an annual index of (1) branching, which is the percentage of the US population living in states that removed branching restrictions; (2) a dichotomous indicator capturing separation of commercial and investment banks, which shows the decrease in regulatory separation of these two types of banks; (3) a dichotomous measure of the existence of interest rate ceilings, which captures the ceilings in effect from 1933 to 1983; and (4) a dichotomous indicator of regulatory separation of banks and insurance companies. I have removed the permissibility of state branching from the measure in order to focus on federal policy. While a national policy change permitted states to change their policy on bank branching, action at the state level was required to actuate that change, so I remove that component of the index here. The same general pattern holds when using the original version of the measure.

8. The VAR estimated here is very simple, including just the two key variables—an annual measure of deregulation from Philippon and Reshef (2013) and top 0.01 percent income share including capital gains (both charted earlier). I have opted for this parsimonious specification since there are few other variables that likely intervene between financial deregulation and income inequality when the direction of causation is from deregulation to inequality. However, there are other political variables that might intervene between inequality and deregulation when the causal arrow is reversed. To consider the potential electoral effects of inequality and how that might change the feedback effect of inequality on deregulation, I have also estimated models that include partisan composition of Congress. Results from that model are substantively similar to the ones reported here and are robust to a variety of assumptions about the causal ordering of contemporaneous shocks. Also note that the model is estimated with one lag of each variable included based on Schwarz's Bayes-

ian Information Criterion for lag length selection (Schwarz et al. 1978). Since both variables in the model are nonstationary, I confirmed the presence of cointegration using Johansen's method prior to estimation (Johansen 1988).

9. Each chart plots an orthogonalized cumulative impulse response function that shows the simulated effect of each variable on the other from the VAR estimates along with 68 percent error bands as suggested by Sims and Zha (1998).

10. Deposit insurance was limited to money held in commercial banks. There was no provision of deposit insurance in investment banks since such insurance would create a moral hazard by encouraging more risky activities on the part of investment banks. That is, if investment losses were protected by government insurance, investment banks could make high-risk, high-reward investments with the government essentially shouldering the risk through deposit insurance.

11. I will compare and contrast the response to the Great Depression to the 2007 crisis more in the concluding chapter.

12. The analysis and discussion below are closely related to previously published work with Eric Keller (Keller and Kelly 2015).

13. As mentioned earlier, I remove the state branching measure from their original index since the focus here is deregulatory activity at the federal level.

14. When neither party has the majority in a legislative chamber, majority party is based on the party having a larger party caucus, including any independents who caucus with one of the major parties.

15. The results are from a regression of annual change in inequality on annual change in party control over the full period analyzed. This initial model is designed to test the general effect of partisan power in the presidency, House, and Senate. Part of the motivation for examining associations between annual change in each variable is to avoid spurious results that can occur when analyzing variables containing unit roots that are not cointegrated, which is the case here. Analyzing annual change ensures that all variables included in the model are stationary.

16. If the analysis includes only years prior to the Carter administration, the effect of presidential partisanship is negative and statistically significant.

17. This result holds even when just years prior to 1980 are analyzed.

18. This is accomplished with the addition of a post-1982 dummy variable (coded 1 from 1982 onward) and multiplicative interactions between the post-1982 dummy variable and variables capturing Democratic control of the presidency and the Senate. The interaction terms provide an ability to assess whether the effect of partisanship changed before and after 1982. I have selected 1982 as the cut point for the analysis presented here. The results are very similar using a range of cut points from 1976 to 1985. The results are strongest using the 1982 cut point, but this presentational decision should not be interpreted as suggesting that partisan convergence happened all at once in 1982.

19. Actually, the first strategy that middle- and low-income American families deployed to cope with stagnating wages was sending additional workers (typically the wife) into the workforce (Warren and Tyagi 2004). Even this was not enough to shelter them from economic insecurity, and credit become the next option.

20. Above, my strategy for figuring out whether the partisan effect was different before and after a particular point in time (1982 turned out to be the best cut point) was to include an interaction term between Senate partisanship and a dichotomous measure coded 0 prior to 1982 and 1 after. Similarly here, I include interaction terms between Senate partisanship and five annual time series measures connected to the

five potential moderators discussed above. The difference here is that the variables interacting with partisan control can take on continuous values rather than being measured dichotomously. For inequality, the income share of the top 0.01 percent income share is included. To assess the effect of credit, total household and nonprofit loans per capita calculated from Board of Governors of the Federal Reserve data is included (this variable is available only since 1945). The proportion of Democratic campaign contributions from the finance sector based on the Database on Ideology, Money in Politics, and Elections (available since 1980) is included to examine the effects of campaign finance (Bonica 2013). Imports and exports as a percent of GDP from the Bureau of Economic Analysis (Bureau of Economic Analysis 2012, table 1.1.5) captures the argument related to trade, and union membership from the US Census Bureau and Bureau of Labor Statistics is included to capture the effect of the decline of unions. A separate model is estimated for each moderating factor in order to avoid issues of collinearity. Each model is an ARIMA model with annual change in financial deregulation as the dependent variable and change in Senate partisan control as the key explanatory variable. The lagged level of each moderating variable along with its interaction with change in Senate partisan control is included. Note that these models implicitly impose some simplifying restrictions on the dynamics of the effects estimated. In particular, it is only the lagged level of the moderator variables that are permitted to shape the effect of partisan control. It could well be that these moderator effects exhibit interesting dynamics of their own, but to keep the models tractable these more complex potential dynamics are set aside.

CHAPTER SIX

1.   To be clear, in the context of the late eighteenth century, the framers were creating a system considerably more democratic than most, and I think it is the case that some of the framers would have preferred a more democratic governing document. But the Constitution was full of compromises that moved the system away from pure democracy. Many of those compromises were driven by the existence of slavery, by far the most undemocratic institution permitted by the Constitution.

2.   In a Republican-controlled Senate, the filibuster-pivot senator could be identified by arraying the Senate from left to right ideologically and identifying the fortieth senator from the *left*. If Democrats controlled the Senate it would be the fortieth senator from the *right*.

3.   Specifically, I use DW-NOMINATE scores (Poole and Rosenthal 1997).

4.   These charts are orthogonalized cumulative impulse response functions from two vector autoregressions, one including Senate polarization and the other including House polarization, along with top 0.01 percent income share and a measure of legislative policy output to capture policy production (J. Grant and Kelly 2008). Error bands are 68 percent intervals as suggested by Sims and Zha (1998). The models include one lag of each variable in the system, with lag length selected based on Schwarz's Bayesian Information Criterion (Schwarz et al. 1978). Since the variables in the model are nonstationary, I confirmed the presence of cointegration using Johansen's method prior to estimation (Johansen 1988). In calculating the impulse response functions I assume a causal ordering that runs from polarization to policy production to inequality. Placing polarization causally prior to policy stagnation seems appropriate on theoretical grounds. I also produced versions of the response

functions placing inequality at the beginning of the causal chain, and the results reported here do not change substantively.

5. McCarty, Poole, and Rosenthal (2006) also find much stronger evidence of the inequality-inducing effects of polarization than any effects of inequality on polarization.

6. The model uses pooled legislator-level data from the House for all Congresses from 1913 to 2014. I estimate a multilevel model of legislators in the House of Representatives nested within Congress. This allows me to isolate the effect of context-level variation in inequality as well as individual-level variation in partisanship on individual-level ideology.

7. The models are robust to the inclusion or exclusion of state and Congress fixed effects as well as a control for the Republican presidential vote share in the district.

8. Results are similar if the top 0.01 percent is analyzed. This period is the focus because it is bracketed by the two largest economic crises in US history. This is important because it is likely that different economic and political processes are at work during financial crises, especially during the Great Depression.

9. The filibuster pivot distance is based on Common Space DW-NOMINATE scores (Carroll, Lewis, Lo, McCarty, Poole, and Rosenthal 2011). These scores provide a measure of the ideological preference of members of Congress and presidents in a common ideological space based on roll-call voting behavior in Congress and public positions of the president.

10. Prior to 1975, sixty-seven votes were required for cloture, so the measure is adjusted accordingly for these years.

11. The measure is also built using Common Space DW-NOMINATE scores.

12. The results are based on a single equation error correction model (ECM). While the applicability of ECMs to political and economic data has recently been questioned (T. Grant and Lebo 2016), such models are appropriate when modeling relationships that evidence cointegration (Enns, Kelly, Masaki, and Wohlfarth 2016, Enns, Kelly, Masaki, and Wohlfarth 2017). ECMs can avoid the risk of spurious regression results when estimating relationships between nonstationary variables (Banerjee, Dolabo, Galbraith, and Hendry 1993, Engle and Granger 1987, Enns, Kelly, Masaki, and Wohlfarth 2016). Johansen's (1988) test for cointegration suggests that an ECM is appropriate here.

13. All variables are mean centered prior to estimation in order to avoid problems of collinearity.

14. The analysis here, of course, is highly aggregated and does not imply that all legislative action is and always will be in the egalitarian direction. But the general story is simply that legislative inaction, on average, increases inequality while legislative action tends to reduce inequality.

CHAPTER SEVEN

1. It is possible that we simply have not yet reached the tipping point at which the public finally generates a serious and sustained backlash against rising inequality, although inequality is already very, very high. We may be seeing signs of such a tipping point in new movements that have gained increasing traction in the first years of the Trump presidency, but that we have not yet hit a clear tipping point raises doubts about whether we ever truly will.

2. Clearly, Democratic legislatures also play the partisan gerrymandering game. But the

recent dominance of Republicans at the state level means that current maps are much more likely to favor Republicans than Democrats.

3. It is important to note that black Americans were initially excluded from most such programs.

4. Remember that these are standardized values to facilitate over-time comparison. The unstandardized top 0.01 share is by definition less than the top 10 percent share at particular point in time, and the Gini is measured on a completely different scale (from 0 to 1) in its unstandardized form.

5. Interestingly, there is no longer a filibuster for supreme court nominations. Progressives would likely point out recent court appointments as a warning against undoing the filibuster. My position is that the filibuster makes sense for court nominations because they are for lifetime appointments. Since these appointments cannot be undone by a change in electoral fortunes, there is a good argument for reinstating a filibuster for Senate approval of lifetime judicial appointments. (Even better would be getting rid of lifetime judicial appointments altogether.) But the argument is not as strong for standard policy choices that can be undone at any time in the future. I favor letting the majority rule when it comes to policy making.

REFERENCES

Abrajano, Marisa, and Zoltan L. Hajnal. 2017. *White Backlash: Immigration, Race, and American Politics*. Princeton, NJ: Princeton University Press.

Achen, Christopher H., and Larry M. Bartels. 2016. *Democracy for Realists: Why Elections Do Not Produce Responsive Government*. Princeton, NJ: Princeton University Press.

Alesina, Alberto, Reza Baqir, and William Easterly. 1999. "Public Goods and Ethnic Divisions." *Quarterly Journal of Economics* 114 (4): 1243–84.

Alesina, Alberto, and Edward Glaeser. 2004. *Fighting Poverty in the US and Europe: A World of Difference*. New York: Oxford University Press.

Ansell, Ben W., and David J. Samuels. 2014. *Inequality and Democratization*. New York: Cambridge University Press.

Ansolabehere, Stephen, John M. De Figueiredo, and James M. Snyder. 2003. "Why Is There So Little Money in U.S. Politics." *Journal of Economic Perspectives* 17 (1): 105–30.

Atkinson, Anthony B., Thomas Piketty, and Emmanuel Saez. 2011. "Top Incomes in the Long Run of History." *Journal of Economic Literature* 49 (1): 3–71.

Bakija, Jon, Adam Cole, Bradley T. Heim, et al. 2012. "Jobs and Income Growth of Top Earners and the Causes of Changing Income Inequality: Evidence from US Tax Return Data." Unpublished manuscript, Williams College.

Banerjee, Anindya, Juan Dolabo, John Galbraith, and David F. Hendry. 1993. *Co-integration, Error Correction, and the Econometric Analysis of Non-stationary Data*. New York: Oxford University Press.

Bartels, Larry M. 2005. "Homer Gets a Tax Cut: Inequality and Public Policy in the American Mind." *Perspectives on Politics* 3 (1): 15–31.

———. 2008. *Unequal Democracy: The Political Economy of a New Gilded Age*. Princeton, NJ: Princeton University Press.

Baumgartner, Frank R., Jeffrey M. Berry, Marie Hojnacki, David C. Kimball, and Beth L. Leech. 2009. *Lobbying and Policy Change: Who Wins, Who Loses, and Why*. Chicago: University of Chicago Press.

Bénabou, Roland. 1996. "Inequality and Growth." In *NBER Macro Annual 1996*, ed. Ben S. Bernanke and Julio J. Rotemberg, 11–76. Cambridge, MA: MIT Press.

Berman, Eli, John Bound, and Stephen Machin. 1998. "Implications of Skill Biased Technological Change: International Evidence." *Quarterly Journal of Economics* 113 (4): 1245–79.

Berry, Jeffrey M. 1984. *The Interest Group Society*. Boston: Little, Brown.

———. 1999. *The New Liberalism: The Rising Power of Citizen Groups.* Washington, DC: Brookings Institution Press.

Bhatti, Yosef, and Robert S. Erikson. 2011. "How Poorly Are the Poor Represented in the US Senate?" In *Who Gets Represented?*, ed. Peter K. Enns and Christopher Wlezien, 223–46. New York: Russell Sage Foundation.

Binder, Sarah. 2003. *Stalemate: The Causes and Consequences of Legislative Gridlock.* Washington, DC: Brookings Institution Press.

Bishop, Bill. 2009. *The Big Sort: Why the Clustering of Like-Minded America Is Tearing Us Apart.* New York: Houghton Mifflin Harcourt.

Boix, Carles. 2003. *Democracy and Redistribution.* New York: Cambridge University Press.

Bolsen, Toby, James N. Druckman, and Fay Lomax Cook. 2014. "The Influence of Partisan Motivated Reasoning on Public Opinion." *Political Behavior* 36 (2): 235–62.

Bonica, Adam. 2013. "Database on Ideology, Money in Politics, and Elections: Public Version 1.0." Computer file. Stanford, CA: Stanford University Libraries.

Bonica, Adam, Nolan McCarty, Keith T. Poole, and Howard Rosenthal. 2013. "Why Hasn't Democracy Slowed Rising Inequality?" *Journal of Economic Perspectives* 27 (3): 103–23.

Bound, John, George Johnson, et al. 1992. "Changes in the Structure of Wages in the 1980's: An Evaluation of Alternative Explanations." *American Economic Review* 82 (3): 371–92.

Box-Steffensmeier, Janet M., John R. Freeman, Matthew P. Hitt, and Jon C. W. Pevehouse. 2014. *Time Series Analysis for the Social Sciences.* New York: Cambridge University Press.

Brady, David W., and Craig Volden. 1998. *Revolving Gridlock: Politics and Policy from Carter to Clinton.* Boulder, CO: Westview.

Brady, Henry E. 2004. "An Analytical Perspective on Participatory Inequality and Income Inequality." In *Social Inequality*, ed. Kathryn Neckerman, 667–702. New York: Russell Sage Foundation.

Brady, Henry, Sidney Verba, and Kay Lehman Schlozman. 1995. "Beyond SES: A Resource Model of Political Participation." *American Political Science Review* 89 (2): 271–94.

Branham, J. Alexander, Stuart Soroka, and Christopher Wlezien. 2017. "When Do the Rich Win?" *Political Science Quarterly* 132 (1): 43–62.

Brewer, Marilynn B., and Madelyn Silver. 1978. "Ingroup Bias as a Function of Task Characteristics." *European Journal of Social Psychology* 8 (3): 393–400.

Brown, Kendrick T., Tony N. Brown, James S. Jackson, Robert M. Sellers, and Warde J. Manuel. 2003. "Teammates on and off the Field? Contact with Black Teammates and the Racial Attitudes of White Student Athletes 1." *Journal of Applied Social Psychology* 33 (7): 1379–403.

Bureau of Economic Analysis. 2012. National Income and Product Accounts. Technical report available at http://www.bea.gov//national/nipaweb/DownSS2.asp.

Campbell, Andrea Louise. 2003. *How Polices Make Citizens: Senior Political Activism and the American Welfare State.* Princeton, NJ: Princeton University Press.

Campbell, Angus, Philip E. Converse, Warren E. Miller, and Donald E. Stokes. 1960. *The American Voter.* New York: Wiley.

Campbell, James E. 2011. "The Economic Records of the Presidents: Party Differences and Inherited Economic Conditions." *Forum: A Journal of Applied Research in Contemporary Politics* 9 (1): article 7.

Carpini, Michael X. Delli, and Scott Keeter. 1997. *What Americans Know about Politics and Why It Matters.* New Haven, CT: Yale University Press.

Carroll, Royce, Jeff Lewis, James Lo, Nolan McCarty, Keith Poole, and Howard Rosenthal. 2011. "'Common Space' DW-NOMINATE Scores with Bootstrapped Standard Errors

(Joint House and Senate Scaling)." http://voteview.com/dwnomin_ joint_house_and _senate.htm.

Chen, Jowei, and Jonathan Rodden. 2013. "Unintentional Gerrymandering: Political Geography and Electoral Bias in Legislatures." *Quarterly Journal of Political Science* 8 (3): 239–69.

Chong, Dennis, Jack Citrin, and Patricia Conley. 2001. "When Self-Interest Matters." *Political Psychology* 22 (3): 541–70.

Converse, Philip E. 1964. "The Nature of Belief Systems in Mass Publics." In *Ideology and Discontent*, ed. David E. Apter, 206–61. Glencoe, IL: Free Press.

Cox, Gary W., and Mathew D. McCubbins. 2005. *Setting the Agenda: Responsible Party Government in the US House of Representatives.* New York: Cambridge University Press.

Cramer, Katherine J. 2016. *The Politics of Resentment: Rural Consciousness in Wisconsin and the Rise of Scott Walker.* Chicago: University of Chicago Press.

Dahl, Robert A. 1961. *Who Governs? Democracy and Power in an American City.* New Haven, CT: Yale University Press.

———. 1967. *Pluralist Democracy in the United States.* Chicago: Rand McNally.

———. 1971. *Polyarchy: Participation and Opposition.* New Haven, CT: Yale University Press.

Dahrendorf, Ralf. 1959. *Class and Class Conflict in Industrial Society.* Palo Alto, CA: Stanford University Press.

Daley, David. 2016. *Ratf**ked: The True Story behind the Secret Plan to Steal America's Democracy.* New York: W. W. Norton.

Danziger, Sheldon, and Peter Gottschalk. 1995. *America Unequal.* New York: Russell Sage Foundation.

Derthick, Martha, and Paul J. Quirk. 2001. *The Politics of Deregulation.* Washington, DC: Brookings Institution Press.

DiAngelo, Robin. 2011. "White Fragility." *International Journal of Critical Pedagogy* 3 (3): 54–70.

Dickey, David A., and W. A. Fuller. 1979. "Distribution of the Estimators for Autoregressive Time Series with a Unit Root." *Journal of American and Statistical Association* 74 (366): 427–31.

Domhoff, G. William. 1990. *The Power Elite and the State: How Policy Is Made in America.* Piscataway, NJ: Transaction Books.

———. 2010. *Who Rules America: Power Politics and Social Change.* 6th ed. New York: McGraw Hill.

Downs, Anthony. 1957. *An Economic Theory of Democracy.* New York: Harper and Row.

Druckman, James N. 2004. "Political Preference Formation: Competition, Deliberation, and the (Ir)Relevance of Framing Effects." *American Political Science Review* 4:671–86.

Durkheim, Emile. 1933. *The Division of Labor in Society.* New York: Macmillan.

Easton, David. 1953. *The Political System.* New York: Knopf.

Edelman, Murray J. 1964. *The Symbolic Uses of Politics.* Urbana: University of Illinois Press.

———. 1971. *Politics as Symbolic Action: Mass Arousal and Quiescence.* Chicago: Markham.

Edsall, Thomas Byrne, and Mary D. Edsall. 1992. *Chain Reaction: The Impact of Race, Rights, and Taxes on American Politics.* New York: W. W. Norton.

Ellis, Christopher, and Joseph Ura. 2011. "United We Divide? Education, Income, and Heterogeneity in Mass Preferences." In *Who Gets Represented?*, ed. Peter Enns and Christopher Wlezien, 277–91. New York: Russell Sage Foundation.

Engle, Robert F., and Clive W. J. Granger. 1987. "Co-integration and Error Correction: Representation, Estimation, and Testing." *Econometrica* 55 (2): 251–76.

Enns, Peter K. 2015. "Relative Policy Support and Coincidental Representation." *Perspectives on Politics* 13 (4): 1053–64.

Enns, Peter K., Paul M. Kellstedt, and Gregory McAvoy. 2012. "The Consequences of Partisanship in Economic Perceptions." *Public Opinion Quarterly* 76 (2): 287–310.

Enns, Peter K., Nathan J. Kelly, Jana Morgan, and Christopher Witko. 2016. "The Power of Economic Interests and the Congressional Economic Policy Agenda." Center for Equitable Growth, Working Paper.

Enns, Peter K., Nathan J. Kelly, Takaaki Masaki, and Patrick C. Wohlfarth. 2016. "Don't Jettison the General Error Correction Model Just Yet: A Practical Guide to Avoiding Spurious Regression with the GECM." *Research and Politics* 3 (2): 1–11.

———. 2017. "Moving Forward with Time Series Analysis." *Research and Politics* 4 (4): 1–7.

Enns, Peter K., Nathan J. Kelly, Jana Morgan, Thomas Volscho, and Christopher Witko. 2014. "Conditional Status Quo Bias and Top Income Shares: How US Political Institutions Have Benefited the Rich." *Journal of Politics* 76 (2): 289–303.

Enos, Ryan D. 2014. "Causal Effect of Intergroup Contact on Exclusionary Attitudes." *Proceedings of the National Academy of Sciences* 111 (10): 3699–704.

Erikson, Robert S., Michael B. MacKuen, and James A. Stimson. 1995. "Dynamic Representation." *American Political Science Review* 89:543–65.

———. 2002. *The Macro Polity*. New York: Cambridge University Press.

Faricy, Christopher G. 2015. *Welfare for the Wealthy: Parties, Social Spending, and Inequality in the United States*. New York: Cambridge University Press.

Fenno, Richard F. 1978. *Home Style: House Members in Their Districts*. New York: Pearson College Division.

Ferguson, Charles. 2012. *Predator Nation*. New York: Crown Business.

Ferguson, Thomas. 1995. *Golden Rule: The Investment Theory of Party Competition and the Logic of Money-Driven Political Systems*. Chicago: University of Chicago Press.

Finocchiaro, Charles J., and David W. Rohde. 2008. "War for the Floor: Partisan Theory and Agenda Control in the US House of Representatives." *Legislative Studies Quarterly* 33 (1): 35–61.

Fortin, Nicole M., and Thomas Lemieux. 1997. "Institutional Changes and Rising Wage Inequality: Is There a Linkage?" *Journal of Economic Perspectives* 11 (2): 75–96.

Frank, Mark. 2009. "Inequality and Growth in the United States: Evidence from a New State-Level Panel of Income Inequality Measure." *Economic Inquiry* 47 (1): 55–68.

Franko, William W. 2016. "Political Context, Government Redistribution, and the Public's Response to Growing Economic Inequality." *Journal of Politics* 78 (4): 957–73.

Franko, William W., Caroline Tolbert, and Christopher Witko. 2013. "Inequality, Self-Interest and Public Support for "Robin Hood" Tax Policies." *Political Research Quarterly* 66 (4): 923–37.

Franko, William W., Nathan J. Kelly, and Christopher Witko. 2016. "Class Bias in Voter Turnout, Representation, and Income Inequality." *Perspectives on Politics* 14:351–68.

Freeman, John R., John T. Williams, and Tse-min Lin. 1989. "Vector Autoregression and the Study of Politics." *American Journal of Political Science* 33 (4): 842–77.

Freeman, Richard B. 1993. "How Much Has De-unionization Contributed to the Rise in Male Earnings Inequality?" In *Uneven Tides: Rising Inequality in America*, ed. Sheldon Danziger and Peter Gottschalk, 133–64. New York: Russell Sage Foundation.

Frymer, Paul. 2010. *Uneasy Alliances: Race and Party Competition in America*. Princeton, NJ: Princeton University Press.

Gaventa, John. 1982. *Power and Powerlessness: Quiescence and Rebellion in an Appalachian Valley*. Champaign: University of Illinois Press.

Gelman, Andrew, David Park, and Boris Shor. 2008. *Red State, Blue State, Rich State, Poor State: Why Americans Vote the Way They Do*. Princeton, NJ: Princeton University Press.

Gerber, Alan S., and Gregory A. Huber. 2010. "Partisanship, Political Control, and Economic Assessments." *American Journal of Political Science* 54 (1): 153–73.

Gilens, Martin. 2000. *Why Americans Hate Welfare: Race, Media, and the Politics of Antipoverty Policy*. Boulder, CO: Westview.

———. 2009. "Preference Gaps and Inequality in Representation." *PS: Political Science and Politics* 42 (2): 335–41.

———. 2012. *Affluence and Influence: Economic Inequality and Political Power in America*. Princeton, NJ: Princeton University Press and Russell Sage Foundation.

Gilens, Martin, and Benjamin I. Page. 2014. "Testing Theories of American Politics: Elites, Interest Groups, and Average Citizens." *Perspectives on Politics* 12 (3): 564–81.

Glaeser, Edward L. 2005. "The Political Economy of Hatred." *Quarterly Journal of Economics* 120 (1): 45–86.

Glazer, Nathan. 2003. "On Americans and Inequality." *Daedalus* 132 (3): 111–15.

Goldin, Claudia Dale, and Lawrence F. Katz. 2008. *The Race between Education and Technology*. Cambridge, MA: Harvard University Press.

Goodin, Robert, and John Dryzek. 1980. "Rational Participation: The Politics of Relative Power." *British Journal of Political Science* 10 (3): 273–92.

Gorton, Gary B. 2012. *Misunderstanding Financial Crises: Why We Don't See Them Coming*. New York: Oxford University Press.

Grant, J. Tobin, and Nathan J. Kelly. 2008. "Legislative Productivity of the U.S. Congress, 1789–2004." *Political Analysis* 16 (3): 303–23.

Grant, Taylor, and Matthew J. Lebo. 2016. "Error Correction Methods with Political Time Series." *Political Analysis* 24 (1): 3–30.

Grim, Ryan, and Sabrina Siddiqui. 2013. "Call Time for Congress Shows How Fundraising Dominates Bleak Work Life." *Huffington Post*, January 8. https://goo.gl/QbpYzL.

Grossback, Lawrence J., David A. M. Peterson, and James A. Stimson. 2006. *Mandate Politics*. New York: Cambridge University Press.

Grossmann, Matt, and David A. Hopkins. 2016. *Asymmetric Politics: Ideological Republicans and Group Interest Democrats*. New York: Oxford University Press.

Gurin, Patricia, Biren Ratnesh A. Nagda, and Gretchen E. Lopez. 2004. "The Benefits of Diversity in Education for Democratic Citizenship." *Journal of Social Issues* 60 (1): 17–34.

Hacker, Jacob S. 2005. "Policy Drift: The Hidden Politics of US Welfare State Retrenchment." In *Beyond Continuity: Institutional Change in Advanced Political Economies*, ed. Wolfgang Streeck and Kathleen Thelen, 40–82. Oxford: Oxford University Press.

Hacker, Jacob S., and Paul Pierson. 2010. *Winner-Take-All Politics*. New York: Simon and Schuster.

Haines, Elizabeth L., and John T. Jost. 2000. "Placating the Powerless: Effects of Legitimate and Illegitimate Explanation on Affect, Memory, and Stereotyping." *Social Justice Research* 13 (3): 219–36.

Hall, Peter A. 1986. *Governing the Economy: The Politics of State Intervention in Britain and France*. New York: Oxford University Press.

Heathcote, Jonathan, Fabrizio Perri, and Giovanni L. Violante. 2010. "Unequal We Stand: An Empirical Analysis of Economic Inequality in the United States, 1967–2006." *Review of Economic Dynamics* 13 (1): 15–51.

Heberlig, Eric S. 2003. "Congressional Parties, Fundraising, and Committee Ambition." *Political Research Quarterly* 56 (2): 151–61.

Herring, Edward P. 1940. *The Politics of Democracy: American Parties in Action*. New York: Rinehard.

Hetherington, Marc J. 2005. *Why Trust Matters: Declining Political Trust and the Demise of American Liberalism*. Princeton, NJ: Princeton University Press.

Hochschild, Arlie Russell. 2016. *Strangers in Their Own Land*. New York: New Press.

Hotelling, Harold. 1929. "Stability in Competition." *Economic Journal* 39 (153): 41–57.

Hughey, Matthew W. 2014. "White Backlash in the Post-racial United States." *Ethnic and Racial Studies* 37 (5): 721–30.

Jacobs, Alan. 2010. "Policymaking as Political Constraint." In *Explaining Institutional Change*, ed. James Mahoney and Kathleen Thelen, 1–37. New York: Cambridge University Press.

Jacobs, David, and Lindsey Myers. 2014. "Union Strength, Neoliberalism, and Inequality Contingent Political Analyses of US Income Differences since 1950." *American Sociological Review* 79 (4): 752–74.

Jacobs, Lawrence R., and Desmond King. 2016. *Fed Power: How Finance Wins*. New York: Oxford University Press.

Jacobs, Lawrence R., and Robert Y. Shapiro. 2000. *Politicians Don't Pander*. Chicago: University of Chicago Press.

Jacobs, Lawrence R., and Joe Soss. 2010. "The Politics of Inequality in America: A Political Economy Framework." *Annual Review of Political Science* 13:341–64.

Jerit, Jennifer, and Jason Barabas. 2012. "Partisan Perceptual Bias and the Information Environment." *Journal of Politics* 74 (3): 672–84.

Johansen, Søren. 1988. "Statistical Analysis of Cointegration Vectors." *Journal of Economic Dynamics and Control* 12 (2–3): 231–54.

Johnson, Simon, and James Kwak. 2010. *13 Bankers: The Wall Street Takeover and the Next Financial Meltdown*. New York: Vintage Books.

Jost, John T., Mahzarin R. Banaji, and Brian A. Nosek. 2004. "A Decade of System Justification Theory: Accumulated Evidence of Conscious and Unconscious Bolstering of the Status Quo." *Political Psychology* 25 (6): 881–919.

Kalla, Joshua L., and David E. Broockman. 2016. "Campaign Contributions Facilitate Access to Congressional Officials: A Randomized Field Experiment." *American Journal of Political Science* 60 (3): 545–58.

Kaplan, Steven N., and Joshua Rauh. 2010. "Wall Street and Main Street: What Contributes to the Rise in the Highest Incomes?" *Review of Financial Studies* 23 (3): 1004–50.

Kay, Aaron C., Maria C. Jimenez, and John T. Jost. 2002. "Sour Grapes, Sweet Lemons, and the Anticipatory Rationalization of the Status Quo." *Personality and Social Psychology Bulletin* 28 (9): 1300–1312.

Keele, Luke, and Nathan J. Kelly. 2006. "Dynamic Models for Dynamic Theories: The Ins and Outs of Lagged Dependent Variables." *Political Analysis* 14 (2): 186–205.

Keller, Eric, and Nathan J. Kelly. 2015. "Partisan Politics, Financial Deregulation, and the New Gilded Age." *Political Research Quarterly* 68 (3): 428–42.

Kellstedt, Paul M. 2003. *The Mass Media and the Dynamics of American Racial Attitudes*. New York: Cambridge University Press.

Kelly, Nathan J. 2005. "Political Choice, Public Policy, and Distributional Outcomes." *American Journal of Political Science* 49 (4): 865–80.

———. 2009. *The Politics of Income Inequality in the United States*. New York: Cambridge University Press.

Kelly, Nathan J., and Peter K. Enns. 2010. "Inequality and the Dynamics of Public Opinion: The Self-Reinforcing Link between Economic Inequality and Mass Preferences." *American Journal of Political Science* 54 (5): 855–70.

Kennedy, Susan Estabrook. 1973. *The Banking Crisis of 1933*. Lexington: University of Kentucky Press.

Kenworthy, Lane. 2010. "How Much Do Presidents Influence Income Inequality?" *Challenge* 53 (2): 90–112.

Kenworthy, Lane, and Leslie McCall. 2008. "Inequality, Public Opinion, and Redistribution." *Socio-economic Review* 6:35–68.

Key, V. O. 1949. *Southern Politics in State and Nation*. New York: Knopf.

Klein, Ezra. 2014. "The Doom Loop of Oligarchy." *Vox*. https://www.vox.com/2014/4/11/5581272/doom-loop-oligarchy.

Krehbiel, Keith. 1998. *Pivotal Politics: A Theory of U.S. Lawmaking*. Chicago: University of Chicago Press.

Krippner, Greta. 2011. *Capitalizing on Crisis*. Cambridge, MA: Harvard University Press.

Krosch, Amy R., and David M. Amodio. 2014. "Economic Scarcity Alters the Perception of Race." *Proceedings of the National Academy of Sciences of the United States of America* 111 (25): 9079–84.

Krueger, Alan. 2012. "The Rise and Consequences of Inequality." Presentation made to the Center for American Progress, January 12. http://www. americanprogress.org/events/2012/01/12/17181/the-rise-and-consequences-of-inequality.

Krugman, Paul. 1994. *Peddling Prosperity*. New York: W. W. Norton.

———. 1996. "The Spiral of Inequality." *Mother Jones* 44:44–49.

Kumhof, Michael, Romain Rancière, and Pablo Winant. 2015. "Inequality, Leverage, and Crises." *American Economic Review* 105 (3): 1217–45.

Kwiatkowski, Denis, Peter C. B. Phillips, Peter Schmidt, and Yongcheol Shin. 1992. "Testing the Null Hypothesis of Stationarity against the Alternative of a Unit Root: How Sure Are We That Economic Time Series Have a Unit Root?" *Journal of Econometrics* 54 (13): 159–78.

Ladd, Everett Carll, and Karlyn H. Bowman. 1998. *Attitudes toward Economic Inequality*. Washington, DC: American Enterprise Institute.

Leighley, Jan E., and Jonathan Nagler. 2007. "Unions, Voter Turnout, and Class Bias in the U.S. Electorate, 1964–2004." *Journal of Politics* 69 (2): 430–41.

Levine, Adam Seth. 2015. *American Insecurity: Why Our Economic Fears Lead to Political Inaction*. Princeton, NJ: Princeton University Press.

LeVine, Robert A., and Donald T. Campbell. 1972. Ethnocentrism: Theories of Conflict, Ethnic Attitudes, and Group Behavior. New York: John Wiley and Sons.

Lewis, Jeffrey B., Keith Poole, Howard Rosenthal, Adam Boche, Aaron Rudkin, and Luke Sonnet. 2017. Voteview: Congressional Roll-Call Votes Database. https://voteview.com/.

Lin, Ken-Hou, and Donald Tomaskovic-Devey. 2013. "Financialization and US Income Inequality, 1970–2008." *American Journal of Sociology* 118 (5): 1284–329.

Lindblom, Charles E. 1977. *Politics and Markets: The World's Political-Economic Systems*. New York: Basic Books.

Lindsey, Brink, and Steven Teles. 2017. *The Captured Economy*. New York: Oxford University Press.

Lowery, David, and Virginia Gray. 1995. "The Population Ecology of Gucci Gulch; or, The Natural Regulation of Interest Group Numbers in the American States." *American Journal of Political Science* 39 (1): 1–29.

Lowi, Theodore J. 1969. *The End of Liberalism*. New York: Norton.

Lupia, Arthur. 2015. *Uninformed: Why People Seem to Know So Little about Politics and What We Can Do about It*. New York: Oxford University Press.

Luttig, Matthew. 2013. "The Structure of Inequality and Americans' Attitudes toward Redistribution." *Public Opinion Quarterly* 77 (3): 811–21.

MacKuen, Michael B., Robert S. Erikson, and James A. Stimson. 1993. "Peasants or Bankers? The American Electorate and the U.S. Economy." *American Political Science Review* 86 (3): 597–611.

Mahoney, James, and Kathleen Thelen. 2010. "A Theory of Gradual Institutional Change." In *Explaining Institutional Change*, ed. James Mahoney and Kathleen Thelen, 1–37. New York: Cambridge University Press.

Mayer, Jane. 2016. *Dark Money: The Hidden History of the Billionaires behind the Rise of the Radical Right*. New York: Doubleday.

Mayhew, David R. 1974. *Congress: The Electoral Connection*. New Haven, CT: Yale University Press.

McCall, Leslie. 2013. *The Undeserving Rich: American Beliefs about Inequality, Opportunity, and Redistribution*. Cambridge University Press.

———. 2016. "Political and Policy Responses to Problems of Inequality and Opportunity: Past, Present, and Future." In *The Dynamics of Opportunity in America*, ed. Irwin Kirsch and Henry Braun, 415–42. New York: Springer.

McCall, Leslie, Derek Burk, Marie Laperrière, and Jennifer A. Richeson. 2017. "Exposure to Rising Inequality Shapes Americans Opportunity Beliefs and Policy Support." *Proceedings of the National Academy of Sciences* 114 (36): 9593–98.

McCall, Leslie, and Lane Kenworthy. 2009. "Americans' Social Policy Preferences in the Era of Rising Inequality." *Perspectives on Politics* 7 (3): 459–84.

McCarty, Nolan, Keith Poole, and Howard Rosenthal. 2006. *Polarized America: The Dance of Ideology and Unequal Riches*. Cambridge, MA: MIT Press.

McDermott, Monica, and Frank L. Samson. 2005. "White Racial and Ethnic Identity in the United States." *Annual Review of Sociology* 31:245–61.

McElwee, Sean, Brian Shaffner, and Jesse Rhodes. 2016. "Whose Voice, Whose Choice? The Distorting Influence of the Political Donor Class in Our Big-Money Elections." Technical report, Demos New York. https://www.demos.org/sites/default/files/publications/Whose%20Voice%20Whose%20Choice_2.pdf.

McGann, Anthony J., Charles Anthony Smith, Michael Latner, and Alex Keena. 2016. *Gerrymandering in America: The House of Representatives, the Supreme Court, and the Future of Popular Sovereignty*. New York: Cambridge University Press.

McNeill, Charles R., and Denise M. Rechter. 1980. "The Depository Institutions Deregulation and Monetary Control Act of 1980." *Federal Reserve Bulletin* 66 (6): 444–53.

Meltzer, Allan H. 2004. *A History of the Federal Reserve*. Vol. 1 Chicago: University of Chicago Press.

Meltzer, Allan H., and Scott F. Richard. 1981. "A Rational Theory of the Size of Government." *Journal of Political Economy* 89 (4): 914–27.

Mendelberg, Tali. 2001. *The Race Card: Campaign Strategy, Implicit Messages, and the Norm of Equality*. Princeton, NJ: Princeton University Press.

Mettler, Suzanne. 2005. *Soldiers to Citizens: The GI Bill and the Making of the Greatest Generation*. New York: Oxford University Press.

———. 2016. "The Policyscape and the Challenges of Contemporary Politics to Policy Maintenance." *Perspectives on Politics* 14 (2): 369–90.

Morgan, Jana, and Nathan J. Kelly. 2017. "Social Patterns of Inequality, Partisan Competition, and Latin American Support for Redistribution." *Journal of Politics* 79 (1): 193–209.

Nielsen, François, and Arthur S. Alderson. 1997. "The Kuznets Curve and the Great U-Turn: Income Inequality in U.S. Counties, 1970 to 1990." *American Sociological Review* 62 (1): 12–33.

Nixon, Richard M. 1970. *Public Papers of the Presidents: Richard M. Nixon, 1970*. Washington, DC: Office of the Federal Register, National Archives and Records Administration.

Nyhan, Brendan, and Jason Reifler. 2010. "When Corrections Fail: The Persistence of Political Misperceptions." *Political Behavior* 32 (2): 303–30.

Offe, Claus, and Helmut Wiesenthal. 1980. "Two Logics of Collective Action: Theoretical Notes on Social Class and Organizational Form." *Political Power and Social Theory* 1 (1): 67–115.

Okun, Arthur M. 1975. *Equality and Efficiency: The Big Tradeoff*. Washington, DC: Brookings Institution.

Olson, Mancur. 1965. *The Logic of Collective Action*. Cambridge, MA: Harvard University Press.

Page, Benjamin I., Larry M. Bartels, and Jason Seawright. 2013. "Democracy and the Policy Preferences of Wealthy Americans." *Perspectives on Politics* 11 (1): 51–73.

Page, Benjamin I., and Martin Gilens. 2017. *Democracy in America?* Chicago: University of Chicago Press.

Page, Benjamin I., and Lawrence R. Jacobs. 2009. *Class War? What Americans Really Think about Economic Inequality*. Chicago: University of Chicago Press.

Page, Benjamin, and Robert Y. Shapiro. 1983. "Effects of Public Opinion on Policy." *American Political Science Review* 77 (1): 175–90.

Page, Benjamin I., and James Roy Simmons. 2000. *What Government Can Do: Dealing with Poverty and Inequality*. Chicago: University of Chicago Press.

Page, Scott E. 2010. *Diversity and Complexity*. Princeton, NJ: Princeton University Press.

Paulson, Henry. 2006. "Remarks Prepared for Delivery by Treasury Secretary Henry M. Paulson at Columbia University." August 1. http://votesmart.org/public-statement /200454/remarks-prepared-for-delivery-by-treasury-secretary-henry-mpaulson-at -columbia-university, accessed October 16, 2016.

Perkins, Edwin J. 1971. "The Divorce of Commercial and Investment Banking: A History." *Banking Law Journal* 88:483–528.

Pettigrew, Thomas F., Linda R. Tropp, Ulrich Wagner, and Oliver Christ. 2011. "Recent Advances in Intergroup Contact Theory." *International Journal of Intercultural Relations* 35 (3): 271–80.

Philippon, Thomas, and Ariell Reshef. 2012. "Wages and Human Capital in the US Finance Industry: 1909–2006." *Quarterly Journal of Economics* 127 (4): 1551–609.

———. 2013. "An International Look at the Growth of Modern Finance." *Journal of Economic Perspectives* 27 (2): 73–96.

Phillips, Kevin. 2002. *Wealth and Democracy: A Political History of the American Rich*. New York: Broadway.

Pierson, Paul. 1993. "When Effect Becomes Cause: Policy Feedback and Political Change." *World Politics* 45 (4): 595–628.

———. 2004. *Politics in Time: History, Institutions, and Social Analysis*. Princeton, NJ: Princeton University Press.

Piketty, Thomas. 2014. *Capital in the Twenty-First Century*. Cambridge, MA: Harvard University Press.

Piketty, Thomas, and Emmanuel Saez. 2003. "Income Inequality in the United States, 1913–1998." *Quarterly Journal of Economics* 118 (1): 1–39.

———. 2006. "The Evolution of Top Incomes: A Historical and International Perspective." *American Economic Review* 96 (2): 200–205.

Piketty, Thomas, Emmanuel Saez, and Gabriel Zucman. 2018. "Distributional National Accounts: Methods and Estimates for the United States." *Quarterly Journal of Economics* 133 (2): 553–609.

Poole, Keith T., and Howard Rosenthal. 1997. *Congress: A Political-Economic History of Roll Call Voting*. New York: Oxford University Press.

Popkin, Samuel L. 1991. *The Reasoning Voter: Communication and Persuasion in Presidential Campaigns*. Chicago: University of Chicago Press.

Preston, Howard H. 1933. "The Banking Act of 1933." *American Economic Review* 23 (4) 585–607.

Rappeport, Alan. 2018. "Republican Bill Curtails Reach of Bank Rules." *New York Times*, January 16, A1.

Reardon, Sean F., and Kendra Bischoff. 2011. "Income Inequality and Income Segregation." *American Journal of Sociology* 116 (4): 1092–153.

Richman, Jesse. 2011. "Parties, Pivots, and Policy: The Status Quo Test." *American Political Science Review* 105 (1): 151–65.

Ritter, Michael, and Frederick Solt. 2019. "Economic Inequality and Campaign Participation." *Social Science Quarterly* 100 (3): 678–88.

Rohde, David, and John Aldrich. 2010. "Consequences of Electoral and Institutional Change: The Evolution of Conditional Party Government in the US House of Representatives." In *New Directions in American Political Parties*, ed. Jeffrey M. Stonecash, 234–50. New York: Routledge.

Ross, Michael, and John H. Ellard. 1986. "On Winnowing: The Impact of Scarcity on Allocators' Evaluations of Candidates for a Resource." *Journal of Experimental Social Psychology* 22 (4): 374–88.

Samuelson, William, and Richard Zeckhauser. 1988. "Status Quo Bias in Decision Making." *Journal of Risk and Uncertainty* 1 (1): 7–59.

Schattschneider, E. E. 1960. *The Semi-sovereign People: A Realist's View of Democracy in America*. New York: Holt, Rinehart, and Winston.

Scheve, Kenneth, and David Stasavage. 2006. "Religion and Preferences for Social Insurance." *Quarterly Journal of Political Science* 1 (3): 255–86.

Schlozman, Kay Lehman, Sidney Verba, and Henry E. Brady. 2012. *The Unheavenly Chorus*. Princeton, NJ: Princeton University Press.

Schwarz, Gideon, et al. 1978. "Estimating the Dimension of a Model." *Annals of Statistics* 6 (2): 461–64.

Shapiro, Ian. 2002. "Why the Poor Don't Soak the Rich." *Daedalus* 131 (1): 118–28.

Sharkey, Patrick. 2013. *Stuck in Place: Urban Neighborhoods and the End of Progress toward Racial Equality*. Chicago: University of Chicago Press.

Shayo, Moses. 2009. "A Model of Social Identity with an Application to Political Economy: Nation, Class, and Redistribution." *American Political Science Review* 103 (2): 147–74.

Sherif, Muzafer. 1966. *In Common Predicament: Social Psychology of Intergroup Conflict and Cooperation*. New York: Houghton Mifflin.

Sims, Christopher A., and Tao Zha. 1998. "Bayesian Methods for Dynamic Multivariate Models." *International Economic Review* 39 (4): 949–68.

Skitka, Linda J., and Philip E. Tetlock. 1992. "Allocating Scarce Resources: A Contingency Model of Distributive Justice." *Journal of Experimental Social Psychology* 28 (6): 491–522.

Skocpol, Theda. 1992. *Protecting Soldiers and Mothers: The Political Origins of Social Policy in the United States*. Cambridge, MA: Harvard University Press.

Skocpol, Theda, and Alexander Hertel-Fernandez. 2016. "The Koch Network and Republican Party Extremism." *Perspectives on Politics* 14 (3): 681–99.

———. Forthcoming. *The Koch Effect*. Chicago: University of Chicago Press.

Smith, Kevin B., and J. Scott Rademaker. 1999. "Expensive Lessons: Education and the Political Economy of the American States." *Political Research Quarterly* 52 (4): 709–27.

Smith, Mark A. 2000. *American Business and Political Power: Public Opinion, Elections, and Democracy*. Chicago: University of Chicago Press.

Solt, Frederick. 2008. "The Standardized World Income Inequality Database." http://hdl.handle.net/1902.1/11992 V3 [Version].

———. 2010. "Does Economic Inequality Depress Electoral Participation? Testing the Schattschneider Hypothesis." *Political Behavior* 32 (2): 285–301.

———. 2011. "Diversionary Nationalism: Economic Inequality and the Formation of National Pride." *Journal of Politics* 73 (3): 821–30.

Soroka, Stuart N., and Christopher Wlezien. 2010. *Degrees of Democracy*. New York: Cambridge University Press.

———. 2008. "On the Limits of Inequality in Representation." *PS: Political Science and Politics* 41 (2): 319–27.

Soss, Joe, Jacob S. Hacker, and Suzanne Mettler, eds. 2007. *Remaking America: Democracy and Public Policy in an Age of Inequality*. New York: Russell Sage Foundation.

Stepan, Alfred, and Juan J. Linz. 2012. "Comparative Perspectives on Inequality and the Quality of Democracy in the United States." *Perspectives on Politics* 9 (4): 841–56.

Stephens, John D. 1979. *The Transition from Capitalism to Socialism*. London: Macmillan.

Stimson, James A. 1999. *Public Opinion in America: Moods, Cycles, and Swings*. 2nd ed. Boulder, CO: Westview.

———. 2004. *Tides of Consent: How Public Opinion Shapes American Politics*. New York: Cambridge University Press.

Stimson, James A., Michael B. MacKuen, and Robert S. Erikson. 1995. "Dynamic Representation." *American Political Science Review* 89 (3): 543–65.

Suarez, Sandra, and Robin Kolodny. 2011. "Paving the Road to Too Big to Fail: Business Interests and the Politics of Financial Deregulation in the United States." *Politics and Society* 39 (1): 74–102.

Taber, Charles S., and Milton Lodge. 2006. "Motivated Skepticism in the Evaluation of Political Beliefs." *American Journal of Political Science* 50 (3): 755–69.

Taylor, Marylee C. 1998. "How White Attitudes Vary with the Racial Composition of Local Populations: Numbers Count." *American Sociological Review* 63 (4): 512–35.

Thelen, Kathleen. 2004. *How Institutions Evolve: The Political Economy of Skills in Germany, Britain, the United States, and Japan*. New York: Cambridge University Press.

Tilly, Charles. 1998. *Durable Inequality*. Berkeley: University of California Press.

Tilley, James, and Sara B. Hobolt. 2011. "Is the Government to Blame? An Experimental Test of How Partisanship Shapes Perceptions of Performance and Responsibility." *Journal of Politics* 73 (2): 316–30.

Tocqueville, Alexis de. 2000. *Democracy in America*. Chicago: University of Chicago Press.

Tomaskovic-Devey, and Ken-Hou Lin. 2011. "Income Dynamics, Economic Rents, and the Financialization of the U.S. Economy." *American Sociological Review* 76 (4): 538–59.

Treeck, Till. 2014. "Did Inequality Cause the US Financial Crisis?" *Journal of Economic Surveys* 28 (3): 421–48.

Truman, David. 1951. *The Governmental Process*. New York: Alfred A. Knopf.

Trump, Kris-Stella. 2013. "The Status Quo and Perceptions of Fairness: How Income Inequality Influences Public Opinion." PhD thesis, Harvard University.

US House Committee on Banking and Financial Services. 1997. "Financial Services Competition Act of 1997, Report of the Committee on Banking and Financial Services on H.R. 10 Together with Additional, Supplemental, and Dissenting Views (105 H. Rpt. 164)."

Uslaner, Eric M., and Mitchell Brown. 2005. "Inequality, Trust, and Civic Engagement." *American Politics Research* 33 (6): 868–94.

Van Arnum, Bradford M., and Michele I. Naples. 2013. "Financialization and Income Inequality in the United States, 1967–2010." *American Journal of Economics and Sociology* 72 (5): 1158–82.

Verba, Sidney, Kay Lehman Schlozman, and Henry E. Brady. 1995. *Voice and Equality: Civic Voluntarism in American Politics.* Boston: Harvard University Press.

Vogel, David. 1989. *Fluctuating Fortunes: The Political Power of Business in America.* New York: Basic Books.

Volscho, Thomas W., and Nathan J. Kelly. 2012. "The Rise of the Super-rich: Power Resources, Taxes, Financial Markets, and the Dynamics of the Top 1 Percent, 1949–2008." *American Sociological Review* 77 (5): 679–99.

Warren, Elizabeth, and Amelia Warren Tyagi. 2004. *The Two Income Trap: Why Middle-Class Parents Are Going Broke.* New York: Basic Books.

Wawro, Gregory John, and Eric Schickler. 2006. *Filibuster: Obstruction and Lawmaking in the US Senate.* New York: Cambridge University Press.

Weber, Max. 1968. *Economy and Society.* New York: Bedminster.

Wells, Donald R. 2004. *The Federal Reserve System: A History.* Jefferson, NC: McFarland.

Western, Bruce. 1995. "A Comparative Study of Working Class Disorganization: Union Decline in Eighteen Advanced Capitalist Countries." *American Sociological Review* 60 (2): 179–201.

———. 1997. *Between Class and Market.* Princeton, NJ: Princeton University Press.

Western, Bruce, and Jake Rosenfeld. 2011. "Unions, Norms, and the Rise in US Wage Inequality." *American Sociological Review* 76 (4): 513–37.

Willis, Henry Parker, and John Chapman. 1934. *The Banking Situation: American Post-war Problems and Developments.* New York: Columbia University Press.

Wilson, Woodrow. 1908. *Constitutional Government in the United States.* New York: Columbia University Press.

Winter, Nicholas J. G. 2006. "Beyond Welfare: Framing and the Racialization of White Opinion on Social Security." *American Journal of Political Science* 50 (2): 400–420.

Winters, Jeffrey A. 2011. *Oligarchy.* New York: Cambridge University Press.

Winters, Jeffrey A., and Benjamin I. Page. 2009. "Oligarchy in the United States?" *Perspectives on Politics* 7 (4): 731–51.

Witko, Christopher. 2013. "When Does Money Buy Votes? Campaign Contributions and Policymaking." In *New Directions in Interest Group Politics*, ed. Matt Grossman, 165–84. New York: Routledge.

———. 2016. "The Politics of Financialization in the United States, 1949–2005." *British Journal of Political Science* 46 (2): 349–70.

Wlezien, Christopher. 1995. "The Public as Thermostat: Dynamics of Preferences for Spending." *American Journal of Political Science* 39 (4): 981–1000.

———. 2004. "Patterns of Representation: Dynamics of Public Preferences and Policy." *Journal of Politics* 66 (1): 1–24.

Wlezien, Christopher, and Stuart Soroka. 2011. "Inequality in Policy Responsiveness?" In

Who Gets Represented?, ed. Peter K. Enns and Christopher Wlezien, 285–310. New York: Russell Sage Foundation.

——. 2017. "Trends in Public Support for Welfare Spending: How the Economy Matters." Paper presented at the Annual Meeting of the Midwest Political Science Association, Chicago.

Yashar, Deborah J. 1997. *Demanding Democracy: Reform and Reaction in Costa Rica and Guatemala, 1870s–1950s*. Palo Alto, CA: Stanford University Press.

Zaller, John R. 1992. *The Nature and Origins of Mass Opinion*. New York: Cambridge University Press.

INDEX

The letter *f* following a page number denotes a figure, and the letter *t* denotes a table.

Printed in Great Britain
by Amazon